From Nairobi to Beijing

DATE DUE

DEMCO 38-296

From Nairobi to Beijing

Second Review and Appraisal of the Implementation
of the Nairobi Forward-Looking Strategies for
the Advancement of Women

Report of the Secretary-General

United Nations, New York, 1995

From Nairobi to Beijing

ns Publications
3, New York, New York 10017 USA

United Nations Publications
Palais desNations, 1211 Geneva 10, Switzerland

U.N. Sales No. E.95. IV. 5
ISBN 92-1-130166-1

Preface

Ten years have passed since the third United Nations conference on women met at Nairobi and adopted the Nairobi Forward-looking Strategies for the Advancement of Women. The first review and appraisal in 1990 sounded the warning that unless urgent action was taken, the Strategies were at risk. Now, on the eve of the Fourth World Conference on Women: Action for Equality, Development and Peace, the second review and appraisal gives another opportunity to look back in order to see how best to move forward.

The balance after 10 years is less disquieting than might have been feared, but less progress has been registered than was hoped. The challenge for the final five years of the Strategies is to build on what has provoked change and address the key obstacles to progress.

Women have taken advantage of greater (though still unequal) educational and economic opportunities to exercise their talents; they have begun to express themselves at the ballot box and determine the outcome of elections; they have organized to struggle for their rights and against violence.

New approaches to providing opportunities for women have been tried at the national level and with the support of international organizations. Non-governmental organizations have proved again to be significant innovators. The review and appraisal shows that, with appropriate priorities and adequate resources, all of the critical areas of concern identified by the Commission on the Status of Women for the Platform for Action to be adopted at the Fourth World Conference can be addressed.

As in the past, the review and appraisal of the Strategies has been a joint effort of the organizations of the United Nations system, coordinated by the Division for the Advancement of Women of the United Nations Secretariat.

The basis for the diagnosis underlying the Platform for Action to be adopted at the Fourth World Conference on Women is the second review and appraisal of the Nairobi Forward-looking Strategies for the Advancement of Women. The review and appraisal has been structured in terms of the critical areas of concern defined by the Commission on the Status of Women. In preparing their national reports, member States were requested to use statistics and indicators that were based on the critical areas. Since the critical areas of concern have also been the focus of considerable analytical work inside the United Nations system, including by the Commission itself, the results of these efforts at diagnosis have also been considered.

The preliminary findings are derived from a review of the *1994 World Survey on the Role of Women in Development*, the statistical analyses being prepared for the update of *The World's Women: Trends and Statistics*, regional reviews and appraisals, analytical work on specific issues undertaken by organizations of the United Nations system and, especially, an initial review of national reports prepared by over 100 countries in all regions. It is these national reports that have shaped the preliminary findings, since they are the most reliable source of information on priorities, conceptual approaches and measures taken.

Overview

Since the adoption of the Nairobi Forward-looking Strategies for the Advancement of Women, the global framework for their implementation has altered in a dramatically. The current political and economic environment, national and international, presents both new challenges and new opportunities for the advancement of women. Specifically:

- The end of the Cold War has permitted a greater use of international approaches to conflict resolution but has also been accompanied by a resurgence in ethnic violence and civil wars;

- The growing tendency to elect governments democratically has provided an opportunity for expression of political preferences and changes in leadership through the ballot box;

- The use of market mechanisms to direct economic behaviour has provided opportunities for economic growth but has also favoured short-term over longer-term economic priorities;

- The increase in global economic interdependence has provided new opportunities for economic growth but has also underscored the vulnerability of States that are carrying heavy burdens of international debt and reduced their ability to compete given the low levels of technology available to them;

- Structural adjustment policies have helped to stabilize the global financial situation but have also reduced the capacity of governments in many countries to provide essential services;

- Successive international conferences have underscored the need for sustainable approaches to development, the universality of fundamental human rights and the critical role of the advancement of women for achieving global objectives in population and development;

- The revolution in communications technology has opened the world to an exchange of ideas and narrowed the distances between countries and cultures.

The growing burden of poverty on women

Poverty has a significant gender dimension. Specifically:

- Poverty among women is directly related to their lack of rights and access to institutional resources and, increasingly, to displacement due to armed conflict or migration for economic reasons;

- The number of women living in poverty throughout the world is growing disproportionately, particularly in countries which are themselves poor;

- The greatest poverty is found in households where women, with their dependants, are the sole income-earners;

- When women obtain the economic means and a conducive environment, they will act on their own to bring themselves out of poverty;

- Targeting anti-poverty interventions on women has a greater impact than traditional approaches to poverty reduction.

Inequality in access to education and training

The situation of education and training can be described as follows:

- Illiteracy rates have been declining for both men and women in most regions as an increasing proportion of young people obtain at least primary education. But among adults, illiteracy is disproportionately high among women;

- Equal access to education has been achieved in some regions, but in others, especially sub-Saharan Africa and South Asia, the lack of adequate schooling facilities, high direct and indirect costs, customary attitudes, early marriages and pregnancies, inadequate teaching and educational materials, poorly qualified teachers and inappropriate curricula impede the education of girls and women;

- Although more women are enrolling in fields once dominated by men, the majority of female students at secondary and higher levels remain clustered in traditional fields of study;

- The successful completion of secondary and higher levels of education is not sufficient to prepare women to enter the labour market, and technical and vocational training for jobs that offer career prospects are lacking.

- While the percentage of female teachers is high at the primary level, women are generally underrepresented in the higher-status and higher paying categories and are generally absent from educational decision-making.

Inequality in access to health

- While many countries have made significant advances in primary health care, general and maternal health care and treatment of complications from pregnancy and childbirth is still very inadequate. The morbidity and mortality rates of women due to reproductive health related causes remain unnecessarily high in many areas of the globe, as do early and too frequent pregnancies. Of the 150-200 million pregnancies that occur each year, about 23 million involve serious complications; half a million end with the loss of the mother;

- HIV/AIDS is increasing among women at a high rate owing to the difficulties they face as a result of their lower status, economic situation and lack of information;

- Life expectancy for women has increased by eight years since 1970 in low and middle income countries and by five years worldwide, a gain less than that enjoyed by men. Between 1990 and 2015, the number of women over the age of 65 will increase from 330 million to 600 million. Reporting on health conditions of the elderly female population is still scanty, especially in the developing countries.

Violence against women

Violence against women has become a major concern everywhere. All national reports on the implementation of the Nairobi Forward-looking Strategies, all regional appraisals and all regional conferences have underscored the importance of dealing with the issue as a matter of health and human rights. Specifically:

- While there are no reliable indicators of its incidence or of changing trends, violence against women is pervasive in all societies, cutting across boundaries of class, ethnicity, religion, age and a society's level of development;

- Greater priority is being given to the problem of violence, and an increasing number of countries have modified their laws to make violence against women in the family a crime with appropriate sanctions;

- Many countries have organized or supported campaigns against domestic violence. Most have set up or supported shelters and other programmes for women who have been victims of violence;

- Increasing international attention is being given to the problem, as reflected in the Declaration on the Elimination of Violence against Women and in the appointment of a Special Rapporteur on violence against women.

Effects of armed or other kinds of conflict on women
Political changes at the end of the 1980s have led to an increase in armed conflict, and in the number of women who are affected by it. Specifically:

- Women continue to be almost completely absent from decision-making on issues related to armed conflict, and from peace-keeping and international conflict resolution. Women, through non-governmental organizations, are only beginning to address the new issues of peace and security and to demand participation in peace negotiations;

- Women are among the main victims of armed conflict and have become refugees, single heads of household and victims of displacement, family disintegration and war-related violence to a scale unknown in recent times;

- Rape and other types of abuse have increasingly been used as "weapons" to humiliate adversaries;

- Measures have been taken at national and international levels to assist women victims of war and women refugees, to assess their needs and to address them through humanitarian assistance, educational programmes, health care, social support policies, self-help and self-reliance schemes.

*Inequality in women's access to and participation in the definition of
economic structures and policies and the productive process itself*

During the past decade women's participation in the economically active population doubled. They have become the workers of choice in many growth industries, and have begun to dominate small- and medium-scale enterprise development. However, they are not yet well represented in economic decision-making in large public or private corporate structures or in national economic policy formulation and programme development, including budgetary processes and resource allocation. Specifically:

- Women tend to be segregated in certain occupations and their average remuneration remains lower than men's;

- Women working in growth sectors continue to experience low wages and precarious conditions, despite their importance in the labour force;

- Women face a "glass ceiling" and even "glass walls" in their efforts to rise to decision-making levels in government and large corporate structures, largely due to the dominant male culture in these organizations and subtle discrimination in hiring and career development;

- Women are emerging as entrepreneurs in the market but face restrictions in obtaining financial resources. They have less access than men to ownership and support services, when those exist, or to training, technology, information and marketing.

*Inequality between men and women in the sharing of power and
decision-making at all levels*

Despite increasing democratization and access to education and employment, women have made little progress in attaining political power in legislative bodies or government and in achieving the "critical mass" target of 30 per cent. Specifically:

- Women constitute only 10 per cent of parliamentary membership and a lower percentage hold ministerial and subministerial positions in government. This is true of almost all regions, except the Nordic countries;

- Women are still not put up as candidates for public office. National and international civil services still maintain barriers to women's advancement;

- Few positive measures, have been taken to remove barriers to women's participation, in the political process.

Insufficient mechanisms at all levels to promote
the advancement of women

Since the United Nations Decade for Women, national machineries have been established in most States, although there is little evidence that they have grown in strength, location or influence. Specifically:

- The political will to integrate women's concerns in all aspects of public action is still lacking;

- Most national machinery for the advancement of women not politically influential and is not mandated to deal with the integration of women's concerns throughout government;

- Resource levels and staffing are usually inadequate and links with non-governmental organizations are often weak;

- There is a general lack of statistical information disaggregated by sex, as well as gender-sensitive appraisals of policy or programme impact.

Lack of awareness of, and commitment to, internationally
and nationally recognized women's human rights

Most reports show an acceptance that women's human rights are universal and indivisible and most States have become party to the Convention on the Elimination of All Forms of Discrimination against Women, but much remains to be done to enable women to enjoy their rights. Specifically:

- Clear-cut guarantees against sex-based discrimination are often absent in national constitutions or fundamental laws or are undermined by the absence of implementation mechanisms or by the persistence of negative customary norms and practices that subordinate women;

- Mechanisms to enforce rights are often absent or are difficult for women to access;

- Despite an increase in information campaigns about women's human rights, there continues to be a lack of awareness about them;

Schools have not made a sufficient effort to teach respect for human rights–women's human rights, in particular. Awareness and respect for equality between the sexes are not being adequately fostered among students.

Insufficient use of mass media to promote women's
positive contributions to society

While the mass media have undergone a technological revolution over the last decade, with significant improvements in overall access to all forms of media, little has changed in the relationship of women to the media. Reports show the following:

- The dominant images of women in the mass media worldwide remain stereotypical and unrepresentative;

- Although the share of women's employment in all forms of media organizations worldwide has increased, women are still clustered in administrative and clerical jobs rather than in decision-making; positions. Given the situation of the mass media since the third conference on women, there has been a steady growth of women's alternative media and networks. They have been effectively used by non-governmental organizations and women's groups to raise social and political consciousness among women and members of the society in general;

- National television and radio have been successfully used in many developing countries to campaign for women's literacy, immunization of children and women's health concerns, and against harmful traditional social practices and violence against women. The media could also be used to transform the traditional images of women.

Lack of adequate recognition and support for women's contribution to
managing natural resources and safeguarding the environment

There is growing recognition that women are affected in specific ways by environmental degradation and that women's practical knowledge of the environmental should be used more effectively. However, reports show that:

- Few efforts have been made to reverse women's underrepresentation in formal government institutions that deal directly with environmental issues;

- There is a lack of coordination between women's non-governmental organization and the national institutions dealing with environmental issues;

- Women lack access to the resources necessary to allow them to maximize their traditional skills and knowledge in managing the environment;

- Poverty, linked with a deteriorated natural environment is having an increasingly negative health impact on women and girls, especially among displaced populations, farm workers, rural women and those living in remote areas under ecologically harsh conditions.

International Action

The organizations of the United Nations system have taken action to implement the Nairobi Forward-looking Strategies create an infrastructure that can assist in mainstreaming women's concerns. However, the structure is too fragile in terms of location, resources and coordination to ensure success. An examination of the work of the organizations of the United Nations system shows that:

- The Commission on the Status of Women has implemented its renewed mandate by analysing priority themes and by developing a new international instrument, the Declaration on the Elimination of Violence against Women;

- Other subsidiary bodies of the Economic and Social Council, especially the Commission on Human Rights, have begun to mainstream gender concerns in their work;

- The Committee on the Elimination of Discrimination against Women has continued to develop its work, and other human rights treaty bodies are beginning to include gender concerns in their review of reports of States parties;

- The specialized agencies have improved both intergovernmental and secretariat structures in order to take gender concerns into account, some by upgrading units, others by creating new units;

- While most organizations of the United Nations system have established targets for increasing the proportion of women in their secretariats, and while the proportion of women has increased since 1985, most organizations are far from achieving their targets, especially at decision-making levels;

- The United Nations has made considerable progress in the research and policy analysis called for in the Strategies, especially in terms of gender statistics and economic and political analysis;

- Organizations such as the United Nations Development Fund for Women (UNIFEM), the United Nations Development Programme (UNDP), the United Nations Population Fund (UNFPA), the United Nations Children's Fund (UNICEF), the International Research and Training Institute for the Advancement of Women (INSTRAW), the World Food Programme (WFP), the Food and Agriculture Organization of the United Nations, (FAO), and the United Nations Industrial DevelopmentOrganization (UNIDO) have developed new and innovative approaches to reaching women through their operational activities;

- Financial assistance through the World Bank, the International Fund for Agricultural Development (IFAD) and the International Monetary Fund (IMF) has begun to target women;

- An effective, if ad hoc, coordination mechanisms has been established, anchored in a system-wide medium-term plan for the advancement of women and regular meetings of focal points on women in the United Nations system.

Introduction

.

1.   By its resolution 36/8 on the preparations for the Fourth World Conference on Women: Action for Equality, Development and Peace, the Commission on the Status of Women decided that the agenda for the Fourth World Conference on Women shall include the second review and appraisal of the implementation of the Nairobi Forward-looking Strategies for the Advancement of Women. The Commission requested the Secretary-General to submit to the Commission, at its thirty-seventh session, a report containing information on data that would be used in the formulation of the second report on the implementation of the Strategies and an outline of the second report, in which special emphasis should be given to the recommendations and conclusions arising from the first review and appraisal - particularly those referring to the condition of women in developing countries - contained in the annex to Council resolution 1990/15.

2.   In its resolution 45/129, the General Assembly urged Governments, international organizations and non-governmental organizations to implement the recommendations and conclusions. It also reaffirmed paragraph 2, on the improvement of the pace of implementation of the Strategies in the crucial last decade of the twentieth century. It stated that the cost of failing to implement the Strategies would be high in terms of slowed economic and social development, misuse of human resources and reduced progress for society as a whole and, for that reason, that immediate steps should be taken to remove the most serious obstacles to the implementation of the Strategies.

3.   The Economic and Social Council acknowledged the obstacles encountered in the preparation of the first review and appraisal, in particular the inadequate response to the questionnaire sent out to all member

States. By its resolution 1990/9 of 24 May 1990, the Economic and Social Council requested that the second review and appraisal should be based on national reports and available analysis of statistical data in the United Nations system and in other pertinent governmental and non-governmental organizations. As stated in the report of the Secretary-General on the preparations for the Fourth World Conference on Women: Action for Equality, Development and Peace, 1/ the preparatory process should be utilized to develop new and innovative approaches to statistics, to be ultimately reflected in the review and appraisal, which should compare women with men and show changes occurring over time.

4.   At its thirty-seventh session, the Commission considered a report by the Secretary-General on the second review and appraisal. In its resolution 37/7, the Commission urged Governments to initiate preparations for their national reports as soon as possible and to ensure that they were submitted to the regional conferences in time to serve as contributions to the regional reviews and appraisals and to the Conference secretariat in time to serve as contributions to the global review and appraisal. It recommended that at all levels the review and appraisal focus on priorities of Governments and highlight the critical areas of concern identified in the structure of the platform for action. It requested the secretariat to prepare a list of the most significant indicators on the basis of the critical areas of concern identified in the structure of the platform for action, taking into account the availability of reliable national statistics, and to circulate the list to national committees and focal points to initiate and promote preparations for the Fourth World Conference. It also requested the secretariat to use the necessary machinery to include the results of the regional conferences in the second report on the review and appraisal.

5.   As requested, the Secretary-General of the Conference circulated, in a note verbale, a model structure for national reports, including the list of indicators. (See annex I.)

6.   The second review and appraisal, also as requested, has been prepared on the basis of information contained in national reports, the results of the regional conferences and information provided by specialized agencies of the United Nations system. It draws heavily on gender statistics

assembled by the Statistical Division of the Department for Economic and Social Information and Policy Analysis, in Women's Indicators and Statistics Database (WISTAT), version 3. 2/ It has made use of information provided by other governmental and non-governmental organizations. A first draft of the document was circulated to all organizations of the United Nations system for comments in their respective areas of competence.

7.   As mandated by the Commission at its thirty-eighth session, the review and appraisal is structured around the platform for action. It should be seen as the factual support for the conclusions and recommendations found in the platform.

8.   Chapter III of the review and appraisal follows the general structure of part V of the Nairobi Forward-looking Strategies for the Advancement of Women and reviews international action.

9.   The review and appraisal has been able to make use of the 130 national reports that were received by the Conference secretariat by 1 December 1994. The table below shows the distribution of reports by region.

Table. National reports received and used in the review and appraisal

Region	Number
Africa	41
Asia and the Pacific	20
Latin America and the Caribbean	29
Western Asia	9
Western Europe and Other	31

Notes

1/   "Preparations for the Fourth World Conference on Women: Action for Equality, Development and Peace" (E/CN.6/1992/3).

2/   The development of WISTAT was made possible by support from the United Nations Population Fund. The statistics are being made available to the Conference in the update of *The World's Women: Trends and Statistics.*

I.
Overview of the Global Economic and Social Framework

1.   Since the adoption in 1985 of the Nairobi Forward-looking Strategies for the Advancement of Women, 1/ the world has experienced far-reaching economic, political and social changes. In response to the economic crisis of the 1980s, greater emphasis was placed on policies of structural adjustment, economic liberalization and improved governance. These policies, together with the expansion of the world trade and international financial markets and with rapid technological innovation, strengthened long-term trends towards globalization, integration of markets and internationalization of production. As a consequence of these trends, the world economy became more interdependent and thus more vulnerable to economic and political upheavals as national economic policies acquired widespread international ramifications. Together, these changes led to economic restructuring that has shaped the development process in recent years and has had a significant impact - both positive and negative - on women's participation in development and on their economic, political and social status.

2.   Perceptions of the meaning, causes and conditions of development have been significantly modified. The development debate now emphasizes sustainability and human-centred and gender-responsive development. In parallel with the evolution of the development debate there have been changes in the perception and content of what are known as Women in

Development issues. The role of women in development is no longer perceived as almost exclusively linked with broad issues of public health and population policies such as nutrition, child-rearing and family planning; women are now recognized as agents of change, as an economic force in themselves and as a valuable resource without which progress in development would be limited. While there have been many global changes over the past decade, the most dramatic for the lives of most individual women have been the changes in the economy.

3.   A number of shifts in economic activity have come to be understood as resulting from the interaction between the allocation by women of their time and incomes and economic variables that include prices, consumption patterns and production techniques. Women's actions in the economic sphere have come to be viewed as actively shaping economic development and not merely being influenced by it. Consequently, within the Women in Development agenda there has been a shift towards greater emphasis on economic growth, sound economic policies and productive employment as the areas of prime concern for the economic advancement of women.

4.   More often than not, the economic reforms of the past decade were part of something larger than the simple restructuring of an economic domain. In many developing economies and economies in transition, economic reforms were part of a movement towards greater democracy, freedom and human rights. Precipitated to some extent by failures in economic development caused by extensive governmental intervention in resource allocation and production decision-making, the rapid process of democratization led to new opportunities as well as to new obstacles for women's advancement.

5.   While providing genuine opportunities for women in transitional and developing economies to participate in the political, economic and social life of their societies on an equal footing with men, democratization unleashed a variety of competitive claims on economic resources and on the political agenda by different political, ethnic, cultural and religious groups. The absence of democratic institutions and the other elements of civil society that serve to separate conflicting interests and turn the power struggle into a truly democratic process for all led, at least initially, to the marginal-

ization of vulnerable groups that lacked a sufficient economic and political power base.

6.   These changes have been found in all regions but have been particularly marked in terms of the situation of women in Eastern Europe, the Commonwealth of Independent States the Baltic States and other transitional States whose economies have deteriorated, especially in terms of ability to influence the process of economic and political decision-making. There, the general absence of the necessary civil institutions, an effective women's movement and of formal women's organizations capable of articulating women's interests and fighting for them in the competitive free-market environment led, at least during the first years of reform, to the exclusion of women from full participation in economic and political decision-making and to a loss of equality in terms of economic opportunities and advancement.

7.   Changes in the work and lives of women all over the world are intricately related to changes in the global economic, social and political environment and to policy responses made within that framework. The traditional division of labour, differential access to factors of production and differences in the consumption patterns of men and women cause apparently gender-neutral policies to have a gender-specific outcome. Numerous studies show that the short-term costs of adjustment and stabilization are often distributed disproportionately so that women come to bear a greater share of the burden. On the other hand, there is evidence of a strong relationship between economic growth and the economic advancement of women. 2/ International economic conditions therefore form a backdrop against which the progress made in the implementation of the Nairobi Forward-looking Strategies for the Advancement of Women should be assessed.

A. Trends in the global economy and in economic restructuring as they relate to the advancement of women

8.   Three interrelated sets of phenomena have shaped the world economy in the recent past and will continue to do so in the foreseeable future. They include:

(a)   The various responses to the economic and political crisis of the 1980s (structural adjustment in developing countries, industrial restructuring and the change of emphasis in macroeconomic policy-making in the developed market economies and economic and political transition in the economies in the former USSR and Eastern Europe);

(b)   Rapid technological innovation and its implications for the organization of work and for income distribution;

(c)   Growing economic interdependence and globalization of markets and production.

Together, these phenomena comprised what was termed a process of economic restructuring. This process affected women's socio-economic position in a complex and multidimensional way, causing changes in the level, patterns and conditions of female employment and modifying women's social roles.

1. Developing countries: structural adjustment and its impact on women

9.   The world recession profoundly affected the majority of developing countries, particularly in Africa, Latin America and the Caribbean, and the Middle East. Those in Asia as a whole proved more resilient, though here,

too, individual countries, such as the Philippines, were adversely affected by external shocks and global developments. Reduced demand for primary products, falling commodity prices, high and rising interest rates, the virtual disappearance after 1982 of private bank lending, and, in the case of the Middle East, the collapse of the regional oil economy in the mid-1980s all contributed to a steady worsening of the balance of payments and the virtual doubling of the external debt burden in the period 1983-1993. For the most part, the response of the developing countries has been to institute programmes of stabilization and structural adjustment designed to bring their economies into line with the new realities of the international marketplace and undertaken, more often than not, under the auspices of the international financial institutions.

10.   In the past decade a large number of developing countries went through the experience of structural adjustment. In fact, the decade came to be known as the "decade of structural adjustment" as the World Bank made 59 adjustment loans between 1980 and 1988 3/ to assist countries with protracted balance-of-payments problems to stabilize their economies and correct distortions causing inefficiency. Policies were thus directed towards allocative efficiency, international competitiveness, market deregulation, "getting prices right", reduction of budget deficits and control of inflation. In the developing countries these policies were employed within the context of structural adjustment, which came to be viewed not only as a response to economic disequilibria but also as a prerequisite for long-term sustainable development. The divergence in economic performance among regions at the end of the decade reflected the varied experience of structural adjustment programmes. In some countries, the reform programme resulted in the resumption of growth, while in others political tensions and the erosion of human capital have hampered growth and decreased the production base. In recent years, some critics have argued that structural adjustment policies have not incorporated country- and gender-specific issues sufficiently.

11.   While structural adjustment policies have been gender-neutral in design and implementation, it is now widely recognized that the social and economic inequalities of women in many countries have rendered them specially vulnerable to the effects of structural adjustment. However, this

recognition has yet to be translated into gender-sensitive development planning. Methodological and theoretical difficulties, together with a lack of proper gender-disaggregated time-series data on the impact on women of structural adjustment, preclude any in-depth empirical assessment of the gender-related aspects. A significant body of analysis nevertheless exists and is based on inferences from the effects of economic policies on main macroeconomic aggregates and a priori knowledge of differences in the ways women and men allocate their labour and income and of differences in their access to productive resources and public services. The uneven distribution of the short-term costs of structural adjustment between men and women is particularly evident with respect to decline in real income, loss of employment opportunities, deterioration of employment conditions and exacerbation of pressures related to reproduction and maintenance of human resources in the context of lagged supply response, rising prices and cut-offs in public expenditure.

12.   The structural adjustment policies of the 1980s lacked gender awareness both at the conceptual level and in implementation. The underlying macroeconomic model did not take account of the fact that women are often unable to respond adequately to the opportunities presented in the context of expenditure-switching policies and to changes in relative prices and the incentives resulting from them for the reallocation of resources, because of persisting inequalities in gender relations and constraints posed by the sexual division of labour. Some analysts suggest that the social costs of adjustment have been shifted from the State to the household and to women in the household. As a result, structural adjustment policies in the 1980s were less efficient in the reallocation of female than of male labour, and less sustainable than they could have been if gender issues were taken into account. Economic development theory and planning have not yet addressed this problem fully.

13.   However, should the emphasis on human investment that is being written into the third generation of structural adjustment packages continue, women could benefit from this new departure. 4/ This however, requires a conscious effort on the part of national and international policy makers to write a gender dimension into all projects and programmes, as much at the formulation stage as at the implementation level.

(a)   Latin America and the Caribbean

14.   Structural adjustment has been particularly intense in the economies of Latin America, where external indebtedness aggravated by falling commodity prices and increased interest rates caused a deep recession throughout the 1980s. The average annual growth rate of GDP in Latin America and the Caribbean in the 1980s was only 1 per cent as against 5.5 per cent in the 1970s. 5/ The decade was indeed "lost" for development as the annual average change in per capita GDP reached -0.1 per cent after having been at 2.0 per cent during the preceding decade 6/ (table 1). These changes were accompanied by worsening of income distribution which is now more inequitable in Latin America and the Caribbean than anywhere else in the world. 7/

15.   In the Latin American region, the adjustment process was both recessionary and regressive, and this was reflected above all in real wages and in employment. Thus, serious problems and difficulties remain, most obviously in the form of persistently high rates of poverty, the inequitable income distribution and, quite often, a deterioration in the provision of social services, which not only renders current democratic processes fragile, but also calls into question the sustainability and indeed the very nature of the economic recovery so far achieved. In addition, only a handful of countries have managed to fully consolidate the adjustment and stabilization policies undertaken, and the process is marked by many interruptions. 8/

Table 1. Growth of world output and per capita GDP, 1971-1994 (annual average percentage changes)

	Growth of GDP						Growth of real GDP (annual rates) per capita (annual percentage change)	
	1971-1980	1981-1990	1991	1992	1993	1994	1974-1983	1984-1993
World	3.9	2.9	0.3	0.8	1.1	2.5		
Developed market economies	3.1	2.6	0.7	1.6	1.0	2.5	2.3	2.1
Economies in transition	5.2	2.5	-9.0	-16.8	-10.0	-6.0	..	-2.9
Developing economies	5.6	3.2	3.4	4.9	5.2	5.0	1.8	1.9
Latin America and Caribbean	5.5	1.0	2.8	2.1	3.3	2.7	0.9	0.5
Africa	4.9	0.5	1.6	0.9	1.7	2.2	0.7	-1.1
West Asia	6.5	-0.2	-0.2	5.7	3.5	3.5	-1.8	-2.9
South and East Asia	5.8	7.0	5.3	5.2	5.4	6.2	3.5	3.8
China	5.9	9.0	8.0	13.2	13.4	10.0	4.9	8.4
Mediterranean	5.3	3.2	-5.6	-1.9	-0.3	4.0	2.2	-0.9

Source: World Economic Survey, 1990 and 1993 (United Nations publications, Sales Nos. E.90.II.C.1 and E.91.II.C.1); World Economic and Social Survey, 1994 (United Nations publication, Sales No. E.94.II.C.1). Forecast is based on Project LINK. Estimates are rounded to the nearest half percentage point. Growth of world output, 1971-1994, and per capita GDP, by country groups.

16.   The impact of the debt problem and the structural adjustment programmes has been especially severe in the Caribbean countries, with direct
consequences for women's unpaid work, migration, human rights violations, domestic violence, sexual exploitation and availability of and access to
health services. As for the particular case of Haiti, it was said that the difficulties were so extreme that they went beyond the parameters of the situation in the rest of Latin America and the Caribbean. 9/

17.   The growth of the informal sector was the main variable in the read-
justment of the Latin American labour market in the early 1980s. The rise in
unemployment and informality was accompanied by massive declines in
wage and a sharp rise in the precariousness of employment. Temporary and
part-time work became increasingly widespread, while the overall quality of
employment declined. Aside from the difficulty of measuring female participation in the informal and precarious sector, it can be said that the poorest
women workers are to be found in the urban informal sector and that, if
domestic employment is added, women's participation is above 70 per cent
in most cases. Information on some countries of the region, based on household surveys, shows that women account for between 8 per cent (Panama)
and 64 per cent (Cochabamba, Bolivia) of the informal sector workforce. 10/

(b)   Sub-Saharan Africa

18.   In Africa, particularly sub-Saharan Africa, economic conditions
remain bleak, despite some modest improvement in current growth.
Economic decline hit bottom in the mid-1980s when even nominal GDP
growth rates turned negative. 11/ Out of the region's 45 countries, 28 suffered a decline in real GDP per capita. The decade of 1990s started with a
minor improvement as growth in 1993 picked up to 1.7 per cent, which is
still, however, well below the average annual population growth rate of 2.9
per cent for the period of 1985-1990. There has also been some modest
improvement in sub-Saharan Africa's terms of trade, which suffered a
decline during the 1980s and the early 1990s.

Table 2. Sub-Saharan Africa: selected economic and development indicators, 1980 and 1990

	1980	1990	Percentage change
Per capita GNP	582	335	-42.4
Per capita consumption	465	279	-40.0
Investment (percentage of GDP)	20.2	14.2	-29.7
Exports of goods	54.9	38.5	-29.9
Total external debt	56.2	146.9	161.4
Per capital food production index	107	94	-12.1
Memo item: Women in labour force	39.3	37.6	-4.3

Source: African Development Indicators (Washington, D.C., World Bank, 1992).

19.   Poverty and deprivation in sub-Saharan Africa continue to deepen. A regional classification by integrated poverty index 12/ reveals that 36 out of the 45 countries in sub-Saharan Africa were in the severe poverty group. 13/ The situation has been aggravated by civil conflicts, 14/ which have destroyed physical capital, institutions and infrastructure in at least eight countries. 15/ To make matters worse, the region has been hit hard by the AIDS epidemic, which is inflicting high costs on the economy and society through its adverse effects on productivity and savings. Africa is home to 50 per cent of all HIV-infected people and the proportion of women among AIDS victims in Africa is larger than in North America and Europe and continues to grow. 16/

20.   Despite the resumption in the early 1990s of the inflow of capital to developing economies, Africa remains excluded from access to international financial resources. In conjunction with the terms-of-trade decline, the persistently negative net financial resources transfer to Africa led to a significant worsening of external balances in African and particularly sub-Saharan economies. In addition, official development assistance may not be as forthcoming as it was in the 1980s because of greater demands on it around the world and the shrinking supply of resources. There is therefore a considerable risk that the inflow of resources to the African region will be inadequate in comparison to its development needs and the restoration of economic stability. This will of course, have serious consequences for investment and growth in the region.   .

21.   General economic decline, deindustrialization and political instability in Africa have inhibited the implementation of the Nairobi Forward-looking Strategies in that region. Government expenditure cuts have led to widespread layoffs in public-sector enterprises. Employment in the private sector is also in decline as a result of aggregate demand deflation caused by stabilization and adjustment policies. The urban unemployment rate is currently between 15 and 20 per cent, up from 10 per cent in the 1970s. Women, although a minority in the public sector, 17/ appear to have fared worse than men as a result of public sector retrenchment. In Benin, for example, women's share in parastatal employment was only 6 per cent, but their share among workers laid off was 21 per cent. 18/

22.   Women in Africa have long been concentrated in the informal sector in such activities as petty trade, small-scale production and personal services. Despite the widespread perception of the informal sector as infinitely elastic with respect to the absorption of female labour, recent figures indicate the opposite. Table 3 shows that the percentage share of women in the informal sector in selected sub-Saharan African countries declined between 1985 and 1990. In 1990 the share of women in the informal sector in these countries was lower than it had been in the 1970s in all but two countries. That the female share of informal-sector employment declined despite the increase in the supply of female labour brought about by the "added worker" 19/ effect of structural adjustment indicates that women may have encountered difficulties in entering the sector that had traditionally provided

them with income-earning opportunities. One explanation might be competition from the men who lost their jobs in the public sector as a result of structural adjustment policies. In most African countries men predominate in public-sector employment and consequently constitute the majority of redundant workers when public expenditures are contracted under policies of structural adjustment. They are better equipped with capital and business contacts, and their entry into the sector may have driven women's businesses out. On the other hand, informal-sector employment is by definition very difficult to measure. Given the low unemployment figures for women in the region and the fact that poor women in Africa simply cannot afford to be unemployed, the declining rates of informal-sector participation may mean greater precariousness for sources of women's income as they resort to informal survival responses at times of economic hardship.

23. The most likely explanation of the declining share of women in the informal sector, however, is the overall economic decline of sub-Saharan Africa. Reduction in real income and contraction of aggregate demand has caused a decline in demand for informal-sector goods and services. The shortage of investable funds and the high cost of credit have not been conducive to the sector's expansion and are likely to drive a number of informal entrepreneurs out of business. Poor access to credit and labour crowding have made women entrepreneurs particularly vulnerable to the decline in informal-sector earnings and loss of business. Despite the limited counteracting influence of the substitution effect (i.e., the increase in demand for the cheaper goods and services of the informal sector owing to the downward pressure on income), the information available (table 3) seems to suggest that the net effect on women's business in the informal sector was that of contraction.

Table 3. Female share of employment in the informal sector,
1970-1990

Country	1970	1980	1985	1990
Congo	26.7	26.9	26.8	24.6
Ghana	32.0	32.0	32.0	27.3
Guinea	31.9	32.0	32.0	26.8
Liberia	42.8	43.2	43.0	39.3
Madagascar	33.3	33.1	32.8	29.0
Kenya	31.3	31.0	31.1	36.7
Nigeria	29.8	30.0	30.0	25.9
Somalia	32.1	31.9	32.0	34.6
Togo	38.6	39.0	39.0	32.2
United Republic of Tanzania	0.3	30.0	30.0	28.4
Zaire	37.3	37.0	37.0	24.9

Source: African Employment Report (ILO, Geneva, 1990). Cited in S. Baden,
"The impact of recession and structural adjustment on women in developing
countries", ILO paper, December 1993.

(c)   Asia and the Pacific

24.   During the recession of the 1980s and early 1990s, the economies of
East Asia as a whole proved relatively more resilient to the worsening of the
external economic environment largely because of greater outward orientation of economic policies and greater diversification of the production base.
The economies of the region grew on average by 7 per cent annually during
the 1980s and have maintained over 5 per cent growth since the beginning
of the current decade. Economic performance has, however, varied from 1.7
per cent growth in the Philippines to 8 per cent growth in Malaysia,
Singapore, Thailand and Viet Nam. 20/ There has been a notable decline in
the dependency of economic growth in the region on the performance of the
developed market economies; as intraregional trade has been growing faster
than the total trade of these economies, the structure of their exports has
continued to veer towards manufactures and the inflow of external capital
has increased. The economies of East Asia are likely to remain the fastest

growing in the 1990s, but rates of growth are expected to slow down as they begin to run into infrastructure and environmental constraints.

25.   The South Asian economies grew on average by 5 per cent annually during the 1980s. Unlike growth in the rest of the developing world, this was an improvement over the proceeding decade. Faced with external financial crises, major economies in the region embarked on structural adjustment and stabilization policies. Future prospects for growth depend on the maintenance and consistency of these reforms. The inward looking import-substitution policies followed by the economies of the region for decades led to the inhibition of factor-market flexibility and, in some cases, to the loss of economic stability. The region continues to be home to the majority of the world's poor. In 1990 the proportion of the population of South Asia whose income and consumption fell below the nationally defined poverty line was 49 per cent. 21/ Most of the region's poor are concentrated in the rural areas, and poverty among women is on the rise. 22/

26.   In the 1980s widespread poverty and unemployment 23/ in the countries of South and South-East Asia prompted a flow of international migration from the region to the capital-exporting economies of Western Asia. A significant number of women from Indonesia, Malaysia, the Philippines, Sri Lanka, India, Bangladesh and Thailand became temporary migrant workers in the Western Asia region. In Kuwait, for example, 103,501 migrant women were employed as domestic workers in 1989, constituting 5.1 per cent of the population of the country. In Saudi Arabia, there were 219,000 non-Saudi Asian female workers in 1986. 24/ However, the collapse of the oil economy, the Gulf crisis of early 1991 and the eight years of the Iran-Iraq war led to a decline of capital surplus in the region. In some cases capital surplus disappeared completely and some countries had to turn to international capital markets to borrow money to finance wars and later reconstruction efforts. The adverse economic and political circumstances in West Asia have caused a decline in opportunities for migrant women and men, thereby worsening the external payments position of the economies from which migration had originated.

27.   If only the quantitative aspect is considered, it is possible to say that Asian women have benefited from the economic success of the region. These

benefits are captured in the increase in labour force participation, sustained over the last two decades, in the increased access to education for girls at all levels, and in an increase in the ratio of women's to men's earnings, as income accruing to women through productive employment has increased.

Table 4. Advancement of women in Asia and the Pacific: selected indicators, 1970-1990

	1970	1980	1990
Education a/			
First level	66.00	78.00	84.00
Second level	58.00	70.00	77.00
Third level	46.00	63.00	84.00
Science and technology b/	33.00	45.00	70.00
Economic activity c/	28.00	42.00	48.00
Employment in professional, technical, administrative and management fields	27.00	47.00	55.00
Wage ratio d/			
Agriculture	74.00	78.00	79.00
Manufacturing	72.00	60.00	64.83

Source: WISTAT, version 3, 1994.
a/   Average ratio of girls to boys in enrolment in schools
(number of girls per 100 boys).
b/   Average ratio of girls to boys in science and technology fields at third level of education.
c/   Average ratio of women to men in the economically active population (number of women per 100 men).
d/   Percentages.

28.   Examined from a gender perspective, the development experience of the East and South-East Asian economies suggests that female advancement is directly related to policies of external openness and export promotion and inversely related to policies of import substitution and protectionism. However, the fact that female employment expansion took place in these

economies in the context of comparative advantage in labour-intensive production should not be overlooked. As countries climb the "ladder of comparative advantage", there is constant pressure to upgrade production and modify micro- and macroeconomic management so as to take account of changes in economic structure and relative prices. In terms of the future of female employment in export-oriented industries in the economies where development in the last two decade has been driven by export expansion, the need for technological upgrading translates into the need for skills acquisition and better education and qualifications for female workers. Otherwise the benefits accruing to women thus far from export-led development will simply vanish with growth. Recent evidence suggests that the share of female labour in export-oriented industries is declining as skill requirements in export industries shift with shifts in comparative advantage. This, together with evidence of poor access for women to retraining, indicates that the gains to women's employment from the expansion of export-oriented industries might have been a short-lived phenomenon. 25/

29.   The emergence of China as a major growth pole and trading power in the region should serve as a catalyst of economic growth and intraregional trade. It should also pose significant competition for already established exporters of labour-intensive manufactures in and outside the region. China's index of comparative advantage correlates significantly with that of four other large developing countries - Egypt, India, Indonesia and Turkey. 15/ Arguably, China's growing exports present a threat to female employment in such industries as electronics, toys, textiles and apparel in the first generation newly industrializing countries where the eventual tightening of the labour market and rising labour costs pushed real wages up. However, economic history shows that, as far as female aggregate employment is concerned, shifts in comparative advantage do not always result in winners and losers. Owing to a strong upward trend in female employment in the non-tradable service sector, women's aggregate employment in the industrialized market economies continues to grow despite increasing cost competitiveness of the developing economies.

30.   The outlook for the developing countries as a whole in the 1990s is considerably brighter than in the previous decade. One indicator of improved growth is the net transfer of financial resources, and this reached

$54 billion in 1993, an amount not seen since the early 1980s. 20/ After years of lost access to foreign credit and of capital flight, the Latin American economies emerged from the depths of the debt crisis as "emerging markets" attracting a considerable inflow of financial resources from the beginning of the 1990s. After almost a decade of being negative figures, net financial transfers to the region reached US$ 12 billion in 1992 and are estimated at almost US$ 19 billion for 1993. The inflow of foreign direct investment and greater access for the economies in question to international credit markets are largely attributed to the success of the Brady Plan in reducing the face value of their commercial debt and to comprehensive macro- and micro-economic reforms that improved their competitiveness and creditworthiness. 26/

31.   The inflow of foreign capital to developing countries creates new jobs and increases the demand for labour, including that of women. Given progress in economic reforms and political stability, the inflow of foreign capital can expand employment opportunities for women in developing countries and thus foster their economic advancement. It should be noted, however, that the conditions underlying competitiveness are changing and are coming to rely less on natural assets like cheap labour and more on created assets in the form of knowledge and skills. Emerging patterns of flows and stocks of foreign direct investment reveal that such assets have become the main determinant of foreign direct investment location. In view of women's poorer educational level - or rather its less appropriate orientation, given modern needs - women in developing countries are less likely to benefit from the inflows of foreign direct investment and the expansion of the export industries associated with it.

2. Economies in transition: 27/ economic and political restructuring and its impact on women

32.   While the former centrally planned economies of Central and Eastern Europe and the Soviet Union were sheltered to some extent from the global economic crisis of the early 1980s by an autarchic trade and production regime, towards the end of the decade they too experienced a decline in economic performance that was caused by a tightening of the resource constraint on extensive growth, the inability to sustain growth through technological progress, severe monetary disequilibria, and attempts at economic

reform in the context of structural rigidities and distortions. Since the end of the 1980s these countries have embarked on the road of transition to a market economy and this has proved to be costly in terms of real income and output decline, loss of employment and security, a rapid deterioration in social conditions and deepening gender inequalities.

33.   The fundamental changes in trading patterns that followed the disintegration of the Council on Mutual Economic Assistance (CMEA) and the internal payments system led to a rapid deterioration in the current account and to an accumulation of external debt. Lack of commitment to tight monetary policy and at times its political infeasibility fuelled inflation rates, which in some countries approached a dangerously high near-hyper-inflation level. In response to high inflation, some countries in the region embarked on "shock-therapy" macroeconomic stabilization. 28/ Where policy makers were able to conduct a consistent monetary policy, this approach worked although inflation still remained relatively high and the decline in output and income continued. Real wage decline took place in all the economies in transition, but its magnitude varied from about 12 to 15 per cent in Hungary and the Czech Republic to around 30 per cent in Poland. 29/

34.   The process of market building in economies in transition involves, *inter alia*, changes in property rights and ownership structures. 30/ Privatization in the transition economies varies in terms of its methods, speed and degree of success. Privatization methods include sales through local auctions, the distribution of privatization vouchers, the use of mutual funds and other financial intermediaries, and sometimes "spontaneous" privatization by the current management. If the privatization of small-scale enterprises, shops and restaurants has been relatively fast and painless, that of large-scale government-owned enterprises has involved many economic problems (such as the difficulty of making an adequate estimate of the market value of the enterprise to be privatized) and social problems (such as the displacement of workers and the loss of social benefits and job security). The emerging private economy covers a wide range of activities, from catering to commercial law; and it takes a variety of forms, from limited liability and joint stock companies to micro-enterprises and sole proprietorship.

Table 5. Rates of growth of GDP and external debt indicators a/ of economies in transition, 1983-1994

	1983-1988	1989	1990	1991	1992	1993	1994 b/
Economies in transition	3.4	2.1	-6.3	-9.0	-16.8	-8.6	-6.0
Eastern Europe	3.3	0.0	-11.8	-12.0	-6.2	0.8	2.2
Albania	-	-	-9.0	-29.4	-6.0	11.0	6.0
Bulgaria	3.7	-1.4	-9.1	-16.7	-13.0	-4.2	-0.5
Former Czechoslovakia	2.0	1.3	-4.7	-15.9	-7.2		
Czech Republic						-0.5	2.0
Slovakia						-4.7	0.0
German Democratic Republic	4.2	2.4	-25.1				
Hungary	1.9	3.8	-4.0	-11.9	-5.0	-2.0	0.0
Poland	4.2	0.2	-12.0	-7.6	0.0	4.0	4.2
Romania	2.4	-5.8	-7.4	-13.7	-15.0	1.0	1.2
Former Soviet Union and successor States	3.5	3.0	-4.0	-8.0	-20.0	-12.0	-9.2

External debt and debt indicators for economies in transition, 1983-1993 b/ (billions of dollars)

Former Soviet Union	27.1	53.9	59.8	67.5	78.7	86.1	
Eastern Europe	65.1	82.6	91.1	99.5	95.4	95.6	

Source: World Economic Survey, 1993 and 1994 (United Nations publications, Sales Nos. E.93.II.C.1 and E.94.II.C.1).
a/   Average growth rates and annual percentage changes.

35.   Privatization raises many complex issues with respect to its impact on the economic status of women. Generally speaking, it tends to increase their chances of being laid off and to worsen their conditions of employment. At the same time, it offers opportunities for higher incomes and for entrepreneurship. Although it is rather difficult to determine with certainty the direction of the impact of privatization on women in transitional economies because the process is still at an early stage and because gender-disaggregated data are lacking, it is possible to identify some early trends. It seems that, so far, privatization undertaken in the context of stabilization policies and slow institutional change has adversely affected women's economic position. Where restructuring is directed at increasing the profitability of privatized and commercialized enterprises, female clerical and administrative jobs tend to be cut before male production-line jobs because of perceptions of female labour as "expensive" owing to the associated social benefits and protective legislation enjoyed by women in the past, and of women as less efficient workers because of the burden of family responsibilities. Consequently, the privatization of large State firms had strong and immediate impact on female employment because of the large numbers of women employed by them in administrative and clerical positions. Because of the special protective measures that underpinned women's participation in the labour force in the past and because of a resurgence of traditional stereotypes of gender relations, women have had difficulty in securing their jobs in privatized firms, or getting new jobs after being laid off. An industrial establishment survey carried by ILO in East-Central Europe in 1990-1993 shows a marked tendency for managers to give pronounced preference in recruitment to men, even in previously "women-dominated" sectors. 31/

36.   In the course of privatization and cost/production restructuring, the sectoral distribution of female employment is changing. An ILO survey of Russian industry shows that, as privatized and commercialized State-owned enterprises undergo restructuring, there is a relatively small decline in the share of female employment in the declining sectors of heavy industry and an increase in the share of female employment in light, "feminized" industries like textiles, garments and food-processing. This trend points towards strengthening the already existing segregation of employment in industry, "which inevitably leads to a decline in their relative wages and benefits".

37.   As transition progresses, female employment dynamics are beginning to resemble those of industrialized market economies. Despite the advantageous position of women in the services sector at the beginning of reform, they seem to be unable to consolidate their advantage in this sector. As trade, banking, insurance and financial services become more profitable men move into these sectors in increasing numbers changing the employment ratio to their advantage. In Poland, for example, in the period 1989-1992 the employment share of women declined in trade, banking, insurance and community and social services, while that of men increased dramatically. Male employment in trade increased by 62 per cent and in banking and insurance by 80 per cent. Similar changes in the female and male shares of employment in trade, banking, insurance and financial services took place in the Czech Republic. There, thus, appears to be a clear tendency towards convergence of high employment shares of women (see table 6) in these branches with those much lower ones in industrialized market economies. The less profitable services like education, health and social care continue to be women-dominated and women's employment share in them is increasing.

Table 6. Share of women in the banking and insurance industries in selected economies in transition, 1993

Country	Women's share (percentage)
Azerbaijan a/	48.80
Belarus a/	88.10
Czech Republic	68.58
Georgia a/	75.50
Hungary b/	74.38
Kazakhstan a/	85.30
Poland	75.00
Romania	79.38
Russian Federation a/	90.20
Slovakia	79.40
Ukraine a/	88.80
Uzbekistan a/	61.10

Source: Economic Commission for Europe, "Regional review and appraisal of Nairobi Forward-looking Strategies" (E/ECE/RW/HLM).
a/   1990.   b/   Financial intermediaries.

38.   Unemployment is becoming a key area of concern for women in the transitional economies. While the steep decline in real income has made women's wages a necessity for the survival of the household, jobs have become scare and competition for them has intensified. The vast majority of women were little prepared for the loss of job security and the need to compete for employment in a market environment. Although highly educated, women appear to be losing jobs to men even in previously "women-dominated" sectors of the economy. The rate of female unemployment is on the rise in all the economies in transition except for the Czech Republic. Women constitute by far the largest share of all those registered as unemployed and are believed to be the majority of those who are not registered. The duration of unemployment is longer for women than for men. In the Russian Federation, for example, the average time of registered unemployment is 4.6 months for women and less than 2 months for men. 32/

Table 7. Women's share in unemployment: selected countries, 1991

Country	Women's share (percentage)
Bulgaria	62.0
Hungary a/	40.0
Kazakhstan b/	70.0
Poland	52.0
Yugoslavia	53.0
Romania	85.0-90.0
Russian Federation c/	90.0
Slovak Republic	58.0
Ukraine d/	65.0

Source: Compiled from several sources, and M. Fong, "Economic restructuring and women's status in Eastern Europe", UNU/WIDER research paper (Helsinki, 1991), pp. 6-9.

   a/   Quoted as "over 40 per cent".

   b/   National report of Kazakhstan.

   c/   1993 figure of ECE, 1994 (E/ECE/RW/HELM/1).

   d/   National report of Ukraine. Quoted as "over 65 per cent".

39.   The position of women in the labour market is further complicated by resurgence of the stereotyping of gender roles and a decline in the availability of social services, particularly in the area of child care, provided in the past by the State and by enterprises. As a result of budgetary pressures and privatization, child-care facilities have become less available and more expansive. The social costs of transition have thus been shifted from the State to the household and ultimately to women.

40.   Growing unemployment among men, lack of child-care facilities and increasing social tensions have precipitated the return of traditional attitudes towards the role of women. A public opinion survey conducted in 1991 in the Russian Federation reveals that a growing number of men feel that women's place is the home. In the media and the press, social problems have been openly blamed on "too much emancipation of women". Measures, such as extended maternity leave and early retirement, have been introduced to encourage women to stay at home. As a result there is little sensitivity to women's issues and to the growing "feminization of unemployment".

41.   So far, women in Eastern Europe, the Commonwealth of Independent States and the Baltic States have had to endure a greater share of the hardship of transition. Their participation in political decision-making has declined, putting them in a poor position to influence the process of reform. At the same time, unemployment among women has grown and they presently account for a greater share of the unemployed. Their incomes have also declined and poverty among women and the households headed by women has increased. The balance between their economic and reproductive roles has shifted towards a greater emphasis on the latter owing to the strengthening of the traditional gender contract. Their distress has been intensified by growing social problems, and rapid criminalization of society in many economies in transition. Sexual harassment against women, sexual abuse and prostitution, previously reported to the United Nations Committee on the Elimination of Discrimination against Women as non-existent, are a reality now. So there is a real danger that women in that area might be further marginalized and find themselves on the periphery of major economic and political structures. This would have serious implications for social equilibrium in the region and for the sustainability of the transition process. Failure to incorporate women would also lead to a less

than optimal economic performance in the transition period as 50 per cent of the labour force that is highly educated and skilled would remain under-utilized.

3. Developed market economies: growing flexibility in markets and women's work

42.   After the recession of the early 1980s, the developed market economies experienced an unusually long period of economic expansion that slowed towards the end of the decade and ended with the shallow recession of the early 1990s (see table 1). The current recovery has been slow: in 1993 growth picked up in the United States and Canada but remained unchanged in Japan and declined in the major economies of Western Europe, except for the United Kingdom, where the economy started to grow again.

43.   Recession and the slow recovery pushed the rate of unemployment up from 6 per cent in 1990 to 7.3 per cent in 1992 and 7.7 per cent in 1993. 20/ While relatively low in the United States and Japan, unemployment has become a major problem in Western Europe, where rates reached 10-12 per cent in 1993. The unemployment rate is expected to increase in 1994 and possibly in 1995.

44.   Among the pressing macroeconomic concerns of the developed market economies are structural fiscal deficits and a resurgence of inflation. Their macroeconomic policies have therefore been directed at fiscal consolidation and they have assumed an anti-inflationary stance that might conflict with the objective of a speedy economic recovery.

45.   The micro- and macroeconomic reforms of the late 1980s and early 1990s encompassed a tightening of fiscal and monetary polices, flexibility and deregulation of financial, product and labour markets, and an industrial restructuring, that in part reflected a longer-term trend of structural shifts involving changes in the roles of industry and services in economic growth. Industrial restructuring was also manifested in the move towards a "flexible firm" to foster competitiveness and greater mobility in an environment of ever-changing markets. These policies have had a distinct impact on women's position in the labour market, and on their rates, quality and conditions of employment.

46.   The long-term trend in the developed market economies has been towards increasing rates of female labour force participation for women and declining rates for men (see figure I). Against this long-term trend, there are cyclical changes in the rates of female labour force participation that are the result of recession, short-term macroeconomic policies and micro-economic reforms.

47.   The general worsening of the employment situation in the OECD economies is currently a major concern for policy makers in these countries. There has been an increase in the rates of long-term unemployment and country reports from the European region indicate that about 50 per cent of the unemployed in some countries has been out of work for 12 months or more. 32/ While there are variations in rates and patterns of unemployment among the developed market economies, it appears that in the majority of OECD countries unemployment rates for women are either comparable to those for men or lower. However, in Denmark, France, Germany, Italy and the Netherlands, unemployment rates for women are significantly higher than those for men. 32/

48.   A consistent increase in the rate of female labour force participation has taken place in the context of the expansion of the services sector. The share of total employment and women's employment in this sector have increased in all the OECD countries, 25/ while the shares of employment in agriculture and industry have declined, which explains the decline in male labour force participation (see figure II).

Figure I. Labour-force participation rates, by sex, total OECD (Percentage)

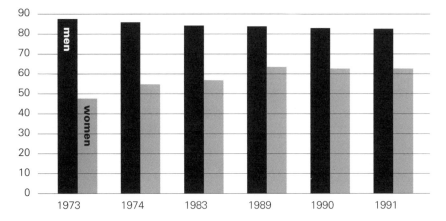

Table 8. Unemployment rates by sex: selected OECD countries, 1973-1992

| | (Percentage share) | | | |
	1973	1979	1990	1992
United States				
Men	2.3	3.1	4.1	6.0
Women	2.3	3.2	3.3	4.4
Japan				
Men	1.0	1.6	1.4	1.4
Women	0.5	1.1	1.3	1.3
United Kingdom				
Men	2.1	3.8	6.3	11.5
Women	0.3	1.3	2.0	3.2
France				
Men	2.3	3.1	5.6	6.5
Women	1.3	3.5	7.8	8.5
Sweden				
Men	1.6	1.3	1.3	5.4
Women	2.1	1.6	1.2	3.5

Source: World Economic and Social Survey, 1994 (United Nations publication, Sales No. E.94.II.C.1).

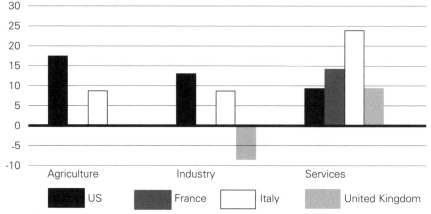

Figure II. Changes in female share of total employment: by sectors, 1973-1992 (Percentage change)

Source: OECD, Labour Force Statistics, cited 1971-1991 (Paris, 1993).

49.   Policies directed at the enhancement of internal and external competitiveness were centred around the deregulation and flexibilization of financial, product and labour markets. They focused primarily on wage-bargaining institutions, tax and social spending policies and employment legislation perceived as hampering wage flexibility. At the micro-level, the flexibilization of markets was matched by industrial restructuring directed at lean production strategies and the evolution of flexible firms, capable of rapid expansion and contraction with a small number of permanent employees and the remainder employed as temporary and casual workers, outworkers and subcontractors. While benefiting female employment in terms of the supply of jobs, flexibilization has led to a trade-off between the quality and quantity of female employment. The positive aspects of the process must be weighted against the potential for undermining existing employment protection, social security provisions, and access to training and for the fragmentation of career prospects. Concern has been voiced that women may have been used as part of deregulation strategy by virtue of their association with flexible employment.

50.   Present data indicate that part-time employment is increasingly a female phenomenon, and the majority of those employed part-time in almost all the developed market economies are women.

Table 9. Women's share in part-time employment: selected OECD economies, 1973-1992

	(Percentage)				
	1979	1983	1990	1991	1992
Austria	87.8	88.4	89.1	89.7	..
Belgium	88.9	84.0	88.6	89.3	..
Canada	72.1	71.3	71.0	70.5	70.0
Denmark	86.9	84.7	75.7	75.5	..
France	82.2	84.4	83.6	83.7	83.7
Germany	91.6	91.9	89.7	89.6	..
Italy	61.4	64.8	67.2	65.4	67.9
Japan	70.1	72.8	70.7	69.9	69.3
United Kingdom	92.8	89.8	86.2	86.1	85.4
United States	68.0	66.8	67.6	67.2	66.4

Source: OECD, Labour Force Statistics, 1971-1991 (Paris, 1993).

51.   The increase in the part-time employment of women has been a factor contributing to increased occupational segregation and persisting inequality in economic rewards, salaries and benefits. While in some economies the proportion of women in "male-dominated" occupations has increased slightly as a result of affirmative action by the Government, employment segregation continues to persist. In France, for example, nurses, midwives, beauticians, secretaries, social assistants, cashiers, switchboard and telephone operators and receptionists are highly "feminized" occupational categories in which women constitute more than 90 per cent of employees. 32/

52.   The increase in female labour force participation has not led to women achieving equal status or bargaining power in the labour market. As wage demands are increasingly being tied to increases in productivity, women's concentration in the services sector has contributed to an overall weakening of their wage bargaining power since increased productivity is not easily measured in this sector. National reports show that women's

earnings are lower than men's in most of the reporting countries. Women earn between 50 and 90 per cent of men's earnings, but rates vary considerably across countries. In 1990, women's wages in non-agricultural industries in Japan were only 49.6 per cent of men's; and in Germany women earned 73.1 per cent of men's wages, while in France the figure was 80.8 per cent and in Australia, 90.8 per cent.

B. Gender aspects of internal and external migration

53.   Migration, involving as it does millions of people around the world, is intricately linked with important economic, social, political, cultural and environmental factors. As such, it has gender-specific characteristics that however are often masked by data aggregates established without regard to gender. The data collected and published under the heading of "migrants and dependents" do not permit a full exploration of the extent, causes and consequences of migration from a gender perspective. Nevertheless, the available data, however limited, suggest that both, internal and external migration may have distinct gender patterns that vary with level of development, development strategies, type of economic growth and political factors.

1. Internal migration

54.   Internal migration, which exceeds external migration by at least an order of magnitude, continues to be viewed primarily in terms of rural-urban flows and the growth of urban areas despite the growing importance of urban-urban and rural-rural flows. The world's urban population is estimated to have grown by about 500 million people over the period 1975-1985 and about half of this gain has been attributed to net rural-urban migration. Recent estimates suggest that 43 per cent of the world's population currently live in urban areas as compared to only 37 per cent in the 1970s. Some projections show that by the year 2005 urban population will reach a staggering 58 per cent. 33/ In recent years average annual population growth rates in urban areas, particularly in sub-Saharan Africa, Latin America and Asia, have been high and positive, while average annual growth in rural areas has, with few exceptions, been low or negative. This suggests that a significant part of population growth is due to migration from rural to urban areas.

Table 10. Ratio of women to men in total, urban and rural population (1990 round)

Region/ age group	Total population	Urban population	Rural population
Africa/15-19	0.997	0.989	1.100
Africa/20-24	1.002	0.885	1.097
Latin America/15-19	0.984	1.061	0.873
Latin America/20-24	1.006	1.089	0.882
Western Europe/15-19	0.956	0.972	0.913
Western Europe/20-24	0.956	0.988	0.865
Asia and Pacific/15-19	0.946	0.930	0.963
Asia and Pacific/20-24	0.944	0.909	0.969
East Asia/15-19	0.938	0.936	0.938
East Asia/20-24	0.935	0.956	0.864
South-east Asia/15-19	0.968	0.987	0.968
South-east Asia/20-24	0.986	1.003	0.982
Eastern Europe/15-19	0.948	0.939	0.934
Eastern Europe/20-24	0.952	0.958	0.929

Source: WISTAT, 1994.

55.   The gender pattern of rural/urban migration can be derived from the population sex ratios given in table 10 below. Although largely insufficient to support any definite conclusions, these ratios suggest that in low-income developing economies with a large agricultural sector men predominate among migrants from rural to urban areas and that in the newly industrialized and highly urbanized economies of Latin America and East Asia women migrate more than men. For example, in Africa, sex ratios in rural areas indicate that more men migrate to cities than women; and in Latin America they indicate that more women than men leave their villages for the city. In Asia, in general, men tend to predominate in the rural-urban migration flow, while in East Asia women in the 20-24 age group slightly outnumber men among rural-to-urban migrants. In Western Asia, rural and urban sex ratios reflect the predominance of males among city migrants.

56.   It should be noted that the patterns of rural-to-urban migration observed in each of these regions are consistent with regional trends in economic development with respect to trade orientation, the inflow of FDI and the gender characteristics of employment in export-processing industries. The creation of EPZs in the context of export-promotion policies has undoubtedly contributed to fostering female migration from rural to urban areas in the first and second generation of the newly industrialized economies of East and South-East Asia and Latin America.

2. External migration

57.   In the past two decades external (international) migration for economic or political reasons has involved millions of people. Census data largely for the 1970s and 1980s suggest that the number of migrants in the mid-1980s exceeded 105 million. 33/   Although more recent data on the extent of external migration are not available, increasing globalization and growing interdependence in the world economy, the greater mobility of capital, regional integration and the reconfiguration of nation States in Europe and the former Soviet Union suggest that external migration may currently involve significantly more people than it did in the 1980s.

58.   There is a general lack of adequate data on the gender composition of the external migration flows, and little attention as yet has been paid to58.such important issues as their gender-specific impact. It is therefore difficult to identify specific ways in which women migrants influence the process of external migration or are impacted by it. Clearly, women migrants may experience a significant change in lifestyle associated with a move to a society with greater gender equality or considerable hardship, when migrating as refugees in the context of war, famine or drought.

59.   With their statistics on foreign-born population, national population censuses provide the most comprehensive data on the extent of female migration. Census data for the 1970s and 1980s show that women accounted on average for slightly more than 50 per cent of the total inflow of migrants into developed countries. In developing countries, they represented 45.4 per cent of the total foreign-born population; and their share in the total number of people living outside their countries of origin averaged 48.1per cent. Of course, these averages mask significant variations within

and between regions. In the Americas and Europe women accounted for more than half of the foreign-born population; in Africa and Asia they were less than half of that category; and they were strongly underrepresented in the countries of Western Asia.

60. In the absence of data for the 1990s it cannot be determined whether the share of women in international migration flows has changed. It is nevertheless clear that women account for about one half of all international migration. Gender-disaggregated reporting of data on international migration and greater attention to its gender-specific consequences are necessary if a better understanding of the process itself and of the role of women in it is to be achieved.

C. Trends in international trade and their influence on the advancement of women

61.   The relationship between the growth of international trade and increasing female participation in productive employment hinges on the employment-creating potential of trade and its influence on the nature and orientation of national economic development by bringing domestic resources allocation into line with comparative advantage. Those developing countries that opened their economies to international trade experienced a dramatic rise in the participation of women in industrial employment.

62.   There are at least three reasons why this happened. First, production for the external market led to an increase in the demand for labour. Secondly, there was a significant expansion in trade flows and a change in their composition. Thirdly, as labour-intensive manufactured exports came to dominate export flows from the developing countries, unit labour cost minimization became a matter of priority for export-oriented industries. In this context, female labour, which is universally cheaper than male labour, enjoyed a unit labour cost advantage. The evidence shows that, in countries with export-oriented production, female labour was systematically preferred over male labour by transnational corporations and domestic export-oriented industries.

63.   As a result of the expansion of international and intra-industry trade, women's participation in industrial production, and particularly in light manufacturing, has increased dramatically. The global average for women's participation in the manufacturing labour force stands today at about 30 per cent, which is almost the same as the share of women in the global labour force. 34/ However, this increase reflects the industrialization

process in developing countries, which typically begins with the production of labour-intensive items as economies begin to diversify away from primary production. In the industrialized and former centrally planned economies, (except for the Asian economies in transition) women's participation in industrial production has actually declined.

64. Trade expansion did not, however, prove to be a zero-sum game in terms of the aggregate female employment as had been predicted. Despite competition from developing countries, female employment continued to rise in the developed economies. The strong and sustained upward trend in women's employment in the non-tradable services sector is thought to have been largely responsible for this development. The decline in female industrial employment was primarily due to the long-term process of structural change in the composition of gross domestic product (GDP) rather than to the competitive pressure from the developing countries only. Some job losses to competition from developing countries, particularly in the manufacturing industries, were, however, inevitable, but the bulk of the burden fell most heavily on low-skilled, overwhelmingly male, labourers.

65. The trade-driven, export-oriented development strategies followed by first- and second-generation of newly industrializing countries 35/ came to be known as "female-led" as much as "export-led" owing to the high share of women in the export-oriented industries. The women-manufactured exports of these countries accounted for most of manufactures exported from South to North. In this sense, South/North trade in manufactures was not only labour-intensive but also "female-labour intensive". In some countries, particularly in East and South-east Asia and Latin America, the share of female employment in export-oriented industries reached as much as 95 per cent in the 1980s. 25/ In Mexico, the share of women's employment in the export-processing zones was 77 per cent in the early 1980s. In the Republic of Korea and Singapore women accounted for between 68 and 83 per cent of the labour force in textiles and clothing and between 59 and 90 per cent in electronics.

66. Although trade liberalization in the developing countries has led to a steep increase in the employment of women in export-oriented industries, providing them with better income opportunities, most of the jobs that went to women were low-wage long-hours production-line jobs or sub-con

tracting jobs with no opportunity for the acquisition of new skills and without wage-bargaining power. That is to say that while trade expansion led to an increase in the supply of jobs for women, the quality of those jobs was often poor and they were insecure, paid only a fraction of male wage for the same job and lacked social protection. 36/ Thus, the increase in the industrial employment of women in the context of outward-oriented development was based on explicitly inferior treatment of female labour. Female employment in export-oriented economies is also highly segregated as the proportion of women employed in "feminized" industries greatly exceeds that in total industrial employment, suggesting that the female labour force is highly concentrated in these industries and underrepresented elsewhere. When the qualitative aspects of this process are weighted against the quantitative indicators of greater job availability, the overall assessment of the impact of export-oriented development is hardly consonant with female advancement.

67.   Recent evidence suggests that the share of women's employment in the export-oriented industries is declining in the "mature" newly industrializing countries. In view of women's relatively poor educational levels - or rather their less appropriate orientation given modern needs - women in developing countries are less likely to benefit from export-oriented production than they were. It is doubtful that trade expansion lays the ground for any special long-term benefits for women in developing countries in terms of their placement in the labour market and of improved access to employment on better terms in the future. As countries move along the development spectrum, they move away from reliance on unskilled labour-intensive manufacturing (as in Singapore) and unless their skills acquisition keeps pace with the country's industrial and technology development, women's employment opportunities will fall away with such growth. 37/

68.   An open trading system is the key to economic growth and prosperity, which in turn is a sine qua non for political stability and democracy. Inasmuch as growth and stability are important factors influencing the economic advancement of women, free trade is instrumental in achieving this objective. There is no doubt that any shrinking of the volume of world trade would do immense harm to the world economy and to prospects for sustainable development in the developing countries. Development experiences

(or rather the lack thereof) in the 1980s showed that the adverse consequences of economic decline often affect women to a greater extent than men. On the other hand, growth based on free trade and principles of comparative advantage has proved to be greatly beneficial to women. The resurgence in the mid-1970s of protectionist pressures and their proliferation in the 1980s under the strain of recession posed a serious threat to free trade and, by extension, to women's jobs and economic advancement.

69.   The main achievement of the Uruguay Round of multilateral trade negotiations was that its successful conclusion served to uphold the principles of free trade. The Round, which took three years to devise and seven to complete, was the most ambitious in the history of GATT. The agreement under the Uruguay Round comes into effect on 1 January 1995, subject to ratification. Although implementation of the major agreements will be spread over the next 10 years and will not be as thorough and swift as exporting countries would have liked, significant new market-opening rules were introduced. The main provisions of the agreement, and those of utmost importance to the developing countries, aim at broadening market access, bringing trade in services and in textiles and clothing under the GATT regulation, providing a comprehensive framework for the future liberalization of trade in agriculture products, and curbing the proliferation of non-tariff trade barriers and unilateral protectionist measures.

70.   The liberalization of trade resulting from the Uruguay Round should lead to a significant increase in world trade and income, which is expected to increase by US$ 213-274 billion annually. It is expected that everybody stands to gain, particularly in the long run. The gender-specific dimensions of these gains (and of the unavoidable short-term losses) are less obvious, however. Some of the largest projected increases in trade are in areas of great importance to developing countries. Trade in clothing is expected to increase by 60 per cent and in textiles by 34 per cent. It should be noted that these are the sectors that usually lead the industrialization process at the early stages when a developing country is just beginning to diversify from primary production. These are also the sectors where production is "female-intensive" - i.e., where the share of women in total employment is high. The dismantlement of the Multifibre Arrangement (MFA), which controlled trade in textiles since 1973 should speed up the shift in comparative

advantage and hence in the global division of labour, leading to the take-off of industrialization process in the least developed countries. As industrialization at its early stages is often "female-led", women stand to benefit in terms of the increase in the availability of productive employment.

71.   In a large number of primary-producing economies, diversification into the production of manufactured exports is nevertheless going to be a slow process. Most of the short- to medium-term gains are likely to accrue to Asian and Latin American exporters of manufactured goods. Given changes in consumer demand, shifts in comparative advantage of established exporters of manufactured goods and gender-related differences in education, it is unlikely that women in these economies will continue to hold onto their share of employment in export-oriented industries.

72.   Primary producers and exporters of tropical products in Africa stand to benefit least from the liberalization of trade, at least in the short run, because of the low-income elasticities of their exports and the already low tariffs on most of them. Furthermore, women in many African countries arenot involved in the production of export crops either because the gender-related division of labour does not permit them to switch to the production of tradable crops or because, as such production becomes profitable, deliberate efforts are made to turn cash-crop production over to men. 38/ Some of the developing countries - net importers of food - might see their terms of trade decline since the prices of their food imports are likely to rise as a short-term result of the Uruguay Round. The increase in trade in services is likely to benefit women, given their high propensity of employment in this sector.

73.   Despite the obvious advantages for women in the liberalization of international trade, the extent to which they benefit will vary with their level of education and the nature of their economic environment. In the short-run, nationally and internationally, there will be winners and losers. Trade-adjustment assistance and skill-building programmes are therefore necessary to assist male and female workers who are displaced as a result of greater competition from abroad. Lately, however, there is some evidence of unequal access to retraining for women. 25/

D. Other factors affecting the implementation of the Nairobi Forward-looking Strategies

74.   The Nairobi Forward-looking Strategies call for equal rights for women in social, legal and economic domains. They specifically emphasize the right to independent and full access to productive resources, and they call for the greater integration of women into every stage of the development process, for the reduction of poverty among women, particularly at the times of economic distress caused by recession or structural adjustment, and for the advancement of women to positions of economic and political power in business and government. They also call for greater recognition in national accounts and economic statistics of women's paid, unpaid and informal-sector work and for the facilitation of women's access to productive employment through the greater availability and the improvement of the conditions of such employment. In that respect, emphasis was also given to the need to reduce widespread employment segregation by encouraging women to work in male-dominated environments.

75.   The World Conference on Human Rights, held at Vienna in 1993, reaffirmed the importance of human rights in relation to all other aspects of global life. It specifically reaffirmed the importance of the equal rights of women and men, as well as a rights-based focus on issues of peace and development. In terms of women's de jure human rights, the provisions of the Vienna Declaration and Programme of Action reflected the considerable progress in placing these in the legal structure. The fact that, by the end of 1994, over 138 States were party to the Convention on the Elimination of All Forms of Discrimination against Women placed the laws of those countries

within the norms set out in the Convention. At the same time, the enjoyment of these rights in terms of women's de facto situation did not improve at the same rate, as is noted below.

76.   The reliance on democratic means for electing and changing governments, through competitive elections, that has characterized recent years, has opened the prospect for women of using the exercise of their political rights to improve their own status. At the same time, enjoyment of these rights has been constrained by the negative effects of previous systems which constitute a base of inequality upon which reform processes have been built. After the shift towards democracy, in the absence of strong and independent national machinery to raise women's issues into public debate, independent women's movements have continued to be excluded from the process of economic and political decision-making. Women's participation in parliament and at all levels of economic decision-making have only increased dramatically in a few countries and in others it has declined.

77.   Where a resurgence of democracy has coincided with the spread of political instability, women continue to be the majority of the countless victims of political and ethnic violence. Much therefore much remains to be done before the world can claim that the objectives of the Nairobi Forward-looking Strategies have been achieved.

II. Critical Areas of Concern

A. Persistent and growing burden of poverty on women

78.   Poverty remains a grave concern for the international community and the issue of its eradication is at the top of the development agenda, particularly in the context of the World Summit for Social Development. This time, in addition to the now customary emphasis on the limitations of economic growth as far as overall development objectives are concerned, the development debate tends to focus, inter alia, on distinctly new dimensions of the issue.

79.   It has become more obvious that economic development does not automatically lead to equitable distribution or redistribution of resources and income, especially to the poorest sections of population. It is further clear that development does not automatically benefit men and women equally. Indeed,there is more and more recognition that women are disproportionately represented among the poor.

80.   It has been explicitly recognized that poverty has a gender dimension. Moreover, research in the past 10 years has shown that in order to eradicate poverty this dimension needs to be addressed in development planning. Micro-studies conducted around the globe have shown that there is a strong correlation between the economic status of women and progress achieved with respect to poverty alleviation in general. There is a growing recognition among development policy makers and practitioners and among international and bilateral donors that it is crucial to improve the economic status of women and to target women in poverty explicitly when designing and implementing anti-poverty policies. These factors are generally not being considered by development planners, who are still reluctant to accept a gender perspective in development planning.

81.   The perception is growing around the globe that poverty is becoming increasingly feminized. It is still a matter of debate whether or not this is a new trend or merely the acknowledgement of a persisting reality and whether or not the feminization of poverty is a world-wide phenomenon. What is clear, however, is that female poverty is a persistent and unevenly distributed burden that threatens the sustainability of the development process and that is, in the long run, likely to translate into slower rates of economic growth.

82.   There is more and more evidence that women are neither a burden nor a cost to development. On the contrary, they constitute a particularly dynamic factor in the eradication of poverty. This realization, however, while reflected in the academic literature and in the agendas of international development institutions, has not been given due weight in the design and implementation of anti-poverty polices. The explicit targeting of poor women as the main thrust of anti-poverty policies is necessary if poverty is ever to be eradicated.

83.   The Nairobi Forward-looking Strategies approached poverty as a significant - albeit indirect - obstacle to the advancement of women. As seen by the Strategies, poverty is a persistent cause of the inequality of women and an obstacle to women's advancement. Just as poverty retards the advancement of women and is an obstacle to equality, it is, along with an adverse economic situation and the general shortcomings of the development process, an impediment to the participation of women in development. However, the Strategies tackle poverty only indirectly as they focus on the three main themes of employment, education and health. The alleviation of female poverty is therefore also addressed indirectly, through measures to eliminate inequality and enhance women's participation in development.

84.   As a means of eliminating inequality between women and men, the Strategies seek to expand women's access to education, training and productive employment. They recommend that anti-discrimination employment legislation and affirmative action, where appropriate, should be implemented to promote equality of opportunity. To ensure women's control of the return to their labour, the Strategies emphasize the need for greater access by women to productive resources - i.e., credit and land.

46

Strategies to increase women's participation in development seek to promote the role of women as a contribution to society rather than as a welfare cost. To emphasize the value of women's participation in development, the Strategies call for women's productive and reproductive work to be adequately reflected in national accounts and economic statistics. The alleviation of poverty is thus addressed through strategies of restructuring the rules governing employment and access to productive resources.

85.   A number of things have happened since the adoption of the Strategies that have changed the order of priority given to the "special areas of concern" and the weight accorded to the poverty issue among them:

(a)   The emphasis within the development debate has once again shifted from economic growth as the principal economic objective of society to human-centred sustainable development, to concerns for the quality of life and hence to poverty alleviation as the main goal of the development process;

(b)   The relationship between women's advancement and poverty has come to be analysed increasingly from the perspective of gender rather than that of cause and effect, focusing on differences in the incidence, causes and dimensions of poverty as experienced by men and women;

(c)   The process of poverty eradication has slowed down significantly since the mid-1980s, the absolute number of people living below the poverty line of US$ 370 increased by 20 per cent over the period 1985-1993 and the number of people living in absolute poverty on a yearly income of less than US$ 300 has also increased;

(d)   If in the past poverty was considered a primarily rural phenomenon, towards the end of the 1980s the analysis had to be broadened to take account of growing impoverishment among the urban population.

86.   These developments, together with the growing perception of poverty as an increasingly female phenomenon have brought poverty priority top among the areas of critical concern for the advancement of women. Since the mid-1980s the issue of female poverty has undergone a transformation in terms of its importance for both the agenda for development and for the advancement of women.

Figure III. Poverty in developing countries, 1985-1993

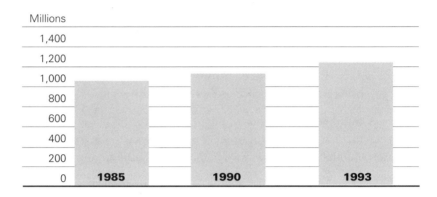

Sources: *World Bank, World Development Report, 1990 and 1992*
(Washington, D.C.); World Survey on the Role of Women in Development,
1994 (United Nations publication, forthcoming).

1. Factors in the feminization of poverty

87.   While urban poverty also increased considerably during the 1980s, poverty in the developing countries continues to be concentrated in rural areas. In 1993, some 939 million of the 1.2 billion people whose incomes were estimated as falling below the poverty line were in rural areas. 13/ The fact that poverty remains a predominantly rural phenomenon in the developing and least developed countries is merely a reflection of the urbanization pattern and does not imply that poverty is less of a problem in the cities. As the proportion of the urban population in developing countries grew from 22 per cent in 1960 to 37 per cent in 1990, rural poor became urban poor. If the rate of urbanization increases as predicted, by the year 2000 the burden of poverty will be transferred from rural to urban areas.

88.   At the same time, there has not been sufficient growth in most developing countries to absorb migrants from the countryside into the paid labour force, leaving many of them impoverished in urban ghettos instead of rural villages. An increasing proportion of the population is living in slums and squatter settlements. It has been estimated that 1 billion people live in very low quality housing, and this number may well double by the year 2000. Many of the poorest urban residents are women. In particular, the growing

number of poor households headed by women experiences the greatest threat to health and safety as a result of urban environmental problems.

89.   Data for 1990 show that the highest poverty rates in terms of absolute numbers and percentage of population are to be found in sub-Saharan Africa and South Asia, followed by the Middle East and North Africa. The poor as a percentage of total population increased between 1985 and 1990 in sub-Saharan Africa, Latin America and the Middle East and North Africa, as economies in these regions struggled with the burdens of adverse internal and external economic circumstances and debt and structural adjustment, which seem to have fallen most heavily on the poor. In Latin America, where poverty was already widespread, the poor as a percentage of the population has reached extremely high proportions. For example, in Ecuador the poor account for 78 per cent of the population, and in Bolivia 70 per cent of all households and 94 per cent of households in rural areas are among the poor.

90.   Despite overall economic growth, the social security mechanisms designed to prevent vulnerable population groups from falling into poverty and the increase in average income in the developed market economies in the 1980s, poverty has been on the rise in some of these countries. In the United States 33.6 million people, some 13 per cent of the population, were estimated to be living below the poverty line, and in Japan, 25 per cent of all households were on the verge of destitution. In the countries of the European Union at the beginning of the 1990s, 44 million people, 18 per cent of the population, were estimated to be living in poverty and 10 million in extreme poverty. 39/

91.   Poverty surged in the transition economies of Eastern Europe, the CIS and the Baltic States as a decline in real wages and the breakdown of social security systems there led to the rapid impoverishment of what appears to be the majority of the population, particularly that part of it living in rural areas and small towns.

Table 11. Poverty in developing countries, by region, 1988

Region	Total number of countries	Severe poverty status a/	Rural population as percentage of total population	Rural population below poverty line Millions	As percentage of rural population
Asia	24	14	74	633	31
Sub-Saharan Africa	45	36	73	204	60
Near East and North Africa	13	2	51	27	26
Latin America and the Caribbean	32	14	29	76	61
Total	**114**	**66**	**68**	**939**	**36**
Least developed countries	42	35	80	253	69

Source: IFAD, 1988.

a/   Severe poverty status is determined on the basis of the integrated poverty index which is calculated on the basis of the percentage of rural population below the poverty line, the income-gap ratio and the range of growth of GNP per capita.

Table 12. The poor as a percentage of population, by region, 1985 and 1990

Region	1985	1990
Sub-Saharan Africa	47.6	49.7
East Asia	13.2	11.3
South Asia	51.8	49.0
Middle East and North Africa	30.6	33.1
Latin America and the Caribbean	22.4	25.5
All developing countries	30.5	25.5

Source: World Bank, World Development Report, 1990 and 1992 (Washington, D.C., 1990 and 1992).

Table 13. Proportion of the total population and of children living in poverty, 1989-1992

Country	Social group	1989	1990	1991	1992
Bulgaria	Population	..	..	..	53.6
Czech Republic	Population	5.7	7.7	19.4	18.2
Hungary	Population	10.1	..	21.3	..
	Children	14.1	..	29.1	..
Poland	Population	20.5	39.7	38.8	42.5
	Children	28.0	53.0	54.7	57.6
Romania	Households	27.3	18.5	28.1	51.1
	Children	38.1	30.7	42.1	70.1
Russian Federation	Population	27.1	24.5	28.7	77.1
Slovakia	Households	8.5	8.9	28.2	30.2
	Children	10.9	11.2	35.6	41.3
Ukraine	Households	33.6	..	21.1	35.7

Source: "The role of women in the transition processes: facing a major challenge" (E/ECE/RW/HLM/5), p. 27.

92.   Recent analyses of poverty in developed and developing countries emphasize the feminization of poverty as a current trend. The term itself appeared in the mid-1980s and was used to describe the growing proportion of women and of households headed by women in the ranks of the poor during the recession of the early 1980s and in the context of cut-backs in welfare programmes. By the end of the 1980s, some 75 per cent of all poverty in the United States was to be found among women, particularly women who were single parents. 40/ A review of the pertinent literature suggests that the number of families headed by poor women has been rising ever since by about 100,000 a year. The greatest incidence of poverty, however, has been found among older black women. 41/

93.   It would be difficult to assert with certainty whether the same trend is at work in the other developed market economies and in developing economies. Evidence from some of the national reports of the European countries (for example, Austria) suggests that the feminization of poverty is not confined to the United States alone. On the other hand, reports from Finland and other Nordic countries suggest that the feminization of poverty has not been a "burning issue" there. Generous welfare systems in these countries prevent large-scale female poverty despite high rates of unemployment among women and a large and growing number of households headed by women. In the Netherlands, for example, more than 70 per cent of all single mothers with dependent children are recipients of benefit payments. Although the mere fact of the primary wage earner being a woman is not by itself an indication of household poverty in these countries, the poverty rate among households headed by women is significantly higher than among households headed by men. In Norway, for example, 13 per cent of all households headed by women live below the poverty level but only 5 per cent of those headed by men.

94.   The complex dimensions of poverty differences between men and women, the lack of data demonstrating changes in the ratio of women to men in the ranks of the poor, and substantial cross-country differences in the gender make-up of poverty make it difficult to substantiate the thesis that the feminization of poverty is a process that currently characterizes the gender composition of poverty in the developed market economies.

(a)   Developed market economies: the feminization of poverty and of labour

95.   An explanation of the feminization of poverty, particularly in the context of developed market economies, may be provided in terms of changing gender-related patterns of employment. The feminization of poverty runs parallel to the other widely discussed process of feminization - that of labour. The feminization of labour took place in the context of the spread of part-time, temporary and other forms of casual or non-standard types of employment across the developed market countries. In the majority of countries, part-time jobs offer little access to training, benefits or occupational mobility and are largely confined to certain industries and occupations that are typically low-skilled and low-paid. The part-time workers generally earn lower hourly rates than their full-time counterparts. The majority of the so-called "working poor" on minimum pay are women, especially in Northern Europe. The distinction between so-called poor women and low-paid women has become blurred. Sectoral data on part-time employment and on the sectoral pattern of the growth of female employment suggests that the majority of those jobs went to women. In 1991-1992 the share of women in part-time employment in the OECD economies varied between 66 and 90 per cent. 25/

96.   Other indicators of the feminization of poverty are the growth of single-parent households headed by women and the long-term decline in transfers to the poor and in government spending on welfare programmes. The feminization of poverty raises complex questions as to the role of the welfare State in the reduction of poverty. It has become apparent that the simple redistribution of income by means of government transfers does not always work towards a solution to the problem of poverty, let alone the reversal or prevention of the feminization trend, and that it often leads to the perpetuation of both. To some extent the feminization of poverty trend can be explained in terms of marginal rates of income taxation and high rates of indirect taxation, minimum-wage polices and income transfers within the social security system.

(b)   Developing economies: trends symptomatic of the feminization of poverty

97.   While in the developed market economies the feminization of poverty presents itself as a growing number of women and women heads-of-household with dependent children in the ranks of low-paid workers and/or in the ranks of the long-term unemployed, in the developing countries it is the harshness of the deprivation experienced by poor women that constitutes the feminization of poverty. Poverty itself is widespread. A number of factors nevertheless point to the disproportionate effect that poverty is beginning to have on women. Poverty among rural women is growing faster than among rural men and over the past 20 years the number of women in absolute poverty has risen by about 50 per cent as against some 30 per cent for rural men. 13/

Table 14. Rural women living below the poverty line, by region, 1988

Region	Number of women (millions)
Asia	374
Asia (excluding China and India)	153
Sub-Saharan Africa	129
Near East and North Africa	18
Latin America and the Caribbean	43
Least developed countries	149

Source: The State of World Rural Poverty (New York, New York University Press, 1992), published in conjunction with IFAD.

98.   Among the factors affecting the increase in the number of women among the poor are the growing share of households headed by women in the total number of households; intra-household gender relations and their impact on the distribution of household income and on the degree of control women have over their earnings; the impact of technology on female wage labour; and the persistent lack of access by women to factors of production, including sometimes the lack of control over the allocation of their own labour.

(c)   Poverty and households headed by women

99.   It is generally agreed that an important interlinkage exists between gender and poverty on the one hand and the situation of households headed by women on the other. An increasing number of surveys and national reports reveal that this is a growing phenomenon world wide.

100.   The World Fertility Survey, conducted in the 1970s, and the Demographic and Health Survey, conducted in the 1980s, both indicate a pronounced increase in the percentage of households headed by women during the past decade in many developing countries. Ghana's national report comments on "the phenomenal increase in the proportion of female-headed households in the country". At the end of the 1980s, households headed by women in Ghana accounted for 35 per cent of the total. Most were headed by women who did not receive any remittances from men for their upkeep, and they were characterized by a high dependency ratio of 1.8 as against 1.2 for corresponding households headed by men. Kenya and Namibia both report high rates, 30 and 40 per cent, respectively, for households headed by women. The highest proportion of households headed by women was registered in Kenya, in Mathare Valley in Nairobi, where 60-80 per cent of all households have women as heads. 42/ In Brazil, the proportion increased from 5 per cent in 1960 to 21 per cent in 1988. Similar increases were reported for Chile, Costa Rica and Colombia, although the proportion of women among the lowest 20 per cent of income distribution increased only in Colombia and rural Venezuela. 43/ The national report of Kenya, however, indicates the highest absolute poverty rates among households headed by single women, namely 52 per cent as compared to 44.3 per cent for households headed by single men. The phenomenon of female-headed households has been on the rise in Bangladesh since the mid-1980s, attesting to a critical decline in the position of women under modernization. 44/

101.   While it is generally true that households headed by women are among the most disadvantaged economically, it is also true that such households are a heterogeneous group in terms of the marital status of their adult members, number of dependents and the circumstances of their formation. The most vulnerable to poverty are the so-called mother-child households where women are single providers for their dependent children. 42/

Table 15. Percentage of households headed by women, by country and year of most recent data [a]

Region	<9 Country	% female	Year	10-14 Country	% female	Year	15-19 Country	% female	Year	20-24 Country	% female	Year	25+ Country	% female	Year
Africa				Burkina Faso	9.70	1985	Madagascar	15.94	1975	Uganda	20.60	1989	Reunion	24.64	1992
				Niger	9.70	1988	Ethiopia	15.50	1984	Benin	21.00	1979	Burundi	24.70	1990
				Sierra Leone	10.80	88/89	Côte d'Ivoire	15.60	1988	Congo	21.09	1984	Rwanda	25.15	1979
				Algeria	11.00	1987	Zaire	16.10	1984	Kenya	22.00	1989	Togo	26.40	1988
				Tunisia	11.30	1988	Zambia	16.20	1992				Malawi	28.80	70/72
				Egypt	12.00	1988	Comoros	16.30	1980				Ghana	32.20	1988
				Guinea	12.70	1983	Morocco	17.30	1987				Zimbabwe	32.60	1989
				Sudan	13.30	1990	Djibouti	18.40	1991				Swaziland	40.30	1986
				Mali	14.00	1987	Cameroon	18.50	1987				Botswana	45.90	1988
							Mauritius	18.53	1983						
							United Republic of Tanzania	18.60	91/92						
							Central African Republic	18.70	1988						
							Liberia	19.10	1986						
Latin America and the Caibbean							Mexico	15.10	1980	Costa Rica	20.00	1992	Dominican Republic	25.00	1991
							Guatemala	16.90	1989	Brazil	20.10	1989	Trinidad and Tobago	25.30	1980
							Paraguay	17.00	1990	Honduras	20.40	86/87	El Salvador	26.60	1985
							Peru	17.30	1991	Chile	21.00	1989	Cuba	28.20	1981
							Argentina	19.17	1980	Venezuela	21.30	1990	Haiti	70.00	1993
										Panama	22.30	1990	Jamaica	33.00	1971
										Colombia	22.70	1990	Guadeloupe	34.24	1982
										Uruguay	23.00	1985	Dominica	37.67	1981
										Nicaragua	24.30	1985	St. Lucia	38.84	1980
										Guyana	24.40	1980	St. Vincent / Grenadines	42.37	1980

Region	Country	% female	Year
Western Europe and others	Spain	15.00	1981
	Greece	15.96	1981
	Portugal	17.91	1981
	Italy	19.94	1981
	Belgium	21.49	1984
	France	21.91	1982
	Luxembourg	22.53	1981
	New Zealand	23.86	1991
	Australia	24.83	1981
	Switzerland	25.06	1980
	United Kingdom	25.24	1981
	Canada	25.38	1981
	Sweden	26.74	1985
	Germany	30.20	90/91
	Austria	31.19	1981
	United States	32.30	1981
	Norway	37.64	1980
	Barbados	43.93	1980
	Grenada	45.25	1981
	St. Kitts and Nevis	45.64	1980
	Antigua and Barbuda	58.50	1991 b
Asia	Pakistan	4.33	1981
	Kuwait	4.77	1985
	Iran (Islamic Republic of)	7.31	1976
	Turkey	10.00	1975
	Philippines	11.30	1990
	Vanuatu	11.40	1986
	Fiji	12.40	1986
	Syrian Arab Republic	12.50	1970
	Indonesia	13.00	1991
	Republic of Korea	15.70	1990
	Myanmar	15.97	1983
	Solomon Islands	16.20	1986
	New Caledonia	16.40	1989
	Thailand	16.45	1980
	Bangladesh	16.83	1981
	Japan	17.00	1990
	Sri Lanka	17.40	1981
	Malaysia	17.70	1980
	Singapore	18.19	1980
	Isreal	18.35	1983
	Tonga	19.90	1986
	Viet Nam	31.90	1989
Eastern Europe	Hungary	19.91	1980
	Czechoslovakia (former)	22.74	1980
	Poland	26.68	1978

Source: a. National report of Haiti, 1994   b. National report of Antigua and Barbuda

Consequently, it is the growth in the number of these households that is indicative of the worsening of female poverty and not the increase in female-headed households in general. Furthermore, the economic situation of households headed by women depend on the circumstances of their formation. A recent study 45/ shows that widowhood remains the main factor underlying female headship in developing countries. The economic situation of such households is quite different from that of female-headed households formed in the context of abandonment or birth out of wedlock, although the degree of economic and social support provided to the former by the extended family and the community is declining with the erosion of traditional values while the social acceptability of the latter is growing.

102.   Nevertheless, the situation with regard to households headed by women is highly indicative of gender and poverty, particularly when the heterogeneity of the group is taken into consideration. The key issue is not headship per se, but rather what it implies about women's detachment from the economic support of other adults, particularly adult men. Recent data show that the percentage of household heads who are single adult providers is much larger among women heads of household than among men. Also, the majority of female-headed households are households with no adult male.

Table 16. Change in the percentage of households headed by women

Region/country	Year	Percentage female, 1970	Year	Percentage female, 1980	Change in percentage female
Africa					
Zambia	1980	27.75	1992	16.20	-11.55
Sudan	1973	22.10	1990	13.30	-8.80
Kenya	1969	29.50	1989	22.00	-7.50
Mali	1976	15.06	1987	14.00	-1.06
Morocco	1971	16.90	1987	17.30	0.40
Botswana	1981	45.15	1988	45.90	0.75
Tunisia	1975	10.40	1988	11.30	0.90
Liberia	1974	14.90	1986	19.10	4.20
Burkina Faso	1975	5.10	1985	9.70	4.60
Cameroon	1976	13.75	1987	18.50	4.75
Ghana .	1970	27.40	1988	32.20	4.80
Latin America and the Caribbean					
Peru	1972	22.50	1991	17.30	-5.20
Honduras	1974	21.60	86-87	20.40	-1.20
Paraguay	1982	18.1	1990	17.00	-1.10
Chile	1982	21.58	1989	21.00	-0.58
Venezuela	1981	21.77	1990	21.30	-0.47
Panama	1980	21.50	1990	22.30	0.80
Uruguay	1975	21.04	1985	23.00	1.96
Costa Rica	1984	17.55	1992	20.00	2.45
Dominican Republic	1981	21.7	1991	25.00	3.30
El Salvador	1971	21.50	1985	26.60	5.10
Brazil	1980	14.43	1989	20.10	5.67
Guatemala	1981		1989	16.90	16.90
Asia and Pacific					
New Caledonia	1983	18.49	1989	16.40	-2.09
Indonesia	1980	14.23	1991	13.00	-1.23
Philippines	1970	10.80	1990	11.30	0.50
Republic of Korea	1980	14.66	1990	15.70	1.04
Japan	1980	15.18	1990	17.00	1.82

Source: WISTAT, 1994

Table 17. Households with only one adult member, by sex, and households headed by women with no adult male in household

Country	(Percentage) One female adult	One male adult	Female head of household with no adult male in household
Sub-Saharan Africa			
Botswana	31	21	56
Burundi	34	10	51
Ghana	31	18	57
Kenya	44	18	63
Liberia	33	12	52
Mali	50	6	68
Sudan	31	2	48
Senegal	16	4	36
Zimbabwe	36	14	51
North Africa			
Egypt	32	1	48
Morocco	34	4	52
Tunisia	30	2	45
Asia			
Indonesia	36	3	55
Sri Lanka	13	2	25
Thailand	20	3	40
Latin America/Caribbean			
Bolivia	51	9	68
Colombia	23	4	44
Dominican Republic	24	10	39
Ecuador	30	6	52
Guatemala	27	4	44
Mexico	26	4	48
Peru	32	7	51
Trinidad and Tobago	23	14	36

Source: Population Distribution and Migration (United Nations publication, forthcoming).

103.   Poverty, as measured by income and consumption, is particularly severe among female heads of household who are single providers for their families and receive no support from a male. Studies indicate that the income of women who are heads of household is significantly lower (sometimes only half or less) than that of male heads of household. The national survey of Chile, for example, showed that in 1988 the average income of female heads of household was only 12,200 pesos while that of males was 24,000. A study of urban household income in Jamaica showed that the average monthly income of households headed by women was 22 per cent less than that of households headed by men. Another study showed that in the mid-1980s in the Kingston metropolitan area 72.6 per cent of female household heads had an income below J$ 400 a week (equivalent to $18) compared to 39.3 per cent of male household heads. 46/

104.   It has already been noted that the economic status of women is indicative of the dimensions of general poverty (i.e. poverty that is non-specific in terms of gender) and correlates closely with the progress made in its reduction. Apparently, the same relationship holds at the household level as well. Studies have found that in poor households where the women's share of income and their economic status were relatively high, the children's needs in terms of nutrition and education were met better and without discrimination between the sexes. It is therefore not surprising that, in households where income is earned and controlled by women the children's health, nutrition and educational attainment was found to be no worse and sometimes even better than in male-headed households even though the households headed by women were poorer. 42/ It is well documented that women heads of households spend a greater proportion of their income on the children's well-being than do men heads of households. This result holds even when, taking Engel's Law 47/ into account, income is controlled for by statistical methods.

(d)   Structural adjustment and poverty among women

105.   Adverse external economic circumstances and distortive domestic macro-policies act as a brake on development and consequently on the advancement of women in the economic and social spheres of life. But even when some progress in development is achieved, research shows that it is often not shared equally by women and men. Some evidence suggests that

men's share of resources and their control over women's lives increases dramatically with economic development. 48/ The greater availability of education in the developing countries has translated into unequal access to it for men and women, and incentives for the production of export cash-crops have been taken advantage of almost exclusively by men whereas women have ended up with responsibility for the production of food for domestic consumption and for helping with cash-crop production while having little or no control over the return on their labour.

106.   As economies around the world responded to the global recession of the early 1980s with policies of structural adjustment, the question was repeatedly raised whether these policies are gender-neutral, gender-blind or outright gender-biased. The argument has been justifiably made that policies of structural adjustment entail a cost that tends to be distributed disproportionately. Women come to bear most of it in the form of loss of income and of control over productive resources, greater pressures in balancing family responsibilities with income generation, and the absence of opportunities to take advantage of price-related changes in production incentives. There have been reports of the distinctly adverse impact of structural adjustment on women in Africa. In Zimbabwe, for example, government health spending fell by one third in the first three years of structural adjustment polices. The number of women dying in childbirth in the capital, Harare, doubled in the two years after adjustment from 101 in 1989 to 242 in 1991. 49/

107.   Concern has been expressed that structural adjustment leads to a perpetuation of the "vicious circle" of female poverty as younger female members of households are drawn into productive and reproductive labour at the expense of school attendance. In Haiti, for example, where 70 per cent of households are headed by women, 10 per cent of girls between 5 and 10 and 33 per cent between 10 and 14 were found to be economically active in 1987. A similar situation was reported in Jamaica, where a decline in school attendance left one quarter of all primary school children, many of them girls, outside the system.

108.   Persuasive evidence had been compiled on the adverse effect of structural adjustment on African women farmers and particularly on poor households headed by women that produce insufficient food and have no access to credit and agricultural inputs and therefore suffer most when food

prices go up. The picture of the consequences of structural adjustment story in Africa is essentially the same for all countries: as incentives arise in the context of structural adjustment for the production of cash-crops and as Governments stop subsidizing agricultural inputs, women lose in terms of access to land and credit and consequently in terms of the income accruing to them and their families. Studies show that the cash-crops controlled by men respond well to increased producer prices, while cash- and food-crops produced by women respond little or not at all. The question is: where does the increase in acreage allocated to men's crops come from? The answer is: from drawing land resources away from women. Given that statistical analyses uniformly show that there is a strong and statistically significant positive relationship between income earned by women and the nutritional status of the family 42/ while in the case of male income it is only the contributed proportion of income which is the best explanatory variable 42/ of family well-being, the impact of the decline in the income accruing to rural African women on poverty is self-evident. A number of empirical analyses of the relationship between these two variables in rural Africa show that subsistence production is a better predictor of children's nutrition than cash-crop production. 50/

109.   However, it would be incorrect and misleading to associate the persistence and, in some cases, worsening of female poverty with the policies of structural adjustment. These policies were introduced into the economies that were already suffering from profound internal and external imbalances which were in themselves detrimental to poverty reduction. To the extent that structural adjustment policies helped to restore financial stability, remove market distortions and improve allocative efficiency they acted as a cure for economic distress and not as a cause. As such, these policies were actually helping towards a long-term and sustainable solution to poverty, including that of women. Furthermore, since "counterfactual" 51/ with respect to women's socio-economic situation cannot be directly observed and no satisfactory methodology exists for its estimation, it would be difficult to conclude with certainty that policies of structural adjustment have had an inevitable negative impact on poor women.

110.   What can be stated is that structural adjustment is about change and change implies costs. It is well documented that the costs of structural adjustment, even if only the short-term ones, have been distributed unevenly

with women being hit hardest. Also, while the policies themselves created opportunities for the reallocation of resources to more productive sectors of the economy, women, owing to existing gender biases, the rigidity of their socially ascribed roles and their limited access to productive resources, were unable to adequately benefit from this reallocation. Thus, when analysing the impact of structural adjustment, it is more appropriate to emphasize the need to alleviate their cost and in connection with that the need for a clear understanding of their gender-specific effects. This, in turn, can be achieved only if a conscious effort is made by policy makers at the national and international levels to trace the impact of macro-policies to the gender level and to capture it in adequate statistical indicators.

111.   Another important aspect of the impact of development on poor women stems from the effect of the introduction of new technology on female wage labour. Generally speaking, the impact of new technologies depends on whether they tend to displace female labour or increase the demand for it; whether they are labour-using or labour-saving; and whether the increase in the demand for female labour falls on family labour on wage labour. Studies of the impact on female wage labour of the introduction of high-yield varieties during the Green Revolution, for example, showed that it increased the demand for it. Poverty rates among female casual labourers in India continue to remain high; at the end of the 1980s, 61 per cent were below the poverty line as compared to 58 per cent of male casual labourers. According to the national report of Bangladesh, the introduction of new technologies in food processing and preservation and in animal husbandry increased the demand for female wage labour. Women nevertheless continue to account for the largest proportion of the poor; the female share of poverty as a percentage of the labour force is currently 87.7 per cent as compared to 74 per cent for males.

112.   According to an ECLAC study, in Latin America and the Caribbean new technologies and the new ways of organizing work could theoretically have been very helpful in reducing gender-based segregation, but these possibilities have not materialized in the region. Where the integration of large numbers of female workers into some of the modernized sectors of the economy has occurred (e.g., in Chile's agro-industry and northern Mexico's electronic maguila industry), it has generally been precarious and workers

in these jobs usually receive low pay, have temporary contracts, lack social security and are not allowed to unionize and engage in collective bargaining. 10/

(e)   Control and allocation of resources within the household
113.   Intra-household gender relations tend to create a disjunction in the translation of the improvement in household and female earnings into the improvement of female and child welfare. The national report of Bangladesh shows that women wage earners in poor households have only 1.03 meals to every 2.4 meals for men. Other studies show that in developing countries household strategies for coping with crises reveal that the bulk of the hardship falls on women, since their consumption tends to be reduced first and their assets are often sold first. In the face of economic hardship, a desperate measure is often the abandonment of the household by the male wage earner, leading to the creation of another female-headed household. Because of its impact on the ability of women to exercise control over their own resources and those of the household, the intra-household gender relationship is an important factor influencing the feminization of poverty in developing countries and in some developed and transitional economies.

114.   Intra-household conflict is undoubtedly a factor that is, *inter alia*, responsible for the distinct gender dimension of poverty. It has been demonstrated at the theoretical and empirical levels that the assumption that households promote joint welfare maximization is useful for the purpose of economic modelling. It is, however, only an assumption, and is also to some extent an oversimplification and as such causes the model to yield a somewhat impoverished construction of social reality. 52/ The growing literature on intra-household distributional inequalities in developed, developing and transitional economies provides further theoretical and empirical refutation of the idea of joint welfare maximization. Research on the issue demonstrates that the economic process is not the result of the interplay of income and prices alone but is strongly influenced by social and cultural factors and factors related to customs and traditions. The inclusion of these factors in a model purporting to explain poverty from the gender perspective is crucial, and otherwise the gender dimension in what at first sight appears to be a gender-neutral process of economic and social deprivation - i.e., impoverishment - goes undetected. However, to emphasize female poverty solely in

terms of gender conflict would be a dangerous trivialization that would inevitably result in masking a more general crisis of the years of gender-blind and at times gender-biased development.

115.   Attempts to assess the extent of the feminization of poverty among the world's poor run into problems of insufficient data. The accessible evidence is based on inferences from the trends that underlie the process of feminization, namely trends in female headship, changes in the pattern and structure of employment and the socio-cultural factors that continue to influence gender relations.

2. Poverty in terms of different groups of women
116.   Women continue to be vulnerable to poverty by virtue of their social status. Social stratification can be affected by migrant and refugee status, age, marital status and ethnicity. Among the poorest of the poor are migrant and/or refugee women who have left home either in search of work or as a result of being uprooted by military conflict and civil strife.

1. Refugees and displaced women
117.   Civil wars in countries as varied as Afghanistan, Angola, Armenia, Azerbaijan, Georgia, Haiti, Mozambique, Rwanda, Somalia, the Sudan and the former Yugoslavia have denied livelihood to millions of people, destroyed infrastructure, driven people away from their homes and reduced millions to destitution and hunger. At the end of 1994, there were some 23 million refugees and millions of displaced persons, all victims of civil war and other forms of armed conflict. According to the United Nations High Commissioner for Refugees, 80 per cent of the refugees and displaced persons are women and children. Recent data shows that mothers and children are disproportionately represented in the refugee population in Africa, Asia and Central America. Two thirds of the total refugee population in Somalia were women, while 90 per cent of the total Ethiopian refugee population in Somalia were women with young children. Eighty per cent of Cambodian refugee families along the Thai-Cambodian border were headed by women, and 68 per cent of the refugee women in one Thai refugee camp headed households with young dependent children. 53/

118.   Having escaped military conflict and/or persecution, refugee women often find themselves trapped in poverty. On resettlement, many

suffer isolation and the lack of employment opportunities except in low-paying, low status jobs, 53/ and they have little or no chance of improving their situation. Despite strenuous efforts to help them, relatively few of these women have managed to escape poverty in any lasting way. Most continue to face adverse conditions owing to the gender bias prevailing in society and economic stagnation in the receiving countries. Any new strategy for eliminating poverty will have to address the special needs of uprooted women not only in the context of complementary actions directed at specially vulnerable population groups but also as part of national efforts directed at poverty eradication.

2. Elderly women

119.   Poverty among elderly women is on the rise, particularly in developing countries where very few of them have pension rights and where rapid urbanization has eroded the traditional system of social support, but it is largely ignored in domestic economic and social policy-making and overlooked by international development donors.

120.   For women in the developed market economies, poverty experienced in the workplace is often extended to their retirement and affects their psychological, physical, economic and social well-being. The retirement income, especially for working-class women, reflects years of disadvantageous positioning in the labour market and the pervasive discrimination that women encounter throughout their lives in schooling, work and housing. As a consequence, many women find themselves in poverty after retirement. 54/ Rural elderly women appear to be particularly vulnerable. Recent research shows that the incidence of poverty among non-metropolitan elderly women in these economies is higher than among metropolitan elderly women. 55/ Poverty among elderly women is mediated by factors such as class, ethnicity and race. The greatest incidence of poverty in the United States, for example, is found among older black women. 56/

121.   Elderly women account for a large proportion of poor in the economies in transition. The national report of Kyrgyzstan, for example, indicates that elderly women constitute the majority of the poor.

3. Indigenous women

122.   Poverty is endemic among indigenous women in Central America,

Africa, New Zealand, Malaysia, Australia, Canada, and the former republics of the Soviet Union. Across the world, indigenous women have higher rates of unemployment, illiteracy, household headship and dependency than non-indigenous men and women and lack of access to health and social services. The national report of Kyrgyzstan, for example, emphasizes the lack of employment opportunities among indigenous women. The national report of Canada indicates that the average income of aboriginal women is the lowest in the country. In 1991, 60 per cent of aboriginal women in Canada had a total income of under $10,000. Twenty-four per cent of indigenous women in Australia are recipients of social security benefits, a rate twice that found for other Australian women.

123.   About 30 million indigenous men and women live in Latin America where their problems cannot be dissociated from the whole range of difficulties experienced by the region. In all Amerindian cultures, identity and culture are closely related to land ownership, which was denied them after the European conquest and which is still the object of a legal battle between indigenous communities and national authorities. As these communities are traditionally categorized as pre-farming self sufficient ethnic groups and farming ethnic groups, it is clear that the loss of their territories greatly affected their living conditions.

124.   Poverty experienced by the indigenous population prompted many of them to seek gainful employment in rural and urban areas. In general, their integration has been marginal, particularly so in the case of women, who find work as household employees, itinerant tradespeople or workers in unstable jobs. They are all the more vulnerable because they migrate at an earlier age than men, when they are still unmarried, and also because their illiteracy rate is higher than that of men (about 3.9 per cent on average). 57/ In Bolivia, for example, where indigenous people account for 60 per cent of the population, 98 per cent of monolingual and 73.5 per cent of bilingual indigenous populations are living in poverty. In Guatemala, the income of the 65 per cent of indigenous men and women, who account for 41.9 per cent of the whole population, falls into the deciles of income distribution corresponding with the lowest share of total national income.

4. Other social factors
125.   Female poverty is also an economic consequence of divorce. Recent

data show that, as a consequence of divorce, women's income drops by 50 per cent compared to 25 per cent for men and that their poverty rate rises threefold, while for men, the rate increases only marginally. Income-to-needs ratios adjusted for family size show a 40 per cent increase for women following divorce, but for men the ratio remains essentially the same. 58/

126.   In light of these trends and the persistence and/or worsening of poverty around the world, the lack of a systematic gender approach to poverty reduction constitutes a threat to the progress of women's advancement. A review of the national reports shows that in many countries measures taken to combat poverty among women are of a somewhat piecemeal nature and lack the context of a coherent, consistent and gender-sensitive strategy.

3. Women, poverty and the environment

127.   The link between women's economic status and environmental problems is complex, problematic and, occasionally, somewhat tenuous. It differs in developed and developing countries, in urban and rural settings, and with the nature of specific environmental problems. Moreover, the connection between environmental problems and women's economic status will vary between the context of global environmental change and that of local environmental problems. The link between the two is also affected by population variables, in particular rapid population growth and migration, which are both a stimulus and a response to environmental change.

128.   The relationship between women, poverty and the environment has taken several conceptual forms since the mid-1970s, when interest in the issue first emerged within the development discourse. Initially, the relationship between female poverty and the environment was seen primarily in the context of fuel shortages and women's responsibilities involving the collection and consumption of wood. As poverty reduction was given greater priority in the development agenda, a new concept, (or rather misconception) emerged, namely, that the poor, in their struggle to survive, tend to exploit whatever natural resources they can appropriate, thus causing greater environmental damage. By the time women in development became a more or less separate field within development studies, women were recognized as being among those who suffer most from environmental degradation

because of their extensive involvement in activities requiring close contact with nature and because of their maternal roles.

129.   Urban women in poverty and their dependents may live in shacks and shanties, hastily developed lodgings, rented rooms, illegal quarters or in shared accommodations in boarding houses. In all cases, cramped and over-crowded quarters increase the risk of transmitting diseases, which is exacerbated by the lack of adequate sanitation, waste collection and access to safe water. Women, who often have to spend more time inside the house than men, are more exposed to both airborne and water-related diseases as well as to respiratory infections from the smoke and fumes of cooking and heating materials. A recent study of women and environment in developing countries 59/ shows that women's exposure to indoor air pollution from biomass fuel combustion often exceeds the WHO peak guideline by as much as 69 to 80 times. Nearly 92 million women in urban areas of the world are affected by lack of access to safe drinking water and more than 133 million by lack of proper sanitation. Most of these live in Asia in highly polluted environments. In Africa, 12 million urban women are estimated to lack access to safe drinking water. In Latin America, the figures are comparable to those for Africa (12 million and 22 million, respectively). 59/ Similarly, 20 per cent of all urban women in Africa, 19 per cent in Asia and 14 per cent in Latin America are estimated to be affected by lack of access to sanitation services.

130.   The same study shows that 68 per cent of rural women in Africa, 77 per cent in Asia and 39 per cent in Latin America are affected by fuelwood scarcity. The largest number of women affected by deforestation and fuel-wood scarcity in absolute terms is in Asia where there are some 494 million when India and China are included and more than 131 million otherwise. The time spent by rural women gathering fuelwood in areas of high deforestation ranges from 2.5 to 5 hours, while in low-deforestation areas women spend an hour or more per day collecting fuelwood.

131.   Rural women in developing countries are also affected by a lack of access to safe water and as a result, have to spend a significant amount of time fetching water. If India and China are excluded, Africa emerges as the region where the largest number of rural women, (56 per cent of those between 10 and 49 years of age), are affected by water scarcity. In Asia, more

than 60 million women, or some 32 per cent, are affected by water scarcity. In Latin America, 46 per cent of all rural women in the same age group are affected by lack of access to safe water. Such a high proportion indicates that, despite the highly urbanized nature of Latin America and the general abundance of water, there are still a significant number of areas where water scarcity, at least seasonally, imposes a burden on women in their daily lives with respect to water procurement. Women in developing countries may spend as much as 1.6 hours a day collecting water in the dry season, and 0.63 hours a day in the wet season. Unfortunately, no studies have been made of the relationships between desertification, deforestation and water collection time.

132.   Finally, any links there may be between environment and fertility will directly involve women. Two types of effect have been emphasized. In urban areas, the degree of exposure to toxic pollutants and other forms of pollution could affect the health of the mother and the foetus. In poor rural areas, the environment may be such that a woman's nutritional level is so low that her health and that of her child are endangered. On the other hand, it has been hypothesized, that as women's workload increases with environmental degradation, they may perceive the benefits of having children to help them as larger than they otherwise would. 60/ A number of studies on the cost and value of children show that inputs by children in peasant agriculture are substantial. 59/

4. Means of eradicating female poverty

133.   Since it is largely true that "what is not counted is usually not noticed", 61/ appropriate measurements of poverty in general and of female poverty in particular are important for determining the nature and dimensions of the phenomenon, and for formulating the anti-poverty policies and monitoring their implementation. There are at least three immediately identifiable problems in measuring female poverty and they concern the choice of indicators, the level of measurement and the degree of aggregation.

134.   The most widely used indicator is income. Poverty is then identified with low income, or with low consumption. The problem with this is that women's consumption is often not a direct function of their income but is governed by complex factors of a socio-cultural nature that are not easy to

quantify. In addition, income accruing to women is systematically underreported owing to the problems of collecting gender-disaggregated data and the concentration of women in informal and non-monetary spheres of economic activity.

135.   Moreover, the income of women is often measured not at the individual level but at that of the household, and this leads to understatement of their poverty status because resource allocation at the household level is not really governed by principles of joint welfare maximization. The calculation of household per capita income is also often based on its number of adult consumers rather than on the actual number of its members. 62/

136.   Finally, while various dimensions of poverty may be closely correlated, they are by no means interchangeable with or reducible to each other. Consequently, their aggregation into a single poverty index may give a misleading picture or bring about the loss of gender-specific information on poverty. This will have serious implications for the way female poverty is addressed. Quantitative analyses also need to be supplemented by qualitative assessment, or such important but unquantifiable dimensions of poverty as self-esteem, empowerment, autonomy, participation in decision-making and security will be overlooked.

137.   Analyses of women's poverty suggest that its main causes stem from the perpetual disadvantage of women in terms of position in the labour market, access to productive resources, education, and income for the satisfaction of their basic needs. They also demonstrate that poor women possess exceptional resourcefulness, initiative and entrepreneurial spirit and show tenacity and self-sacrifice in trying to take a long-term view of their adverse economic situation and in safeguarding their livelihoods. The agenda for the eradication of female poverty should therefore begin with the recognition of women's economic potential and should aim at enhancing women's capabilities. Conversely, the agenda for development should begin by targeting women in poverty, because experience has shown time and again that any approach to poverty alleviation that leaves the economic status of women unchanged tends to fall short of its goal.

138.   Attempts to provide a conceptual foundation for policies directed at reducing of female poverty have produced at least three approaches, all

aimed at improving women's capabilities and creating the appropriate environment for their utilization. One approach, popular with international development institutions, emphasizes the role of the market as a sine qua non in creating income-generating opportunities for women providing that its functioning is not distorted by interventionist policies. Another important aspect of this approach is its recognition of the fact that it is not the rate of economic growth but rather its nature and its sources that determine whether or not women will benefit from it or end up being marginalized by it. Policy recommendations formulated on the basis of this approach emphasize sound micro- and macroeconomic policies together with non-distortive public intervention directed at the provision of social services.

139.   A second approach to anti-poverty policy is on the expansion of the rights of the poor "so that rights of social security can be made to stand as guarantees of minimal protection and survival". 63/ The strength of this approach is that it emphasizes that the alleviation of female poverty cannot rely exclusively on either "the operation of market forces or on some paternalistic initiative on the part of the State ... or other social institution". 64/ Markets are not always hostile to women and government interventions are not always beneficial for the advancement of their economic status. In light of this approach, the policy challenge is therefore to maximize the market's potential by creating income-generating opportunities for women, to minimize its hostile influences and to provide public assistance and social services in the least distortive way.

140.   A third approach emphasizes "growth with equity" as the main premise in the formulation of anti-poverty policies and it is also based on the firm rejection of the "trickle-down" principle of GNP growth. In its attempt to reconcile market efficiency with equity as embodied in policy interventions, this approach is close to that couched in terms of the entitlement and endowments of the poor, except that the emphasis here is not so much on the inefficiencies resulting from distorted markets, as on failure to ensure the just distribution of the fruits of growth. Anti-poverty policy measures based on this approach emphasize responsible price and market polices together with policies for distributing assets and expanding productive employment opportunities.

141.   During the 1980s, policies of poverty reduction reflected the differing conceptual approaches to their formulation. In the early 1980s, in the face of widespread macroeconomic difficulties and debt problems, anti-poverty policies aimed at restoring growth. In the late 1980s, they began to highlight the importance of environmental protection and of targeting female poverty in the fight against poverty in developing countries. The participatory approach directed at women's empowerment and the rejection of "welfarism" became central to the formulation of policies directed at the reduction of female poverty. This approach emphasizes the interdependence of women's advancement and development and also seeks to modify development policies so as to transform unequal gender relations and account for their gender-specific effects. In other words, it seeks to incorporate gender into development planning.

142.   The policy prescriptions put forward by international development agencies reflect the conceptual approaches to poverty outlined above. There is a significant degree of similarity and overlap between these prescriptions. All of them pay attention to the role of markets in addressing female poverty, and all conform to the notion of the importance of well-functioning, undistorted markets and prices, although the degree of emphasis on the role of markets varies. All are concerned with access to productive resources, and particularly to credit. Access to education and health services is recognized by all as important for a solution to female poverty and references to better employment opportunities are frequently made.

143.   The policy recommendations most frequently made are the following:

(a)   Target resources to poor women and facilitate access by women to credit (group lending schemes) and to new technology (using women extension workers to reach groups of women farmers);

(b)   Ensure access to education and health services (safe motherhood programmes, nutrition programmes etc.);

(c)   Change laws where necessary to ensure women's access to land, assets and employment;

(d)   Provide adequate safety nets;

(e)   Redefine priorities for resource allocation within national budgets to reflect priority social services;

(f)   Supplement the economic approach to female poverty with the elimination of social and legal gender inequalities;

(g)   Enable the rural and urban poor to analyse their situation and express their own priorities through a community participation approach (participatory rural appraisal, for example).

144.   The common difficulty with such recommendations is that they address what is required without specifying how it is to be achieved. Also they do not adequately reflect gender relations and do not provide a comprehensive strategy for dealing with female poverty. And finally, they do not adequately address the role of the State, except in terms of restructuring public expenditure.

145.   At the national level, approaches to female poverty are even less coherent and lack the context of a comprehensive strategy for dealing with the problem. Most of the national reports reviewed so far lack a coherent, balanced agenda for combating female poverty. Piecemeal measures, such as the introduction of a quota system for women in the recruitment policy of the public sector in Bangladesh or tax breaks for single mothers with children in the Russian Federation, are reported as measures taken towards the reduction of poverty among women. Nowhere is the issue addressed by gender-sensitive development planning, and due consideration is nowhere given to the role of Government and the market in the alleviation of female poverty. In light of the apparent feminization of poverty in developed, developing and transitional economies alike, the lack of specific policies that are well balanced in terms of emphasis is a threat to development and to democracy, because in the long run the low economic status of women is likely to translate into slower rates of economic growth.

Notes

1/   Report of the World Conference to Review and Appraise the Achievements of the United Nations Decade for Women: Equality, Development and Peace, Nairobi, 15-26 July 1985 (United Nations publication, Sales No. E.85.IV.10), chap. I, sect. A.

2/   See the discussion in Women in the World Economy: the 1994 World Survey on the Role of Women in Development.

3/   F. Nixson, "The third world and the global economy: recent trends and future prospects", Developments in Economics: An Annual Review, vol. 6 (1990), p. 34.

4/   Since early 1994, the International Monetary Fund has placed greater emphasis on social sector policies. Recognizing the important developmental gains from improving the status and quality of life of women, in the context of both programmes and the policy dialogue with member Governments the Fund has underscored the importance of improving women's access to education, health care, and family planning. The Fund is exploring, in close consultation with the Bank, the modalities of providing gender-sensitivity training for Fund staff, in order to enhance their effectiveness in both the design of adjustment programmes and the provision of technical assistance.

5/   World Economic Survey, 1990 (United Nations publication, Sales No. E.90.II.C.1), p. 3.

6/   World Economic Survey, 1993 (United Nations publication, Sales No. E.93.II.C.1), p. 209.

7/   ECLAC, Panorama social de America Latina y el Caribe, 1993 ed. (Santiago, 1993).

8/   _____, "Women in Latin America and the Caribbean in the 1990s: diagnostic elements and proposals" (LC/L.836; CRM.6/4).

9/   _____, "Report of the Regional Conference on the Integration of Women into the Economic and Social Development of Latin America and the Caribbean, Mar del Plata, Argentina, 25-29 September 1994" (PLE/2/Rev.1).

10/   _____, 1994. "Women and urban employment in Latin America: the significance of changes in the 1990s" (DDR/3). See also M. Pollack, "Feminization of the informal sector in Latin America and the Caribbean?" Mujer y Desarrollo, No. 11 (LC/L.731).

11/   "Population distribution and migration. Proceedings of the United Nations Expert Meeting on Population Distribution and Migration, Santa Cruz, Bolivia, 18-22 January 1993" (ESA/P/WP.12).

12/   The Integrated Poverty Index is calculated by combining the head-count measure of poverty and the income-gap ratio, income distribution below the poverty line and the annual rate of growth per capital GNP.

13/   I. Jazairy, M. Alamgir and T. Panuccio, The State of World Rural Poverty. An Introduction into its Causes and Consequences (New York, New York University Press, 1992).

14/   Civil strife in Algeria, Burundi, Kenya, Liberia, Rwanda, Sierra Leone, Sudan and Zaire and the civil war in Angola reduced or brought to a halt economic activities, displaced population, destroyed infrastructure and precluded economic reforms.

15/   Global Economic Prospects and the Developing Countries (World Bank, Washington D.C., 1994).

16/   Report on the World Social Situation, 1993 (United Nations publication, Sales No. E.93.IV.2), p. 39.

17/   G. Standing, "Feminization through flexible labour", World Development, vol. 17, No. 7 (July 1989).

18/   V. Moghadam, "An overview of global employment and unemployment in a gender perspective" (UNU/WIDER, 1994).

19/   The effects of structural adjustment on women are often described in terms of "added worker effect" and the "discouraged worker effect". The "added worker effect" is increase in the supply of female labour in response to a decline in household income. The "discouraged worker effect" results from the decline in employment opportunities.

20/   World Economic and Social Survey, 1994 (United Nations publication, Sales No. E.94.II.C.1).

21/   World Development Report, 1992. Development and Environment (New York, Oxford University Press, 1992).

22/   I. Jazairy, M. Alamgir and T. Panuccio, op. cit., p. 84.

23/   In Sri Lanka and the Philippines, for example, the rates of unemployment among women have been higher than among men throughout the period since the Nairobi Conference. (See "Review and appraisal of the implementation of the Nairobi Forward-looking Strategies for the Advancement of Women" (E/ESCAP/RUD/SOCWD/1).)

24/   "Violence against migrant women workers" (A/49/354).

25/   S. Baden, "The impact of recession and structural adjustment on women's work in developing countries", paper prepared for the ILO, 1993.

26/   Current debt-service to export ratio of major recipients of private capital among developing countries is 0.22 as compared with 0.29 in the period 1982-1987. Their debt to export ratio in 1990-1992 declined to 1.75 from 1.86 in 1982-1987 (Global Economic Prospects and the Developing Countries..., p. 11).

27/   Economies in transition include the countries of Eastern Europe (Albania, Bulgaria, Croatia, the Czech Republic, Hungary, Poland, Romania, Slovakia, Slovenia and the Federal Republic of Yugoslavia), the republics of the former Soviet Union cooperating within the Commonwealth of Independent States, and the Baltic States of Estonia, Latvia and Lithuania.

28/ "Shock therapy" involves a sharp cut of budget deficits, liberalization of prices and imports, devaluation of exchange rates, interest rate increases and tight control of money supply growth.

29/ "The role of women in the transition processes: facing a major challenge" (E/ECE/RW/HLM/5).

30/ J. Musil, "New social contracts: responses of the State and the social partners to the challenges of restructuring and privatization", Labour and Society, vol. 16, No. 4, p. 1.

31/ L. Paukert, "Women's employment in East-Central European countries during the period of transition to a market economy system", working paper prepared for the

32/ "Regional review and appraisal of the Nairobi Forward-looking Strategies for the Advancement of Women" (E/ECE/RW/HLM/1).

33/ Population Distribution and Migration (United Nations publication, forthcoming).

34/ About 854 million women were estimated to be economically active in 1990, accounting for 32.1 per cent of the global labour force. See Women in Manufacturing: Participation Patterns, Determinants and Trends (Vienna, UNIDO, 1993).

35/ Recent trends suggest that Malaysia, Thailand, Indonesia, the Philippines and China have replaced four original newly industrializing countries as the engine of growth in the region.

36/ J. Henshall Momsen, "Attitudes to women factory workers in Malaysia" in Women and Development in the Third World (London, Routledge, 1991).

37/ "Productive employment: women workers in a changing global environment", ILO contribution to the World Survey on the Role of Women in Development, 1994 (United Nations publication, forthcoming).

38/ B. Rogers, The Domestication of Women (London, Tavistock, 1986), p. 142.

39/ M. Gaudier, "Poverty, inequality, exclusion: new approach to theory and practice", Série Bibliographique, No. 17, Institut international d'études sociales (Geneva, 1993), pp. 48-49.

40/ B. Simon, "The feminization of poverty: a call for primary prevention", Journal of Primary Prevention, vol. I, No. 2 (1988), pp. 6-17.

41/ V. Wilson-Ford, "Poverty among black elderly women", Journal of Women and Aging, vol. V (1990), pp. 5-20.

42/ J. Mencher and A. Okongwu, eds. Where Did All the Men Go? (Boulder, Colorado, Westview Press, 1993).

43/ N. Kabeer, "Women in poverty: a review of concepts and findings", paper presented to the Seminar on Women in Extreme Poverty: Integration of Women's Concerns in National Development Planning, Vienna, 9-12 November 1992.

44/   S. Alam, "Women and poverty in Bangladesh", Women's Studies International Forum, vol. 8, No. 4 (1985), pp. 361-371.

45/   Living Arrangements of Women and Their Children: A Demographic Profile (United Nations publication, forthcoming).

46/   L. Beneria and S. Feldman, eds., Unequal Burden. Economic Crises, Persistent Poverty and Women's Work (Boulder, Colorado, Westview Press, 1992).

47/   The proposition that the proportion of income spent on basic necessities is inversely related to income is known as Engel's Law.

48/   Barbara J. Nelson and Najma Chowdhury, eds., Women and Politics Worldwide (New Haven, Yale University Press, 1994), p. 5.

49/   IPS Daily Journal, vol. II, No. 120 (1994), p. 4.

50/   Raie Lesser Blumberg, "Income under female versus male control: hypotheses from a theory of gender stratification and data from the third world", Journal of Family Issues, vol. IX, No. 1 (1988), pp. 51-84.

51/   "Counterfactual" is defined as the situation that would have taken place in the absence of a programme.

52/   N. Kabeer, "Benevolent dictators, maternal altruists and patriarchal contracts: gender and household economics" in Reversed Realities, N. Kabeer, ed. (London, Verso, 1994).

53/   Cited in P. DeVoe, "The silent majority: women as refugees", Women and International Development Annual, vol. IV (1994), p. 35.

54/   K. Perkins, "Recycling poverty: from workplace to retirement", Journal of Women and Aging, vol. V (1993), pp. 5-23.

55/   D. McLaughlin, "Nonmetropolitan elderly women: a portrait of economic vulnerability", Journal of Applied Gerontology, vol. XII, No. 3 (1993), pp. 320-334.

56/   V. Wilson-Ford, "Poverty among black elderly women", Journal of Women and Aging, vol. IV, No. 4 (1990), pp. 5-20.

57/   ECLAC, "Integration of the feminine into Latin America culture: in search of a new social paradigm", Mujer y Desarrollo, No. 9 (LC/L.674).

58/   R. Finnie, "Women, men and the economic consequences of divorce: evidence from Canadian longitudinal data", Canadian Review of Sociology and Anthropology, vol. XXX, No. 2 (1993), pp. 205-241.

59/   R. Bilsborrow and T. Keshari, "Statistical indicators on women and environment in developing countries". Mimeo (Chapel Hill, North Carolina, Carolina Population Center, 1994).

60/   M. Nerlove, "Population and environment: a parable of firewood and other tales", American Journal of Agricultural Economics, vol. 73, No. 5 (1991), pp. 1,334-1,347; J. Jacobson, "Gender bias: roadblock to sustainable development", Worldwatch Paper 110 (Washington, D.C., 1992).

61/   J. Galbraith, "The economics of the American housewife", Atlantic Monthly, vol. 232, No. 2 (August), p. 79.

62/   N. Kabeer, "Women in poverty: a review of concepts and findings", paper prepared for the Seminar on Women in Extreme Poverty, Vienna, 9-12 November 1992.

63/   J. Drexe and A. Sen, Hunger and Public Action (Oxford, Clarendon Press, 1989), p. 20.

64/   Ibid., p. 17.

B. Inequality in access to education and other means of maximizing the use of women's capacities

1.   The Universal Declaration of Human Rights asserts that everyone has a right to education. This has often been neglected in the list of basic human needs and has only recently received more attention, when economists and development planners recognized that education and human resource development are key factors in promoting development. There is evidence that education has an impact on health, mortality, productivity, household income and fertility rates. The social returns to a woman's education go far beyond individual welfare and are vital to national development. Potential economic gains result from the expansion of women's income earning capacities. Special efforts need to be made to reach the excluded and the vulnerable, in particular, girls in some regions and countries, girls with disabilities, girls of ethnic minorities and indigenous groups.

2.   Several international instruments put forward the rights of girls and women to education. The Convention on the Elimination of All Forms of Discrimination calls for the elimination of discrimination against women in order to ensure equal rights with men in the field of education. 1/ It asks for the same conditions for career and vocational guidance, for access to studies and obtaining of diplomas at all levels of schooling. The Convention requests access to the same curricula and examinations, to scholarships and other study grants, to programmes of continuing education including adult and functional literacy programmes and to information on family planning. It addresses the drop-out rates of female students and asks for the provision of special programmes for girls who leave school prematurely. It stresses

that girls should be given the same opportunities to participate actively in sports and physical education. It recognizes the need to eliminate stereotyped roles of men and women at all levels and in all aspects of education. 2/

3.   The World Conference on Education for All, held in Jomtien (Thailand) in 1990, drew attention to the gender gap in educational opportunities and its consequences for human development. Article 3.3 emphasizes that the education of girls and women constitutes a priority. It calls in particular for the elimination of all gender stereotyping in education and in particular for a supportive policy con text. 3/

4.   The Convention on the Rights of the Child 4/ contains provisions to the right to education, including the right to compulsory and free primary education and access to all to secondary, vocational and higher education. It also claims equal rights for girls and boys to education and asserts the importance of education as a social and cultural right. It affirms that every child has the right to a non-discriminatory education that fully respects cultural identity and language needs.

1. Education and the Nairobi Forward-looking Strategies

5.   The Forward-looking Strategies consider education to be "the basis for the full promotion and improvement of the status of women". 5/ Recommendations related to education for women are set out as an area of development, but references to the need for formal and non-formal education and training are made in many other sections of the Nairobi Forward-looking Strategies. Governments agreed to encourage public and private schools to examine educational materials and textbooks and to eliminate discriminatory gender-stereotyping, to redesign textbooks that reflect a positive and dynamic image of women and to include women's studies in the curricula. They also agreed to take steps to diversify women's vocational training and to create integrated systems for training that have direct links with employment needs and future trends. The Forward-looking Strategies do not call for parity of women's enrolment in primary, secondary and university education but rather for "equal opportunities" in access to resources, especially education and training, and do not consider the issue of completion (repetition and drop-out) and the need for teacher training on gender issues.

6.   The first review and appraisal of the Nairobi Forward-looking Strategies in 1990 gives evidence that changes have taken place in formal education. 6/ In the decade from 1970 to 1980, programmes to improve women's access to education were effective in many regions, especially for younger women. Equality between men and women in school enrolment was achieved in several regions, although not in those where the majority of the world's population is located. However, it shows that this change affected only a small number of countries. Modest progress had been achieved in Africa, which could be largely attributed to national development plans and the fact that education at the primary level had been free in many countries. In Asia and the Pacific, the pervasive influence of traditional social attitudes and feudal patriarchal systems were identified as the main obstacles to women's emancipation and education. In Latin America and the Caribbean, major differences exist between countries and between rural and urban areas. Indigenous populations have less access, while opportunities at higher-income levels were nearly equal. Few countries seemed to have engaged in a comprehensive strategy to advance women's education.

7.   Following the 1990 first review and appraisal of the implementation of the Strategies on education and training, the Economic and Social Council adopted the following conclusions:

> "**Recommendation III.** In the area of education, both formal and non-formal, Governments should promote the training of teachers on gender issues, co-education and professional counselling. Governments should complete the revision of textbooks expeditiously, if possible by 1995, in accordance with national law and practice, in order to eliminate sex-biased presentations and should, in conjunction with women's groups, take steps to reduce the stereotyping of women in the mass media, whether by self-policing on the part of the media or by other measures.

> "Governments, non-governmental organizations, women's groups and all other entities concerned should take steps to amend formal and informal educational systems at all levels to promote change in the psychological, social and traditional practices that are the foundation of the de facto obstacles to women's progress.

> "The United Nations Secretariat, the United Nations Educational, Scientific and Cultural Organization and other appropriate organizations of the United Nations system should continue to analyse the extent and effects of stereotyping of women and implement innovative programmes to combat it."

> ...

"**Recommendation X**. Governments that have not already done so should reorient resources to ensure women's equal access to education and training at all levels and in all fields and, in collaboration with women's groups and non-governmental organizations, should make special efforts to remove all gender-related differences in adult literacy by the year 2000. Programmes should be established to ensure that parents and teachers provide equal educational opportunities for girls and boys. In particular, encouragement should be given to promoting the study by girls of scientific and technological subjects, particularly those corresponding to national development priorities, and to preparing girls for full participation in the economy and in public life. In order to fulfil these commitments, appropriate measures should be taken at the national and international levels to ensure revitalization of growth on a long-term basis.

"The United Nations Educational, Scientific and Cultural Organization and other organizations of the United Nations system should give special priority to eliminating female illiteracy and to monitoring efforts to ensure that women have equal access to all levels of education and training." 7/

2. Progress achieved and persistent gaps in female education and training
(a)   Literacy

8.   Nine hundred and five million men and women are estimated to be illiterate world wide; 65 per cent of whom are women. 8/ In all regions of the world, the illiteracy rate of women has been steadily declining. With the exception of Africa, important progress has been made in eliminating both adult illiteracy and the differentials between female and male illiteracy. High illiteracy rates in Africa and Asia and the Pacific are a reflection of past discrimination and lack of opportunities. In the present age group 15-24 years, illiteracy rates are significantly lower due to higher levels of school enrolment.

9.   Global figures on literacy mask disparities between countries within a region and between rural and urban areas. In the Caribbean region, for example, very low levels of illiteracy are reported for the majority of countries (Cuba, 2 per cent, Barbados, Guyana, the Netherlands Antilles, 10 per cent), whereas a few continue to have consistently high rates (Haiti, 65 per cent in 1985, Saint Lucia, a 54 per cent illiteracy rate in 1991). Countries with high numbers of indigenous populations have higher illiterate ratios, in particular among women. Guatemala reports that 80 per cent of the indigenous women are illiterate. Despite a general improvement in Asia and the Pacific - for example, female illiteracy in south-eastern Asia has decreased to 24 per cent - the significantly high illiteracy rates among

women still persist in that region. There are 62 per cent of female illiterates in South Asia, indicating a 5.5 per cent increase compared to the 1985 figure. In the developed countries, the number of people who have no literacy or numeracy skills is minimal and reaches higher percentages only among immigrant populations and people living in poverty.

10.   Figures on illiteracy do not reflect the level of functional illiteracy. As a result of low levels of schooling and educational achievements, functional illiteracy is growing among men and women in many countries, even some of the most developed, thus leaving large numbers of the population partially illiterate and with no or little knowledge of history, current events on societal problems. Evidence suggests that considerable numbers of the adult populations in some developed countries are having difficulties with the basic skills of reading, writing and basic mathematics, although women score better than men in literacy and numeracy. These functional illiterates often lack the knowledge of basic skills, such as how to operate machines and equipment. Functional literacy has an impact on income-generating activities, hygiene and protection of the environment.

Table II.B.1. Average percentage of men and women who were illiterate in 1980 and 1990 census rounds, by region

Region	1980 round Men	1980 round Women	1990 round Men	1990 round Women
A. Over 15 years of age				
Africa	51.8	71.8	44.6	61.1
Latin America and the Caribbean	18.2	23.3	14.3	16.0
Western Europe and other	5.7	11.4	8.7	9.9
Asia and the Pacific	31.8	49.3	21.7	34.3
Eastern Europe	1.5	4.9	0.9	2.3
B. 15-24 years of age				
Africa	35.8	55.7	35.6	51.0
Latin America and the Caribbean	9.0	10.3	7.5	6.9
Western Europe and other	1.0	1.0	2.6	1.2
Asia and the Pacific	19.7	32.6	10.3	17.9
Eastern Europe	0.5	0.9	..	..
C. 25-44 years of age				
Africa	50.7	74.4	35.3	58.3
Latin America and the Caribbean	14.1	19.4	5.3	7.3
Western Europe and other	2.5	4.7	5.5	3.7
Asia and the Pacific	26.7	44.7	20.2	35.8
Eastern Europe	0.7	2.4	..	..

Source: Division for the Advancement of Women, United Nations Secretariat, based on information contained in Women's Indicators and Statistics Data Base (WISTAT), version 3, 1994.

11.   Many national reports suggest that illiterate women have a great desire for learning. This strong motivation coupled with attractive programmes is a driving force for the acceptance and success of literacy programmes. Illiterate women are reported to regret that they have not been in school and consider illiteracy a major obstacle to their advancement. Even if women are not specifically targeted by literacy programmes, there is a considerable increase in the number of female participants in some countries. There is evidence that the illiteracy rate among women is dropping at a faster rate than that of men. In Egypt, for example, urban illiteracy for men remained constant between 1976 and 1986, while it dropped by 9.5 per cent for women during the same period. In the Caribbean, more women than men have been attracted to adult education literacy programmes geared at educating adults and exposing them to income-generating opportunities, developing positive attitudes and sensitizing youth to the dignity of work.

12.   Mass literacy campaigns constitute one effective strategy for elimination of widespread illiteracy among adult women within a set time-frame. Such campaigns have been carried out in the past in China, the former USSR, Viet Nam, Cuba and the United Republic of Tanzania, among other countries. India is one of the countries undertaking mass campaigns for literacy in various districts. Literacy campaigns are successful when they take into account the social condition of women and are linked to income-generating activities. Some countries report on the obstacles they have encountered. Major obstacles for successful implementation of literacy campaigns are the discontinuity of funds, the financial and material incapacity of communities to take charge of the training, the decreasing motivation of volunteers and irregularities in the follow-up activities. If there are no continuing education opportunities, women who already know how to read and write cannot apply and further develop their skills. Trainers play a catalyst role in literacy campaigns. Some countries recognize the necessity to clearly define literacy policy and to involve young people and especially women as instructors in the literacy process.

(b)   Primary education and secondary education
13.   In the past decade, substantive and successful efforts were made to achieve universal primary education and to attract girls to primary schools.

On a regional level, girls' enrolment has achieved parity with boys', except in Africa and Asia (see table II.B.2). The lowest rates persist in sub-Saharan Africa and Central and Southern Asia. In the ESCAP region as a whole, mean years for schooling for girls have increased from 2.99 in 1980 to 3.58 in 1990, while in South Asia, girls spent on average only 1.26 years in school in 1990 (1980: 1.16). Some countries report significant increases in female enrolment, which reflects a political will to promote girls' education. As an example, Bhutan has increased primary school enrolment for girls by 68 per cent since 1984, to 93 per cent, while boys registered a growth of only 11 per cent. The report explains that a special effort has been made to constantly gain the confidence of the parents to send their daughters to school in a country where the value of education in a modern environment was not fully appreciated before 1984, and the first modern school opened in the 1950s.

14.   Enrolment in secondary education is reaching parity in the developed countries and Eastern Europe (see table II.B.3). In Latin America and the Caribbean, the ratio of girls to boys is higher, indicating that more girls now remain in secondary education than boys. In 11 countries within the region, girls' enrolment rates exceed those of boys. The increase in the ratio of girls to boys in the African and Asia and Pacific region in only one generation (1970-1990) is considerable but is still far from reaching parity.

Table II.B.2. Average ratio of girls to boys in primary education, by region, 1970-1990

Region	1970	1980	1990
Africa	65	74	79
Latin America and the Caribbean	94	95	95
Western Europe and other	95	95	95
Asia and the Pacific	66	78	84
Eastern Europe	94	94	96
World	77	84	87

Source: Division for the Advancement of Women, United Nations Secretariat, based on information contained in Women's Indicators and Statistics Data Base (WISTAT), version 3, 1994.

Table II.B.3. Average ratio of girls to boys in secondary education, by level and region, 1970-1990

Region	1970	1980	1990
Africa	46	57	69
Latin America and the Caribbean	98	107	109
Western Europe and other	90	98	98
Asia and the Pacific	58	70	77
Eastern Europe	97	91	94
World	67	80	85

Source: Division for the Advancement of Women, United Nations Secretariat, based on information contained in Women's Indicators and Statistics Data Base (WISTAT), version 3, 1994.

Some developed countries report significant increases, which are not due only to the expansion of the educational opportunities at secondary level. In Australia, the number of girls staying in school to year 12 has increased from less than 37.3 per cent in 1980 to 82 per cent in 1992 (compared with 72.5 per cent for boys). In the United States, women have been narrowing the education gap. The figure of women completing their high school increased from 53 per cent in 1970 to 75 per cent in 1990.

15.   In Latin America, the quantitative progress achieved does not take into account the increment in late enrolments, grade repetition, temporary and definitive drop-outs. Access to schooling and appropriation of educational and cultural benefits is affected by urban or rural residence and by social class. Poor and rural women are more likely to be illiterate, to have no access to training programmes and higher education. Since the public educational system is fragmented, the poor attend low-quality schools, and vulnerable groups are most affected. Great disparities continue to persist among countries and within them, between urban and rural zones, among different ages and social classes.

16.   The African region remains the region with the lowest levels of education.

Almost half of the children of primary school age are out of school, the majority of them girls. Nevertheless, the countries of the African region have made an important effort on the supply side to cater for the educational needs of their growing populations. On a global level, primary enrolments in Africa more than tripled between 1960 and 1989, while they have doubled in Asia and Latin America. This expansion was subsequently reduced in the 1980s. In many countries with high population growth, the planning of new educational facilities did not meet the actual need. The educational sector in Nigeria, for example, has continued to expand rapidly. The number of primary schools doubled from nearly 20,000 in 1975/76, when the universal primary education was launched, to over 37,000 by 1982/83. The number of pupils, however, increased from 6 million to 14.5 million during that period. An increase of 85 per cent of the supply side stands against an increase of 140 per cent on the demand side.

17. The economic crisis and measures of structural adjustment in the eighties had their impact on the educational system. Expressed as a proportion of their national income during the 1980s, developing countries in general maintained the public expenditures on education. However, the significant population growth with the low level of national incomes actually brought the budgetary cuts in public expenditures on education. Thus, public expenditures on education per capita in sub-Saharan Africa fell by more than one half between 1980 and 1989. In Zaire, for example, a decrease from 3.6 per cent in 1980 to 1.7 per cent in 1985 and to 1.4 per cent in 1988 brought with it a decrease in the quality of education and lower enrolment. In Togo, such a situation caused the closure of schools and consequently a decrease in enrolment.

18. The political will to encourage girls' education is a prerequisite for increasing enrolment. There is evidence that the increase in per capita GNP positively affects female enrolment rates and women generally move towards parity with men. However, this does not occur automatically. If there are no gender-specific educational policies, the countries even with relatively high per capita GNP show disappointing achievements in terms of progress in female enrolment; whereas the countries with low per capita GNP show remarkable success because of deliberate educational policies taken to promote female education. For example, in Indonesia, through

affirmative action programmes the female/male disparity at secondary level was reduced by more than half during the 1980s. In Malawi, 33 per cent of the total secondary school enrolment slots are reserved for girls. In Bangladesh, taking into account the cultural constraints, separate secondary schools for girls were established at sub-district level.

19.   An important contributor to low female enrolment rates in education is the cost factor. The annual cost per pupil for primary education may be as high as a rural family's annual cash income. The annual cost of educating a child in secondary school is even greater. If a family decides to educate a child, culture and economics may favour the male. In some countries, the introduction of free secondary education considerably benefited the girls; previously if there were not sufficient family resources for education, they were kept at home.

20.   The enrolment of girls differs significantly in rural and urban areas. In Mali, for example, where only 17-20 per cent of girls are enrolled, the difference between rural and urban areas ranges from 13 to 59 per cent, respectively.

21.   Many countries reported on high drop-out rates. In some countries of Latin America and the Caribbean the drop-out rates for boys are higher than for girls. Boys are leaving school in order to earn an income. In countries with low levels of girls' schooling, drop-out rates for them are higher. Customs and traditions also have an impact on girls' school attendance.

22.   There are socio-economic and cultural obstacles for girls' access to education. These obstacles and a generally low perception of the value or utility of educating girls have an impact on their educational performance. Poor health and nutrition, early pregnancy and marriage, traditional practices such as circumcision, for example, further aggravate the situation. In some countries, only a small percentage of girls passes the primary school-leaving examinations. Several projects have been launched to remedy this situation, such as the abolishing of school fees for girls who do not repeat classes, social mobilization campaigns and the introduction of a bursary scheme for girls which provides tuition, uniforms and learning materials. Where equal access for girls is achieved and guaranteed and women's education is not considered a low priority, girls achieve better results and

higher scores than boys in a number of countries. In the Caribbean and in some Latin American countries, girls perform better than boys in terminal examinations at the secondary level. In the United Kingdom, girls currently out-perform boys in science subjects in examinations in the age group 16-18.

23.   On a global level, the rate of distribution among various subjects of specialization reveals a large gap in the female/male ratio in arts, literature, science and mathematics. Female secondary students are clustered in traditional fields of study. This is a decisive factor in determining whether women enrol in university to major in non-traditional areas and pursue vocational and technical or industrial training. When selecting their fields of specialization, girls tend not to focus as much as boys on long-term planning and not to take into account career choices and labour-market conditions.

(c)   Tertiary education

24.   Women are increasingly entering colleges and universities. However, progress in that area depends on the region. In developed countries women and men are approaching parity in higher education. In Latin America and the Caribbean and in Eastern Europe, women outnumbered men at that level; in Africa they are far behind (table II.B.4). However, even in the African region measures are being taken to correct the situation. In Uganda, for example, due to the implementation of special measures, the share of girls in the national university increased from 25 per cent in 1985-1990 to 33 per cent in 1993 .

25.   In China, the number of female postgraduates increased by 157 per cent from 1985 to 1992; of female college and university graduates, by 143 per cent; and of female graduates from secondary vocational schools, by 157 per cent. The national reports cite various reasons for the increases besides the general expansion of the educational system. In some cases, the elimination of gender-exclusive admission practices opened the door to educational establishments which had been closed to women. Other countries undertook reforms of their higher education systems and incorporated in them various post-secondary study programmes that attracted women. One reason given for the predominance of female students is the early entrance of men into the labour force, which prevents them from completing their degree of higher education.

26.   A few countries with low female enrolment rates in tertiary education reported on measures of affirmative action taken to encourage young women to pursue their education. Australia is linking funding allocations to institutions of higher education to the progress achieved towards equity goals, while setting specific targets for the increase of the number of women in non-traditional courses and postgraduate study by 1995. In Sweden, the Government approved a 10-point programme for monitoring efforts to promote equality between women and men in higher education which proposed steps to increase the number of female graduate students.

27.   The majority of female students are still enrolled in the traditionally "female" fields of studies. The highest increase in the number of female graduates has continued to occur in fields such as humanities, fine arts and education. In the United States, where college enrolment of women now exceeds that of men, the majority of women still choose subjects of study that are less likely to lead to higher paying jobs.

28.   However, more and more women are entering formerly male-dominated fields such as law, medicine and business administration. There is an increase in the number of women studying law and business in Latin America and Caribbean (table II.B.5). In science and technology women are catching up to men almost in all regions, except Africa, though even in that region there is a positive shift (table II.B.6).

Table II.B.4. Average ratio of girls to boys in tertiary education, by region, 1970-1990

Region	1970	1980	1990
Africa	20	30	32
Latin America and the Caribbean	72	74	106
Western Europe and other	53	72	94
Asia and the Pacific	46	63	84
Eastern Europe	78	106	104
World	46	61	75

Source: Division for the Advancement of Women, United Nations Secretariat, based on information contained in Women's Indicators and Statistics Data Base (WISTAT), version 3, 1994.

Table II.B.5. Average ratio of girls to boys in law and business in tertiary education, by region, 1970-1990

Region	1970	1980	1990
Africa	12	43	36
Latin America and the Caribbean	30	92	97
Western Europe and other	25	54	85
Asia and the Pacific	25	56	70
Eastern Europe	64	134	124
World	25	63	102

Source: Division for the Advancement of Women, United Nations Secretariat, based on information contained in Women's Indicators and Statistics Data Base (WISTAT), version 3, 1994.

Table II.B.6. Average ratio of girls to boys in science and technology fields in tertiary education, by region, 1970-1990

Region	1970	1980	1990
Africa	24	21	24
Latin America and the Caribbean	37	54	80
Western Europe and other	29	49	67
Asia and the Pacific	33	45	70
Eastern Europe	61	81	74
World	32	43	56

Source: Division for the Advancement of Women, United Nations Secretariat, based on information contained in Women's Indicators and Statistics Data Base (WISTAT), version 3, 1994.

29.   Scholarships are one means of encouraging and enabling girls to pursue their education and of guiding them into non-traditional fields. Some developing countries criticize the attribution of scholarships by donor countries on a purely merit basis for those priority areas of study identified

for future labour needs. Traditional attitudes often prevail in decisions concerning whether female students should be sent abroad to study. Mentoring programmes have been initiated in a number of developed countries. Senior women scientists mentor schoolgirls and young scientists on how to develop career strategies and paths and how to sustain motivation and inspiration. Vocational counselling and guidance are additional means used to encourage girls to opt for non-traditional career paths. France, for example, launched important campaigns in 1992 and 1993 encouraging girls and young women to pursue technical specializations and professions.

30. The increased number of women in higher education has started to have a visible effect in certain careers that were until recently closed to women. Women who have completed higher degrees are also having an impact on the economy. In Bulgaria, for example, 56 per cent of all economically active persons with academic qualifications are women. Reports from all regions indicate that equal education does not mean equality in professional qualifications or remuneration. In general, the majority of well educated women with university degrees are employed in lower-level jobs, despite higher educational qualifications than men. The low level of quality of the educational results and the loss of contact between education, training and the modern requirements of the labour market have been noted. Wage differences between men and women are greater among young adults with similar education. There is a growing distortion between the qualifications and expectations of young women, who are more and more educated, and their effective participation in the labour market.

(d)   Non-formal education
31.   Although formal education is the norm and is advocated for children aged 6-14 years, many children - in particular, girls - fall through the net of formal education because of its inaccessibility, high cost and perceived irrelevancy. The role of non-governmental organizations in non-formal and basic education is being increasingly recognized. In developed countries, non-governmental organizations carry out research and educational campaigns.

32.   Non-governmental organizations are essential partners in the provision of basic education in developing countries with low levels of enrolment and urban-to-rural disparities. In many developing countries, non-govern-mental

organizations are working in a complementary fashion to the public education system. They receive increasing support from multilateral and bilateral donor agencies for their work in the field of education and are dependent on financing from abroad.

(i)   Pre-school education

33.   Pre-school education has grown rapidly over the past 10 years in many regions. Globally, there seem to be no gender differences between girls and boys with regard to enrolment in pre-school education, where and when it is available. Available figures in Latin America and the Caribbean show that supply for pre-school education is directed primarily towards the middle and upper socio-economic strata.

34.   With more mothers and fathers both employed and the disappearance of extended families, there is growing need for child care of good quality. Research findings indicate that a child's environment from birth to age three helps to determine his or her cognitive structure and ability to learn. Infants and toddlers need intellectual stimulation, emotional nourishment and social guidance for healthy development. The shaping of gender roles also takes place during this period, and pedagogical interventions - in particular, in kindergartens - can have an impact on later attitudes and behaviour patterns.

35.   In many countries, projects have been undertaken to remove gender stereotyping from pre-school education and to make pre-schoolteachers aware of gender bias in attitudes and behaviour.

(ii) Alternative forms of teaching

36.   Non-traditional programmes for out-of-school children provide a non-institutional environment based on a learner-centred curriculum and flexible schedule. They have been advocated by many educators as a temporary measure to improve access and performance, in particular for girls and groups of children that cannot be reached by or integrated into the formal educational system.

37.   Programmes in non-formal education have been carried out in many countries - Bangladesh, Dominican Republic, India, Nepal, Thailand, United Republic of Tanzania and others. Specific conditions for success are

the location of the classrooms in the local community, competent teachers recruited locally, free education with no hidden costs, and convenient class schedules that take into account the girls' household and agricultural responsibilities. Girls in regions and cultures most resistant to female formal education are most eager to attend those schools and perform very successfully. One example is the Bangladesh Rural Advancement Committee, which started non-formal primary education in 1985 and has expanded to 4,500 experimental schools, teaching 100,000 children; 70 per cent are girls from rural landless families.

(iii) Adult education

38.   Activities in the field of continuing education for women are abundant and rich in their diversity and range from literacy, income generation and politics to creative and spiritual programmes. They are carried out by a variety of organizations, including non-governmental organizations, political parties, educational institutions and foundations. Educational activities for adult women are a major component to awareness-raising and increasing self-confidence among women. Training in legal literacy, for example, has gained importance since it is a necessary tool for making women aware of their human rights. Vocational training, training on the job, and training for income generation and self-employment are important features.

39.   Adult education programmes have been a vital resource for educationally disadvantaged women and young adult females, even if they are not specifically targeting women. Life-long learning needs more attention in times of rapid social and technical changes. Women are increasingly taking advantage of training opportunities offered to them.

(e)   Vocational training

40.   The successful completion of education at the secondary level is not sufficient to prepare women to enter the labour market; technical and vocational training is usually considered necessary. Compared to the career paths of men, women's professional life is characterized by frequent interruptions and changes of orientation, voluntary or not. Women still take responsibility for the bulk of the work done in the home, so they are looking for possibilities to reconcile working and family duties. Women who interrupt their careers for maternity leave and care-taking or who are displaced by unemployment

need training and retraining in order to re-enter the labour market. A life cycle approach to employment is therefore needed and requires training and frequent retraining. However, many education and training policies for women are not sufficiently adapted to the changing patterns of demand in the labour market. Women frequently do not have the same access as men to ongoing training in the workplace so as to upgrade skills and promote their career development. Many training and retraining schemes designed to increase women's access to jobs remain insufficiently developed. In addition, they often direct women to a limited number of fields where career opportunities are limited. Few countries give special regard to the training of single parents and women re-entering the labour market as well as unemployed women. Some countries conduct special programmes to enhance long-term employability of certain target groups, such as young teenage mothers.

41.   Obstacles to the technical and vocational education of women include inadequate knowledge of mathematics and science, limited opportunities for women to study technical subjects, inadequate policies for promoting technical and vocational education for women, and a reluctance by employers to recruit qualified women for technical jobs. Many training programmes for women have been restricted to traditional domestic activities such as sewing, cooking, embroidery and child care. In developing countries, many vocational training programmes are concentrated in the capital cities and a few provinces. Although many women attend these programmes, they remain clustered in typical female jobs, and only a few enrol in technical schools which are oriented towards the modern industrial sector, engineering, agriculture, forestry and handicrafts.

(f)   Education for special groups of girls and women
42.   In many countries, there has been markedly less educational improvement among particular groups of girls such as migrants, aborigines, girls with disabilities, or girls living in poverty. Many countries report on the special needs of immigrant women, visible minority women and female single parents and have adopted special programmes. Australia, for example, is paying attention to the special needs of girls from non-English-speaking backgrounds, isolated rural areas, aborigines, and economically disadvantaged groups. Canada is providing special scholarships for indigenous persons who want to pursue full-time or part-time post-secondary

education. Two thirds of the students who receive such support are women.

43.   Countries affected by civil strive, occupation and war report on the suspension of all forms of education. In many cases, primary schools, intermediate, secondary, vocational and teacher training centres are closed for long periods. The effects of these interruptions in education on women and girls become visible only in the long term. In situations of frequent curfews and closures of schools, the number of girls who drop out of the educational system has increased, especially if additional cultural restrictions are put on their mobility.

44.   Girls with disabilities often lack access to education and training, because educational facilities cannot cater for their special needs. The cost of providing equal opportunities for girls and women with disabilities is an obstacle that prevents many political decision makers from providing adequate and needed services. Few countries reported on the efforts to provide special educational facilities for girls and women with disabilities.

3. Women in teaching and educational decision-making

45.   In all regions the male-to-female ratio in teaching varies according to the level of teaching. The percentage of female teachers is high at the primary level, decreases at the secondary level and declines further in universities and equivalent institutions (see table II.B.7). Women are generally underrepresented in the higher status and higher paying categories. They are still underrepresented in educational administration and as teachers of science, where they can have an image-shaping function on boys and girls. In Africa the number of female teachers is especially low, even at the primary level, though there is a positive trend in that area.

46.   Although the number of female academics in higher education is increasing globally and has even doubled in some developed countries over the past 20 years, tenure is still heavily concentrated among older, more senior male academics. Female university staff tends to be employed in support positions which lack promotional opportunities, such as specialist or instructor. In other cases, women have been promoted into new fields of studies, and thus the figures increased. The Netherlands reports on an increase in the number of female professors of 4 per cent which can be mainly attributed to newly appointed professors in women's studies.

Table II.B.7. Percentage of teachers who are female, by level taught, 1990

	Percentage of female teachers, by level taught, 1990			Numbers of countries/ areas included in averages		
	First Level	Second Level	Universities	First Level	Second Level	Universities and equivalent
Developed regions	75	51	26	38	29	29
Eastern Europe a/	78	53	31	15	11	12
Western European others	73	50	23	23	18	17
Western Europe	74	52	23	18	13	12
Other developed	72	47	23	5	5	5
Africa	40	25	16	46	38	28
Northern Africa b/	48	35	23	5	5	3
Sub-Saharan Africa	39	23	15	41	33	25
Latin America and Caribbean	73	52	32	28	22	18
Latin America	74	51	27	17	12	8
Central America	74	46	27	6	5	3
South America	74	54	28	11	7	5
Caribbean	72	54	35	11	10	10
Asia and Pacific c/	54	43	24	34	33	29
Eastern Asia d/	67	45	26	6	5	6
South-eastern Asia	57	51	31	7	7	5
Central and Southern Asia	34	26	20	6	6	5
Western Asia	56	45	22	13	13	11
Oceania e/	54	40	23	11	10	4

Sources: Calculated from UNESCO education statistics database and Statistical Yearbook (Paris, various years up to 1993); Statistics Division of the Economic Commission for Latin America and the Caribbean; national statistical yearbooks; national census reports; and reports of national education ministries or departments.

a/ Albania, Belarus, Bulgaria, the former Czechoslovakia, former German Democratic Republic, Hungary, Poland, Republic of Moldova, Russian Federation, Romania, the former USSR, Ukraine and the former Yugoslavia.

b/ Not including the Sudan, which is included in sub-Saharan Africa.

c/ In obtaining unweighted averages for Asia and the Pacific, only two countries in Oceania are considered: Fiji and Papua New Guinea.

d/ Excluding Japan, which is included under "Developed regions".

e/ Excluding Australia and New Zealand, which are included under "Developed regions".

47.   Many countries have taken measures to ensure a greater representation of women in the teaching professions at higher levels. In 1991, Austria enacted changes in the law on university organization which encourage the minister for science and research and the executive bodies of the universities to work towards achieving gender balance in universities.

48.   There are few figures on women's active participation in educational planning and decision-making. Some countries have realized that women have to be actively involved in the implementation of educational campaigns. The involvement of women in the formulation of formal educational policies and their active participation in the design of policies and educational projects are key elements for successful literacy campaigns and means of empowerment. In the African region, high-level women educators organized and regrouped in the Forum of African Women Educationalists, which is striving for the achievement of universal primary education and education for all the children in Africa by mobilizing resources, developing and comparing strategies and raising awareness on the importance of girls' education and influencing attitudes of parents and society as a whole.

4. Measures to remove gender bias in education and training

49.   The quality of education is a question that goes beyond issues of access and performance. It extends beyond the satisfaction of basic educational needs to improved completion rates, critical awareness and empowerment. Much research has been done on gender stereotypes and bias in education and training in the past decade. The establishment of women's studies programmes at the undergraduate and graduate levels is the most visible acknowledgement of the need to examine gender issues in society and gender bias in education, training and research. Most countries claim to have

at least the beginnings of a women's studies curriculum in progress, while in as many as 30 countries of the world women's studies centres and programmes function both inside and outside the formal educational system.

50.   The first step undertaken by many developing countries is the removal of gender bias in textbooks. Official textbooks mostly transmit gender-stereotyped values and attitudes and portray women as weak and passive and in traditional roles as mothers and housewives. Beyond the general recognition that the stereotyping of women should be eliminated from textbooks and curricula and policy declarations on the issue, few Governments have taken far-reaching steps. Some countries have taken action aimed at balancing illustrations and removing gender-biased texts from schoolbooks. Others regret that further guidelines have not yet been established. Few countries have made a systematic attempt to change syllabi and course content or to take further measures to foster non-stereotyped gender roles. The most common curricular innovation is the inclusion of technical and home management subjects at the middle-school level as common learning areas for boys and girls. Reforms of the curricular nomenclature are reported. Some countries have invited school administrators to evaluate the curricula to root out gender bias and sexist language.

51.   Separate classes for boys and girls in particular fields of study have been introduced. To create an interest in technology among young girls, summer courses in technology for girls are proposed in some European countries. In a pilot project in Sweden, girls are taught how to speak freely and to present their opinion while boys are taught to write and to listen. Experience has shown that equality must be mainstreamed in the teaching process in order to give boys and girls equal opportunities in education. Teachers and school managers must learn about different conditions for boys and girls at school so that they can take the action necessary to counteract prejudice and gender-related problems.

52.   Some Governments have activated a number of instruments to promote gender awareness in education, such as courses for teachers, development of teaching materials, experimental projects and training centres that focus on various actors, including the girls and their parents, teachers and administrators. In some countries, schools use federal funds to implement

professional development programmes providing teachers with effective strategies for gender-fair and culturally sensitive teaching.

53.   A few countries have established national plans of action to promote greater equality in education. In Sweden, the long-term objective is that neither sex should constitute less than 40 percent of the students in any educational programme and that the proportion of female school leaders should be increased to at least 20 per cent during the first five-year period, a goal that was fully attained and exceeded by 35 per cent by 1993. Since 1985, current education policy in Uganda is encouraging affirmative action in favour of women until gender balance is attained. This policy is being implemented in terms of enrolment in governmental institutions of higher learning.

54.   Different forms of awareness-raising programmes and pilot projects are being carried out. Many countries in developed and developing countries have conducted information campaigns to increase girls' awareness of the need for and advantages of continued education. Non-governmental organizations are playing a critical role in carrying out mass public campaigns for awareness-raising. In some countries, special activities for girls have been organized in response to research that shows that girls seem to struggle and suffer more than boys as they move into adulthood. In the United States, the event "Take our Daughters to Work Day" mobilized parents, educators, employers and other caring adults and millions of girls who participated in 1993 and 1994. Similar activities which challenge and prevent stereotyped career choices of girls have been organized in other countries. Non-governmental organizations have also made contributions in the form of scholarships and awards programmes for training assistance to women who need to upgrade their skills (especially single parents).

5. Action by the international community

55.   The most important joint activities of the international community in the field of education was the World Conference on Education for All, convened jointly by the United Nations Children's Fund (UNICEF), the United Nations Development Programme (UNDP), the United Nations Educational, Scientific and Cultural Organization (UNESCO) and the World Bank, in Jomtien (Thailand) in 1990. It represented a global consensus on an expanded vision of basic education and a commitment to ensure

that the basic learning needs of all children, youth and adults are met effectively in all countries. 3/

56.   With regard to children in emergency situations, such as refugee children, the United Nations High Commissioner for Refugees (UNHCR), as well as UNESCO and UNICEF, is providing for educational projects within the limits of its budget. The mandate of the United Nations Relief and Works Agency for Palestine Refugees in the Near East (UNRWA) comprises explicitly the provision of education in addition to relief and health services for Palestinian refugees. UNRWA has carried out a variety of educational programmes, including vocational training for women. For a transitional period, students from South Africa are being granted awards through the United Nations Educational and Training Programme for Southern Africa.

57.   The bilateral donor community has made significant advances in promoting a gender perspective on basic education. Donors have implemented a variety of projects supporting basic education while focusing on questions of educational access and retention, supporting student and female teachers, assisting in curricula and textbook production and providing teacher training, literacy and vocational training.

Notes

1/   General Assembly resolution 34/180, annex, art. 10.

2/   As of 3 November 1994, there were 138 States Parties to the Convention, including all of the States of Latin America and the Caribbean, almost all the States in Europe, South-eastern and Eastern Asia, and a majority of the States in the other regions.

3/   World Declaration on Education for All and Framework for Action to Meet Basic Learning Needs, World Conference on Education for All, Jomtien, Thailand, 5-9 March 1990.

4/   General Assembly resolution 44/25, art. 28.

5/   Report of the World Conference to Review and Appraise the Achievements of the United Nations Decade for Women: Equality, Development and Peace, Nairobi, 15-26 July 1985 (United Nations publication, Sales No. E.85.IV.10), chap. I, sect. A, paras. 163-173.

6/   "Progress at the national, regional and international levels in the implementation of the Nairobi Forward-looking Strategies for the Advancement of Women" (E/CN.6/1990/5).

7/   Economic and Social Council resolution 1990/15, annex.

8/   UNESCO, World Education Report (Paris, 1993).

C. Inequality in access to health and related services

1.   In the Nairobi Forward-looking Strategies for the Advancement of Women, health is one of the three sub-themes, along with employment and education, of the three goals - equality, development and peace - of the United Nations Decade for Women. In designing measures for the implementation of the basic Strategies at the national level, a number of areas for specific action were identified.

2.   With the recognition of the vital role of women as providers of health care and the need for strengthening basic services for the delivery of health care came the need both to promote the positive health of women at all stages of life and to recognize the importance of women's participation in the achievement of Health for All by the Year 2000. The Strategies stressed the need to increase the participation of women in managerial and higher professional positions, through appropriate legislation, training and supportive action and to change the attitudes and composition of health personnel.

3.   They also emphasized the necessity for providing health education to the entire family and the need to combine promotional, preventive and curative health, and access to water and sanitary facilities that involved women in all stages of planning and implementation. They stressed as well the need to comply with the International Code of Marketing of Breast Milk Substitutes, forbidding any commercial pressures that interfered with the priority of breast-feeding, the application of vaccination programmes for children and pregnant women and the elimination of any differences in coverage between boys and girls, as well as the eradication of the marketing of

unsafe drugs and of practices detrimental to health and the provision of access to essential drugs.

4.   The Strategies called for the provision of adequate nutrition for women and children and the promotion of interventions to reduce the prevalence of nutritional diseases such as anaemia in women of all ages, particularly young women.

5.   They also stressed recognition of the fact that the ability of women to control their own fertility was an important basis for the enjoyment of other rights. The Strategies called for the provision of appropriate health facilities, adapted to women's specific needs, and the reduction of the unacceptably high levels of maternal mortality. The need was also expressed to strengthen maternal and child health and the family-planning components of primary health care, and to produce family-planning information and create services, pursuant to the basic human right of all couples and individuals to decide freely and informedly the number and spacing of their children. The urgency of developing policies to encourage delay in the commencement of child-bearing was indicated, since pregnancy in adolescent girls had adverse effects on morbidity and mortality, as well as the need to change discriminatory attitudes towards women and girls through health education. There was a need for providing adequate fertility-control methods, consistent with internationally recognized human rights, as well as with changing individual and cultural values.

6.   The need to encourage participation of local women's organizations in primary-health-care activities was part of the focus of the Strategies, as were the application of gender-specific indicators for monitoring women's health and the necessity of enhancing the concerns with occupational health and the harmonization of work and family responsibilities.

7.   The Economic and Social Council, in its resolution 1990/15 (adopted by the Council upon the recommendation of the Commission on the Status of Women, at its thirty-fourth session), adopted the recommendations and conclusions arising from the first review and appraisal of the implementation of the Nairobi Forward-looking Strategies, contained in the annex to that resolution. The following constitute the most detailed recommendations arising out of the review process.

"**Recommendation XII**. "15. Since the beginning of the 1980s, there has been a decline in the standard of health and nutrition of women in parts of every developing region due, inter alia, to a decline in per capita expenditure on health. This is a particularly alarming situation since maternal and neonatal health are crucial to infant survival. Infant and child mortality rates have been rising in a number of countries after having declined for decades.

"**Recommendation XIII**. Governments, international organizations, non-governmental organizations and the public in general should be aware of the decline in women's health in developing countries. Improvement of women's health by the provision of appropriate and accessible health services should be a priority within the goal of health for all by the year 2000.

"Women constitute the majority of health-care workers in most countries. They should be enabled to play a much larger role in decision-making for health. Governments, international non-governmental organizations and women's organizations should undertake programmes aimed at improving women's health by ensuring access to adequate maternal and child health care, family planning, safe motherhood programmes, nutrition, programmes for female-specific diseases and other primary health care services in relation to the goal of health for all by the year 2000.

"The World Health Organization and other organizations of the United Nations system should further develop emergency programmes to cope with the deteriorating conditions of women's health mainly in developing countries, with particular attention to nutrition, maternal health care and sanitation.

"16. Women's access to information and services relating to population and family planning are improving only slowly in most countries. A woman's ability to control her own fertility continues to be a major factor enabling her to protect her health, achieve her personal objectives and ensure the strength of her family. All women should be in a position to plan and organize their lives.

"**Recommendation XIV**. Governments, non-governmental organizations and women's movements should develop programmes to enable women to implement their decisions on the timing and spacing of their children. These programmes should include population education programmes linked to women's rights and the role of women in development, as well as the sharing of family responsibilities by men and boys. Social services should be provided to help women reconcile family and employment requirements.

"Family planning programmes should be developed or extended to enable women to implement their decisions on the timing and spacing of their children and for safe motherhood.

"The United Nations Secretariat, the United Nations Population Fund, the World Health Organization and other organizations of the United Nations system should develop collaborative programmes to link the role of women in development to questions related to population.

"17.   During the past five years, women's health, both physical and psychological, has been increasingly affected in many countries by the consumption and abuse of alcohol, narcotic drugs and psychotropic substances.

"**Recommendation XV**. Governments and other competent national authorities should establish national policies and programmes on women's health with respect to the consumption and abuse of alcohol, narcotic drugs and psychotropic substances. Strong preventive as well as rehabilitative measures should be taken.

"In addition, efforts should be intensified to reduce occupational health hazards faced by women and to discourage illicit drug use.

"18.   The emergence, since the Nairobi Conference, of new threats to the health and status of women, such as the alarming increase in sexually transmitted diseases and the acquired immunodeficiency syndrome (AIDS) pandemic, requires urgent action from both medical and social institutions.

"**Recommendation XVI**. Greater attention is also needed with respect to the issue of women and AIDS. Efforts in this regard should be an integral part of the World Health Organization Global Programme on AIDS. Urgent action and action-oriented research are also required by social institutions at all levels, in particular the United Nations system, national AIDS committees and non-governmental organizations, to inform women of the threat of AIDS to their health and status."

1. Women's health: an overall view

8.   In the 1991 progress report on women, health and development of the Director-General of the World Health Organization (WHO), 1/ presented to the Forty-fourth World Health Assembly, it was recognized that women's health was influenced by biological, environmental, social, economic and cultural factors. 2/ It was further recognized that women's health, their status and their multiple contributions were pivotal links between the health of a population and its prospects of sustainable development - prospects which, despite the remarkable progress of the 1960s and 1970s, had been dimming in the 1980s. 3/

9.   Setting an agenda for women's health must begin with a recognition of the fact not only that the health situation of women is different from that of men, but also that the systems identifying and determining that health situation are fashioned according to gender-biased models. Gender discrimination has tended to be hidden within the general issue of poverty and underdevelopment. In practice, women and girls suffer disproportionately because of their low status in society.

10.   While most of the world's poor suffer from poor health and nutrition, in many countries, particularly those of South Asia, rates of malnutrition are generally higher among females than among males of the same age group. In many countries, food is distributed within the household according to a member's status rather than according to nutritional needs.

11.   Low health status is the outcome of biological as well as social, political and economic factors acting together. Many women suffering from poor health status are found to lack knowledge, information, skills, purchasing power, income-earning capacity and access to essential health services. Health must be considered in a holistic manner.

12.   Reliable and high-quality health services promote sustainable development. The greatest reduction in fertility rates have resulted from a combination of women's improved economic and social status, education and access to reproductive-health-care services.

13.   Despite the fact that in households and sometimes in the community, women are the primary providers of health care, they often lack access to

outside health care for themselves. For example, data show that in many countries there are fewer women than men who are treated in hospitals, receive prescriptions for medication, receive timely treatment from qualified practitioners and survive common diseases. Restricted access to health services leaves women less capable of taking care not only of their own health, but also of that of their children, thereby perpetuating a trend of high child mortality.

14.   Ensuring women equal access to the benefits of public health care is critically dependent upon gender-specific health strategies. This is true because men and women tend to suffer from different illnesses. Women are far more likely to suffer from reproductive role-related illnesses such as sexually transmitted diseases, anaemia, and the complications resulting from child-bearing. Targeting these health problems clearly involves different strategies for men and women.

15.   Under increasing economic pressure in the past four years, 37 of the poorest countries have cut health-related spending by 50 per cent. Some countries report on the implementation of social compensation programmes to offset the impact of structural adjustment policies.

16.   A major factor mentioned by many countries is the focus on primary health care, promoted by most developing countries. To provide equal care to both rural and urban women, many countries have adopted the system of primary health care including family planning, maternal and child care, vaccination and reinforcement for the curing of diseases, including prevention of sexually transmitted diseases and human immunodeficiency virus (HIV)/AIDS.

17.   In Asia and the Pacific, the focus of policy in the area of women's health has generally been within the context of reproductive health. Fertility control and family planning have been the major set of issues around which health policies and programmes have generally evolved in the past.

18.   Some countries report that the fact that women have come to dominate the teaching and health professions has resulted in the feminization of those professions, and a consequent lowering within them of prestige and pay. Several national reports acknowledge the skills of women in the areas of birth attendance and traditional medicine practices, and various areas of

self-healing, although these practices have not yet been duly incorporated in the medical system.

19.   In many countries, there is not yet a policy for women's health, except for reproductive health. The reports often link improvements in the overall situation of women's health to demographic trends and improvement in infrastructure. Health is considered an outcome of combined factors promoting quality of life.20.   Many countries note the contribution of specific health programmes, like the expanded programme of immunization, to women's health, and the contribution of local non-governmental organizations in health campaigns.

21.   Rural health centres are in general on the decline, and in much poorer condition than urban ones. For instance, one country reports that a person in the rural areas consults the health centre about twice a year, versus four times a year in the urban areas.

2. Environmental health

22.   Sustaining the global cycles and systems upon which all life depends is a first requisite of health. The combination of population and production growth and unsustainable consumption patterns has, however, heavily depleted natural resources, threatening the environmental base upon which health and survival depend.

23.   In developing countries, where populations are still expanding, pressure on scarce resources has made it very difficult to improve living conditions. In 1990, an estimated 1.5 billion people did not have access to safe water, and almost 2 billion people lacked sanitary means for disposing of excreta.

24.   Many countries have subscribed to the goal of universal access to safe water for the year 2000. Some reports indicate that improvements have been made in sanitary education and in the application of low-cost technologies. One country refers to an initiative to save on wood energy, for example, through cheaper production of charcoal and improved charcoal stoves.

3. The life-cycle perspective

25.   In the case of women's health, the using of a lifelong perspective that takes into account the whole life-span is of paramount importance, since

health conditions in one phase of a woman's life affect not only its subsequent phases but also future generations. It is also useful to look at common issues or themes so as to identify a useful framework from which a feasible agenda for action can be elaborated.

26.   For every 100 females delivered into the world, there are 105 males born. The female human being is biologically more resistant, and the surplus of male infants is nature's way of balancing the sex ratio in the population. Ordinarily, the number of surviving girls soon surpasses that of boys. However, there are parts of the world where this male-to-female imbalance is never overcome.

27.   Human intervention, in the form of neglect of girls, favours the survival of males. In several countries in the Asian and Pacific region, the preference for sons over daughters has resulted in a differential treatment of infants by sex. The data show that there is a higher risk that girls, as compared with boys, will die before age 5, in spite of the natural biological advantage of girls. In Bangladesh, the under-five mortality rate for girls was recorded as 175 per 1,000 live births, as against 160 for boys, and in Nepal, 187 for girls as against 173 for boys. The pattern is much more alarming in regions within large countries like India and China, known for their strong preference for sons. In India, there are 957 females aged four years or under for every 1,000 males in the population.

28.   Preference for sons is most marked in South Asia and the Middle East, but is not confined to those regions alone. In Colombia, the number of deaths of boys between the ages of one and two is 75 as against a figure of 100 for girls in the same age group. Recent empirical evidence suggests that excess female mortality during childhood also occurs in Latin America and the Caribbean, particularly in the less developed countries with low life expectancy.

29.   Globally, at least 2 million girls per year are at risk of having to submit to genital mutilation. WHO estimates that 90 million women in the world today have - at some time between the ages of 2 and 15, depending on local custom, and most commonly between the ages of 4 and 8 - undergone one of the procedures that fall under this category. Most live in Africa, a few in Asia, and, increasingly, due to migration processes, some in Europe and North America.

30.   Many Governments have publicly denounced the practice. Some have translated their concerns into laws prohibiting female genital mutilation or into programmes to persuade people to abandon the practice. Several countries report on the existence of harmful traditional practices and their impact on women's health. One report, on the other hand, highlights coexisting cultural practices that are beneficial, including respect for and assistance to elders, mutual assistance networks and breast-feeding.

4. Adolescents

31.   More than 50 per cent of the world population is under age 25, and 80 per cent of the 1.5 billion young people between the ages of 10 and 24 live in developing countries. Although fertility levels have been decreasing in many regions, the fertility rates of adolescents are very high and in some cases increasing. At present, it is estimated that close to 15 million infants per year (10 per cent of total births) are born to adolescent mothers.

32.   Adolescents girls are more vulnerable to reproductive health problems than young men. The age of the first sexual encounter is declining everywhere. For example, a survey in Nigeria found that 43 per cent of schoolgirls in the age group 14-19 were sexually active. During the 1980s, 30.2 per cent of female adolescents in Jamaica and 12.7 per cent in Mexico were sexually active before they were 15 years of age. The proportion of females under 20 years of age who used contraceptives at first coitus was 40 per cent in Jamaica, 21 per cent in Mexico and 8.5 per cent in Guatemala.

33.   The rate of pregnancy among girls in the age group 15-19 is 18 per cent in Africa, 8 per cent in Latin America, 5 per cent in North American and 3 per cent in Europe. In Venezuela, the number of births to girls under age 15 rose by 32 per cent between 1980 and 1988. In the Caribbean, 60 per cent of first births are to teenagers, most of whom are unmarried.

34.   One quarter of the 500,000 women who die every year from pregnancy-and-childbirth-related causes are teenagers. A survey in Bangladesh found that maternal mortality in age group 10-14 was five times higher than in age group 20-24.

35.   The sense of urgency in addressing the situation is justified by the sheer numbers of girls involved. In 1990, girls aged 15 or under constituted

40 per cent of the female population in Egypt and Morocco, 44 per cent in Algeria and Mauritania, 45 per cent in Ethiopia and Mali, 46 per cent in Djibouti and Somalia, 48 per cent in Nigeria, Uganda and the United Republic of Tanzania, 50 per cent in Côte d'Ivoire, and 52 per cent in Kenya. Increasing concern for the status of women and girls prompted the South Asian Association for Regional Cooperation (SAARC) to declare 1990 the Year of the Girl Child.

36.   Some countries report an increase in the life expectancy of girls over that of boys. One country reports that owing to the availability of medical facilities and health units in all villages, life expectancy at birth for girls increased from 2 to 66 per cent, or at a rate of 127 per cent, from 1981-1982 to 1992-1993.

37.   Many countries indicate strong policies of readmitting teenage mothers into secondary schools. Many have included courses on family-life education at school. One country reports a peer approach counselling programme at the Young Women's Christian Association (YWCA).

5. Reproductive health

38.   The health of women in the years 15-45 is influenced predominantly by their reproductive and maternal roles. Despite progress in a number of key areas, the morbidity and mortality rates of women due to reproduction remain unnecessarily high in many areas of the globe. Maternal mortality is the indicator that exhibits the widest disparity among countries. Of the 150-200 million pregnancies that occur world wide each year, about 23 million lead to serious complications such as post-partum haemorrhage, hypertensive disorders, eclampsia, puerperal sepsis and abortion. Half a million of these end with the loss of the mother.

39.   Ninety-nine per cent of these deaths take place in developing countries. The incidence of maternal death ranges from almost non-existent to very high (the rates in some poor countries reach as high as 1,600 times those in industrialized countries). Scattered information suggests that in some countries, one fourth to one half of all deaths of women of child-bearing age result from pregnancy and its complications.

40.   Maternal mortality rates in central and eastern Europe, apart from

Romania and Albania, are about twice as high as the average for Europe as a whole. In Romania and Albania, maternal mortality has fallen dramatically since the legalization of abortion, as previous rates were largely due to unsafe abortions. Unsafe abortions are among the top causes of maternal mortality in all countries except Azerbaijan. Azerbaijan's exceptional status might be due to the way it defines such practices. In the Russian Federation, nearly 200 abortions are reported for every 100 births.

41.   Comparing new information on maternal mortality with that available five years ago suggests that pregnancy and childbirth have become safer for women in most of Asia and in parts of Latin America. Nevertheless, data are still too scattered and more needs to be done to have a more complete picture. However, frequent child-bearing, which can seriously compromise the health and nutrition of a woman's children, continues to be characteristic of large numbers in many areas of the world.

42.   One reason for the lack of progress is the tendency to look for rapid solutions to deep-seated problems. It has been found that safer motherhood requires a massive and simultaneous attack on all the elements contributing to the problem, including those under the headings of legislation, social services, rights of women. As regards the health sector alone, the system's entire infrastructure - including community mobilization, pre- and post-natal care, clean and safe delivery with trained assistance and above all timely referral for management of complications - needs strengthening in most countries where maternal mortality is high.

43.   International commitments setting goals for reduction of maternal mortality by 50 per cent for the year 2000 have been endorsed by most countries. Many countries mention the Safe Motherhood Initiative, adopted by WHO, the United Nations Development Programme (UNDP), the United Nations Population Fund (UNFPA), and the United Nations Children's Fund (UNICEF) in 1987. Many countries report that the increased provision and improvement of existing maternity services at all levels of the health system is the most effective means of reducing maternal mortality. In addition, quality reproductive-health-care services, including family planning, together with good primary health care represent important interventions. Many countries report increments in health care to address the matter of maternal mortality. Several reports mention a national programme for

maternal health, with campaigns on reproductive health and family planning. Several countries report the inclusion in their expanded programmes of immunization of antitetanus campaigns.

6. Fertility

44.   Fertility levels, measured by the total fertility rate, have continued their tendency to decline in all regions. World fertility fell by 10.5 per cent, from 3.8 to 3.4 births per woman, between the periods 1975-1980 and 1985-1990. The total fertility rate varied from 8.5 (the highest) in Rwanda, to 1.27 (the lowest), in Italy.

45.   Sub-Saharan Africa is the only region of the developing world that has not yet undergone a widespread decline in fertility. A decline has started in three countries of the area: Botswana, Kenya and Zimbabwe. Ethiopia reports a fertility rate of 7.5 births per woman in 1992.

46.   The total fertility rate continued to decline in all subregions of Asia and the Pacific throughout the post-Nairobi Conference era. Between 1985 and 1992, it dropped from 2.42 to 2.19 in developing East Asia and from 3.69 to 3.37 in South-East Asia. In South Asia, it fell from 4.71 to 4.36 and in the Pacific Islands, from 4.92 to 4.61. The developed countries of the region, namely, Australia, Japan and New Zealand, which had already achieved a total fertility rate of 1.71 by 1985, experienced a further decline to 1.56, by 1992.

47.   In the Caribbean, many countries have experienced nearly a 50 per cent drop, from about 6.0 to 3.0, in total fertility rate levels within the last 30 years, and the rate is expected to decline further in the next decade.

48.   Although fertility rates have gone down world wide, many women still lack access to information and services, or cannot make use of them because of economic limitations or cultural norms. Only 27 per cent of couples use contraception; 140 million women in developing countries become pregnant although they did not want a child. Every year, over 20 million women terminate unwanted pregnancies through unsafe abortions, as a result of lack of access to relevant care and services such as family planning, costly contraceptive methods, lack of information, and restrictive legislative practices. Of these, 15 million survive, but with a wide range of long-term disabilities. Some 60,000-100,000 die.

49.   One country reports that in 1992, for the first time since the intro-duction of family planning, the gender-differential participation ratio became 55 to 45 in favour of men, owing to a broader public awareness of the relative seriousness of the side-effects of contraceptive measures taken by women. Some countries consider that with respect to utilization of con-traceptives, universal coverage has been reached: only 4 per cent of sexual-ly active women are without any such coverage. The protection and monitoring of maternity programmes have been further reinforced in the last years. One country reports the establishment of family counselling ser-vices, with a counsellor-to-woman ratio of 1.4:2,000.

7. Cervical cancer and sexually transmitted diseases

50.   Cancers of all types among women are increasing. Those affecting women more frequently in both developed and developing countries are stomach cancer, breast cancer, cervical cancer and colorectal cancer.

51.   Cervical cancer is the most common form of cancer in women in most developing countries and the second most common form of cancer in women in the world as a whole. There are an estimated 450,000 new cases (a realistic figure including undiagnosed early cases would go as high as 900,000), and a death toll of 300,000, each year.

52.   Breast cancer is one of the major causes of female mortality in devel-oped countries. The number of women developing breast cancer and dying from the disease is growing steadily every year. As in cervical cancer, early detection plays a major role in reduction of mortality.

53.   Prevalence rates of sexually transmitted diseases are higher among females than among males in those aged 20 years or under. In one industri-alized country, 6 million women, half of whom are teenagers, acquire a sex-ually transmitted disease.

54.   A number of countries report the launching of national aware-ness-raising campaigns. Several countries report the establishment of national programmes of early detection of breast cancer.

8. HIV/AIDS

55.   AIDS emerged as a major health problem in the mid-1980s, in both the developed and the developing countries, threatening to undermine

major gains in the reduction of morbidity and mortality. A decade ago, women seemed to be on the periphery of the AIDS epidemic, but today almost half of newly infected adults are women. Women are more susceptible to contracting the disease for biological reasons and because of their lower social status.

56.   WHO estimates that well over 14 million adults and children have been infected with HIV since the start of the pandemic, and projects that this cumulative figure may reach 30-40 million by the year 2000. It is estimated that over half a million children have been infected with HIV from their infected mothers. The epidemic incapacitates people at the ages when they are needed most for the support of the young and the elderly. WHO estimates that by the year 2000, 13 million women will have been infected with AIDS.

57.   The AIDS pandemic is most devastating in sub-Saharan Africa. WHO had estimated that by 1992, 1.5 million adults in the region would develop AIDS, and more than 7 million would be infected with HIV. In this region, HIV transmission is predominantly through heterosexual relations, and among the infected population, almost the same proportions of men and women are represented. In the 15 countries in Eastern, Central and Western Africa where by 1990 above 1 per cent of the adult population was infected, the already low level of life expectancy at birth (about 50 years in 1985-1990) is projected to remain unchanged through the year 2000. Because as many women as men carry the virus, WHO estimates that child mortality may increase by as much as 50 per cent through mother-to-child transmission in much of sub-Saharan Africa during the 1990s. In Ethiopia, the trend between 1987 and 1993 (2.4:1 compared with 1.4:1) indicates that the male-to-female ratio is narrowing.

58.   At the beginning, transmission of HIV in North America, Europe and Australia occurred basically through homosexual contact, but increasingly heterosexuals and drug-users are becoming the agents of transmission, especially in North America. According to WHO estimates, 1.6 million cases of HIV and close to 350,000 cases of AIDS might occur by 1992. In Latin America, the Caribbean and the urban sections of Brazil are the areas most affected. It is estimated that currently about 1 million people in the region may be affected by HIV.

59.   Asia and the Pacific has exhibited the highest growth rate in HIV/AIDS among women, many of whom are married women with a single partner. India and Thailand are the countries worst affected. There are no estimates available for the region as a whole, but the estimate for India is up to about 1 million, and for Thailand about 400,000.

60.   A Global Programme on AIDS was established by WHO in 1987. By 1990, more than 150 countries had established national AIDS committees to coordinate national control programmes. Part of the problem that has to be faced concerns the reluctance of national authorities to acknowledge the existence of HIV infection, and its real magnitude. Another challenge is the discrimination against people with HIV/AIDS, a response often connected with the stigma attached to sexually transmitted diseases, and the mistaken belief that HIV can be transmitted through casual social contacts.

61.   The Global Programme on AIDS strategy stresses a gender-specific approach, emphasizing women's social, physical and economic vulnerability. In most countries where HIV/AIDS has become a serious threat or is expected to become one, national AIDS committees have been established to formulate prevention programmes. Several countries are devoting resources to research, guidance, educational material and technical assistance. National campaigns of education and prevention have been developed in many countries. Several have included prevention components in school curricula. A few countries report close collaboration with non-governmental organizations in training peer leaders as a way of improving service delivery.

9. Health consequences of violence

62.   Although grossly underreported, violence against women has assumed alarming proportions, as can be seen in section D below. Only recently have domestic violence and rape been viewed as a public health problem, yet they are a significant cause of female mortality and morbidity. Violence against women leads to psychological trauma and depression, injuries, sexually transmitted diseases and HIV, suicide and murder.

63.   Accurate figures on the prevalence of domestic violence and rape are not available, but from existing data it is known that rape and domestic violence account for about 5 per cent of the total disease burden among women

aged 15-44 in developing countries. In industrialized countries, where the total disease burden is much smaller, this share rises to 19 per cent. In these countries, assaults have been reported to cause more injuries to women than vehicle accidents, rape and mugging combined.

64.   In Asia, non-governmental organizations have played a pivotal role in publicizing the situation. They have collaborated with Governments in many countries in efforts involving the provision of legal aid and legal counselling to victims of violence, and the running of trauma centres and shelters for abused women.

10. Health issues related to ageing

65.   Life expectancy for women has risen by eight years since 1970 in the low-and middle-income countries, and by five years world wide, though this gain has been less than that enjoyed by men.

66.   In the years to come the number of women over age 65, in both industrialized and developing countries, will increase; and the total number of these women will rise from 330 million in 1990 to 600 million in 2015. Women over age 50 constitute more than one third of the entire female population of the United States of America. In addition, women constitute about 59 per cent of the United States population aged 65 or over, and 72 per cent of the population over age 85. In contrast, in Lithuania, female life expectancy decreased, as it did in Poland and some of the newly independent States.

67.   Of these elderly women, many will suffer from the chronic diseases associated with ageing such as osteoporosis and dementia, or from the consequences of neglect such as malnutrition, alienation and loneliness. Reporting on health conditions of the elderly female population is still scanty, especially in the developing countries. Osteoporosis affects 10 per cent of women world wide above age 60. In one industrialized country, osteoporosis is responsible for 1.3 million bone fractures per year. Most of the women affected become totally dependent as a result of the illness.

68.   When women do seek care for their health problems, the result is often overprescription of tranquillizers - especially to older women - instead of further investigation. A North American study found that physicians prescribed psychoactive drugs 2.5 times more often to women over age 60 than to men in the same age group.

69.   Many industrialized countries are concerned with the rising demand for health-care services on the part of their growing population of elderly people. Some developing countries are restating the importance of the traditional family and community networks in caring for the elderly.

11. Malnutrition

70.   Adequate nutritional intake is particularly important for girls and women. Discriminatory feeding practices in childhood sometimes lead to protein-energy malnutrition, anaemia and other micronutrient deficiencies in young girls. Higher rates of malnutrition generally exist among females than among males in the same age group. In many developing countries, food is distributed within the household according to a member's status rather than according to nutritional needs.

71.   Problems caused by malnutrition in girls are responsible for subsequent problems during childbirth, like obstructed labour, fistulas and birth asphyxia. Because women need more iron than men, and because they tend to receive a lower share in the distribution of food, globally 43 per cent of women and 51 per cent of pregnant women suffer from anaemia. A third of women of reproductive age who are not pregnant have anaemia. In developing countries, 56 per cent of pregnant women are anaemic and up to 7 per cent suffer from severe anaemia. Virtually all adolescent girls in developing countries suffer from iron deficiency.

72.   Because their mothers lack iodine, 30,000 babies are stillborn every year, and over 120,000 are born cretins. Iodine deficiency is the most common and preventable cause of mental retardation. At least 25 per cent of adolescent girls are affected. This deficiency leads not only to goitre but to brain damage as well, and also affects women's reproductive function. In developing countries, stunting caused by energy-protein malnutrition in girls affects 43 per cent of all women aged 15 or over.

73.   Many countries mention the adoption at the World Summit for Social Development of the goal of a one-third reduction in iron-deficiency anaemia by the year 2000. Some countries have improved their nutrition-surveillance system. Many report a direct impact of structural adjustment programmes on the nutritional situation.

12. Mental health

74.   Community-based studies and treatment studies indicate that women are disproportionately affected by mental health problems and that their vulnerability is closely associated with their marital status, their work and their roles in society. Epidemiologic evidence is accumulating that links mental disorders with alienation, powerlessness and poverty, conditions most frequently experienced by women.

75.   Several reports indicate a tendency in health services to shift their emphasis from the provision of curative services to the prevention of ill health. Although most health measures still focus on physical ill health, well-being-related measures are becoming increasingly important.

13. Substance abuse

76.   Over the next 30 years, tobacco-related deaths will more than double, so that starting from the year 2020 well over 1 million adult women will die from tobacco-related illnesses annually. Women are smoking in increasing numbers in developing countries and are a special target of cigarette advertising world wide. In France, a recent survey among students showed that girls today smoke more than boys. There is also a rapidly growing trend among girls towards the use of other drugs.

77.   Some 30 million women have contracted diseases due to alcohol intake. Alcoholic cirrhosis is the cause of 300,000 deaths among women each year. The ill-treatment of 50 per cent of battered wives is alcohol-related.

78.   Illicit drug-abuse problems among females have been underestimated, as statistics in many countries are not gender-disaggregated. A few countries report a new bio-psycho-social approach in health services, distinct from the focus only on maternal and child health.

Notes

1/   Document WHO/FHE/WHD/92.5.

2/   Ibid., para. 16.

3/   Ibid., para. 10.

D. Violence against women

1.   The Nairobi Forward-looking Strategies place violence against women under the basic strategies for addressing the issue of peace. Reference was made to specific groups of women deserving special concern, including abused women, women victims of trafficking and involuntary prostitution, and women in detention and subject to penal law. The strategies state that violence is a major obstacle to the achievement of peace and the other objectives of the Decade. Women victims of violence should be given comprehensive assistance, with legal measures, national machinery, preventive policies and institutional forms of assistance. These should be specially applied in the case of the groups of special concern.

2.   In Economic and Social Council resolution 1990/15, on recommendations and conclusions arising from the first review and appraisal of the Nairobi Strategies, adopted at the recommendation of the Commission on the Status of Women at its thirty-fourth session, the Council states that:

> "23. The recognition that violence against women in the family and society is pervasive and cuts across lines of income, class and culture must be matched by urgent and effective steps to eliminate its incidence. Violence against women derives from their unequal status in society.
>
> "**Recommendation XXII.** Governments should take immediate measures to establish appropriate penalties for violence against women in the family, the work place and society. Governments and other relevant agencies should also undertake policies to prevent, control and reduce the impact of violence on women in the family, the work place and society. Governments and relevant agencies, women's organizations, non-governmental organizations and the private sector should develop appropriate correctional, educational and social services, including shelters, training programmes for law enforcement officers, the judiciary and health and socialservice personnel, as well as adequate deterrent and corrective measures. The number of women at all levels of law enforcement, legal assistance and the judicial system should be increased."

3.   A preliminary review of the national reports prepared for the current review and appraisal reveals that, in contrast to the previous review and appraisal, most countries have reported on violence against women and the problem has been largely recognized. Most reports indicate that the issue has attracted national attention and emphasis has been placed on legal reforms, by considering violence against women as a crime and increasing the penalties for it. A large number of countries indicated the adoption of programmes intended to prevent domestic violence or provide assistance to victims of violence. Most of these programmes were initiated by non-governmental organizations and subsequently supported by the Governments concerned. Other reports acknowledged a need for these kinds of programmes but indicated that funds were lacking.

Trends

4.   The issue of violence against women became a matter of priority in the second half of the 1980s. The increasing concern about victims of violence and the need for change was voiced both by bodies within the United Nations and by non-governmental organizations. The adoption, by the General Assembly, in resolution 48/104, of the Declaration on the Elimination of Violence against Women, signalled an intention to deal with the problem in its full complexity and to give appropriate priority to domestic violence.

5.   Debates relating to women and development in the South led to the identification, frequently by grass-roots women, of various manifestations of violence against women. 1/ Concentration by activists and scholars in both the North and South was initially on sexual violence by those outside the family, including sexual harassment in the workplace and elsewhere, forced prostitution and trafficking. 2/ This was followed by attention to violence against women in the family, often described as domestic violence. Perhaps because violence in the family context challenges the universal image of the family as a supportive and loving haven, the natural and fundamental group unit of society, 3/ and because violence against women in the family represents the most fundamental example of the persistentinequality between women and men and, at the same time, serves to entrench that inequality in other spheres, violence against women in this context has remained the central focus of activism and scholarship within the general issue of violence against women.

6.   Attention to issues of sexual and domestic violence resulted in the revelation of further manifestations of violence against women. These different manifestations occur within the family but are tolerated or, indeed, condoned, by the community and State. These include female foeticide 4/ and infanticide, the neglect and physical and sexual abuse of girl-children, often by family members, and marital rape. Forms of violence related to custom, culture or religion, some of which are a source of cultural pride, including the practice of sati (self-immolation by widows), 5/ female genital mutilation and other initiation practices, widowhood rites and violence related to the custom of dowry were also revealed as risks to women.

7.   Economic, social and political developments, some post-dating the adoption of the Forward-looking Strategies, led to the identification of other areas where women are at particular risk of violence. In some countries, structural adjustment policies have caused women to move from employment in the formal sector to that in the informal sector. There they are frequently subject to poor and unregulated working conditions and vulnerable to physical and sexual abuse. The increasing participation of women, predominantly from the South and Eastern Europe, in international labour migration, legal and illegal, the conditions of which are frequently unsatisfactory, has also provided a setting for physical and sexual abuse, 6/ with illegal immigrants most at risk. Poverty and lack of alternative employment has encouraged many women to turn to prostitution, both in their own countries and abroad. One of the results of HIV/AIDS has been increased sexual violence against girl-children, who are the subjects not only of victimization by individuals but also of forced prostitution and trafficking, as men seek younger and younger sexual partners so as to avoid infection. 7/

8.   Ethnic, religious, communal and political conflicts have marked the end of the Cold War, and these conflicts have proved to be the setting for much female victimization. Female activists have been subject to physical and sexual violence, frequently by State agents, such as members of the military or the police. 8/ Women who are detained have been abused, most often sexually, by prison officers, the police and the military. During armed conflict, women have been the victims of terrorism and specific targets for rape and other sexual assault. Clear evidence exists suggesting that sexual

abuse by soldiers is widespread and that rape, sexual slavery and forced pregnancy are used systematically in some conflicts. 9/ Most women who are subject to violence during wars take no active part in the conflict, but their abuse, which is very often sexual, is a deliberate tactic to intimidate or undermine the "enemy" and often aims to inflict deep and lasting damage on entire communities. Frequently, like women in detention, women subjected to violence in conflict situations are abused because they happen to be the wives, mothers, daughters or sisters of the men the authorities cannot capture. These women become substitutes for the men in their families, with soldiers or governmental agents victimizing them in order to shame their male relatives or to coerce them into surrendering. Many women who are abused during conflicts, moreover, are often from the most marginalized and vulnerable sectors of society, such as indigenous or peasant women, 10/ refugees or displaced women.

9.   Conflicts, political and economic insecurity, and environmental degradation have resulted in large refugee flows, with women forming the bulk of the refugee population. Refugee women and girls, particularly those with inadequate documentation or who are single and unaccompanied, are vulnerable to physical and sexual abuse during flight, on arrival in refugee camps and in the country of ultimate settlement. 11/ Perpetrators of such violence include pirates, border guards, and army and resistance units, as well as male refugees. 12/ Systematic sexual violence against women and girls, in the context of armed conflict and otherwise, and the sexual victimization of individual women is one of the major causes of internal displacement and the decision to seek asylum abroad. 13/

10.   In sum, the focus on violence against women since the formulation of the Forward-looking Strategies has shown that women are subjected to three main forms of violence: physical abuse, sexual abuse, and psychological abuse. They are at risk of these abuses in all settings and contexts. The major site of violence against women is the family - where physical, sexual and psychological violence is a risk factor for girls and women throughout their lives and even from before birth. The community not only constitutes a site of violence against women but also supports aspects of the family which make it the major site of victimization for women. So also, the State constitutes a site of violence against women when, for example, it condones or tolerates the rape and torture of women in detention.

11.	The Nairobi Forward-looking Strategies, in the areas of special concern, identify gender-specific violence as a form of abuse of women. Evidence suggests that men and women experience violence differently. Women, irrespective of context, are at much greater risk of sexual violence than men, and the harm caused by violence is usually determined by their sex. The violence is often motivated by gender concerns, since violence is often used to enforce male power. As a result, violence is increasingly being recognized as linked to the social, economic and political inequality that women experience as part of their daily lives while, at the same time, reinforcing that inequality.

2. Action at the international level

12.	Until the beginning of the 1990s international action on violence against women concentrated on the family. However, in response to growing claims by women for equality in all areas, the issue of violence has broadened, to address other forms of violence.

13.	Thus, although the focus of the work of the United Nations in the field of violence against women has been on the domestic sphere, violence against women in other contexts has also been acknowledged. The Economic and Social Council has adopted, on the recommendation of the Commission on the Status of Women, several resolutions that relate to violence against detained women which is specific to their sex 14/ and has requested the Secretary-General to compile reports on this subject. 15/ The General Assembly has adopted two resolutions on violence against women migrant workers. 16/ The issue of female genital mutilation has been considered by the Working Group on Contemporary Forms of Slavery, 17/ the Sub-Commission 18/ and Commission on Human Rights 19/ and the Working Group on Traditional Practices Affecting the Health of Women and Children. 20/ Forced prostitution and trafficking in women has been the concern of the Working Group on Contemporary Forms of Slavery, which in 1991 elaborated the Programme of Action for the Prevention of Traffic in Persons and the Exploitation of the Prostitution of Women, which has been endorsed by the Subcommission and the Commission on Human Rights. 21/ Specialized agencies of the United Nations, including the United Nations High Commission for Refugees (UNHCR), and UNIFEM, part of the United Nations Development Programme (UNDP), have also addressed the question of violence against women. The UNHCR Executive Committee has adopted a number of resolutions concerning violence against refugee women 22/ and in 1990 adopted the Policy on Refugee Women. General guidelines have been developed by UNHCR to help organizations working with refugees to ensure that women are protected against manipulation, exploitation and sexual and physical abuse and that they are able to benefit from protection and assistance programmes without discrimination, 23/ while specific guidelines concerning the prevention of and response to sexual violence among refugees have just been completed. UNIFEM has linked the various forms of violence against women to development. 24/

14.   Coordination of the work of the United Nations and its specialized agencies with respect to the problem was one of the first factors contributing to this shift in approach, as was the emergence of violence against women as a priority for United Nations bodies dealing with women's issues, including the Commission on the Status of Women and the Committee on the Elimination of Discrimination against Women. 25/

15.   The Commission on the Status of Women adopted a number of recommendations regarding violence against women, leading, inter alia, to the adoption of the Declaration on the Elimination of Violence against Women. 26/

16.   The Convention on the Elimination of All Forms of Discrimination against Women was elaborated by the Commission on the Status of Women prior to the World Conference of the United Nations Decade for Women, held in Copenhagen in 1980. The terms of the treaty bind States Parties to condemning discrimination against women in all its forms and to takingimmediate and appropriate steps, in public and private life, to eliminate such discrimination. Although the obligation to eliminate discrimination against women imposed by the treaty is broad, encompassing "discrimination in all its forms", part II of the Convention addresses particular areas of discrimination. At no point does the Convention specifically mention violence against women, although article 6 obliges States Parties to take "all appropriate measures, including legislation, to suppress all forms of traffic in women and exploitation of prostitution of women".

17.   The substantive work of the Committee on the Elimination of Discrimination against Women coincided with the revelation of the endemic nature of violence against women and the identification of this violence as related to the inequality of women with men. The absence of the mention of violence against women in the terms of the Convention encouraged States Parties to regard the issue, if they considered it at all, as outside their international treaty obligations. The Committee, concerned, first, that States Parties frequently did not include information with respect to the problem in their treaty reports, thereby indicating that violence against women was not regarded as an issue of inequality and, secondly, that States Parties might justify inaction because of the silence of the Convention on the matter, adopted, at its eighth session in 1989, general recommendation 12. Recommendation 12 suggested that articles 2, 5, 11, 12 and 16 required States Parties to act to protect women against violence of any kind in the family, the workplace or in any other area of social life and that States Parties report on legislative and other measures that have been taken to address violence against women, to protect the victims by providing support services and to compile statistics on incidence and victims. The following year, the Committee adopted general recommendation 14, concerned with female circumcision and other traditional practices harmful to the health of women. This recommendation suggested various strategies, predominantly of an educational nature, that States Parties might take to eradicate, specifically, female circumcision.

18.   General recommendations 12 and 14 were tentative steps by the Committee to relate violence against women to discrimination and its elimination. In 1992, at its eleventh session, the Committee formulated the far more comprehensive general recommendation 19, which specifically categorized gender-based violence, which it defined as violence that is directed against a women because she is a women or that affects women disproportionately, as a form of discrimination that supports other forms of discrimination and, accordingly, as a breach of the general obligations of the Convention. Unlike general recommendations 12 and 14, general recommendation 19 firmly places gender-based violence within the rubric of human rights and fundamental freedoms and makes clear that the Convention obliges States Parties to eliminate violence perpetrated by pub-

lic authorities and by private persons, organizations or enterprises. The general recommendation, further, elaborates programmatic measures States Parties should employ to address various manifestations of gender-based violence.

19.   Prioritization by the Committee of the issue of gender-based violence, particularly in general recommendation 19, was informed by the second factor that led to the broadening of the issue of violence against women within the United Nations namely - the categorization of violence against women, because of its scale and gender dimension, as an issue of human rights. In order to concretize this categorization and because international and regional human rights instruments and mechanisms, although implicitly concerned with gender-based violence, did not explicitly relate to the issue and had, in general terms, not been interpreted as concerned with it, the Commission on the Status of Women recommended the formulation of an international instrument on violence against women.

20.   The Declaration on the Elimination of Violence against Women, the result of the Commission's recommendation, locates violence against women within the framework of violation of human rights obligations, inequality and discrimination and sets out strategies that member States and the organs and specialized agencies of the United Nations should employ to eliminate its occurrence. The Declaration's adoption was facilitated by the recognition by the World Conference on Human Rights, six months earlier, of the egregious nature of violence against women and the human rights dimensions of the problem. 27/ Further analysis of the issue within this framework occurred in October 1993 at the Expert Group Meeting on Measures to Eradicate Violence against Women, convened by the Division for the Advancement of Women as part of the preparation of apriority theme for the Commission on the Status of Women. The recommendations were made with respect to human rights, law and justice, development, health and education and peace, peace-keeping, emergencies and conflict. 28/

21.   The final step towards the broadening of the issue within the United Nations occurred in March 1994, when the United Nations Commission on Human Rights condemned all acts of gender-based violence against women and appointed a special rapporteur on violence against women 29/ to seek

and receive information on violence against women, its causes and consequences; recommend measures at the national regional and international levels to eliminate violence against women; work with other mechanisms of the Commission on Human Rights and the Commission on the Status of Women and to report to the next session of the Commission on Human Rights.

3. Existing strategies to confront violence against women

22.   Coinciding with the identification of violence against women as gender-based, policy has broadened, and the problem has come to be considered a matter of human rights and a dimension of discrimination between women and men. Basically, at all levels, strategies fall into three broad categories: raising awareness of the various forms of violence against women, advocating legal change, and providing services for victims.

a.   International level

23.   Action at the international level with respect to violence against women has included the establishment of policy, the formulation of recommendations for member States and United Nations activity.

24.   Comprehensive recommendations relating to violence against women in the family, incorporating very specific suggestions for legal reform, with a concentration on a criminal justice approach to domestic violence, the role and training of the police, prosecutors and the health sector, social and resource support for victims and the compilation of research and data were made by the (1986) Expert Group on Violence in the Family, with special Emphasis on its Effects on Women. Important recommendations were also made by the Group with regard to public awareness of violence against women, education at all levels and in all forms,and the elimination of images in education and the media entrenching the subordination and violation of women. Similar recommendations were made in the general recommendations of the Committee on the Elimination of Discrimination against Women with regard to family violence. As has been noted, general recommendation 19 was drawn more widely than the two earlier recommendations on violence against women and thus included suggestions relating to trafficking and sexual exploitation, sexual harassment, female circumcision and violence against rural women and domestic workers.

25.   Strategies elaborated in the Declaration on the Elimination of Violence against Women contain recommendations found in existing United Nations documents. Thus, recalling paragraph 258 of the Forward-looking Strategies, States are urged to consider the development of national plans of action to promote the protection of women against any form of violence and, if appropriate, cooperate with non-governmental organizations in that regard, entrench appropriate legal provisions, introduce training for relevant sectors, address issues of education and the portrayal of images of women, promote research and adopt measures directed to the elimination of violence against women who are especially vulnerable to violence. Unusually, however, the Declaration specifically addresses the organs and specialized agencies of the United Nations. They are requested to promote awareness of the issue and encourage coordination within the Organization with respect to efforts to eliminate gender-based violence.

26.   It is the clear categorization by the Declaration of gender-based violence against women as both an issue of human rights and of discrimination, however, which establishes the framework for the development of future strategies at the international level. Within the Declaration itself, States are urged to condemn violence against women and refrain from invoking custom, tradition or religion to avoid this obligation. States are also urged to refrain from engaging in violence against women and to exercise due diligence to prevent, investigate and punish acts of violence against women, whether perpetrated in the public or private sphere. This language not only sets strategic objectives for member States but encourages the interpretation of existing international standards and methods of implementation so as to address the issue of violence against women.

b.   National level

27.   Measures that have been introduced at the national level to confront violence against women fall into three broad categories: service and support provision, substantive and procedural law reform, and training and education for specific groups as well as for the general public.

28.   Not all countries have introduced measures in this context, but most have provided information in their national reports. Where they have done so, it has usually been as a result of advocacy and activism by women's

non-governmental organizations. Accordingly, the focus of the measures and their level of development reflect the primary focus of attention of such non-governmental organizations. Until very recently, the primary focus of activist attention in individual countries was violence against women which occurs in the private sphere. Thus, sexual assault generally and all forms of violence against women in the family received primary attention and, accordingly, at the national level measures in those contexts were most developed. Sexual harassment in the workplace and elsewhere had also attracted attention, as had particular forms of violence based on culture, tradition or religion. Since the beginning of the decade, and particularly with the identification of gender-based violence against women as an issue of human rights, activist attention has expanded to encompass violence against women in the public sphere. Although activism relating to violence against women in this setting has largely been devoted to achieving better application of extant international standards and procedures of implementation in this context, in some countries specific measures have been introduced which relate to violence against women in this sphere.

29.   Existing national measures to confront violence against women do not approach the various manifestations of such violence as the result of a uniform structural cause but, rather, address each form of violence separately, generally in accordance with where the violence occurs. Thus, different measures have been employed to address violence in the family, the community and elsewhere. Government measures have been initiated to confront a number of forms of violence against women: violence against women in the household; sexual harassment; sexual assault; violence related to tradition and culture; and violence perpetrated against women in the public sphere. Where each is concerned, the text will examine legal approaches, service provisions, and the research, training and educational measures that have been utilized.

30.   Where all forms of violence against women are concerned, national strategies have concentrated predominantly on legal and service measures with, to a lesser extent, attention being paid to sector-specific and public-education programmes or campaigns which address values, attitudes and actions related to gender violence. In the main, it has been unusual for countries

to implement an integrated, holistic response to gender-based violence against women. Thus, in general, responses have been reactive, with the protection of the victim and the punishment of the perpetrator as their primary concerns. Exceptional in this regard are Australia and Canada where some attempt has been made to take a comprehensive approach to violence against women. In Australia, a National Committee on Violence Against Women, which has formulated a national strategy with respect to violence against women has been established, 30/ and Canada has set up the Canadian Panel on Violence Against Women, which has formulated a national action plan. 31/

31.   Responses have often been law-centred, predominantly concerned with law reform. However, many laws are based on a model of gender neutrality in what is, in fact, a gender-specific area, and the laws do not take account of the reality of victimization and the systemic inequalities in society. Very often the laws are still based on outdated sexual stereotypes and result in unfair and unequal treatment of women.

32.   For each type of measure chosen, there has to be a distinct evaluation. What has appeared in national legal systems is a broader definition of what is considered physical or sexual violence against women. The national reports suggest that most countries have provisions in their constitutions or in their legislation about violence in the family or in terms of sexual assault.

33.   The central question that has emerged in the evolution of strategies to confront the problem is whether the penal or criminal justice system is appropriate for the management of violence against women. In some cases, the criminal law was believed to be inappropriate when Governments reported their intention to undertake reforms of legislation. In other cases, reports stressed the need to create or enlarge facilities for victims, anapproach that dominated the measures taken. However, a number of countries noted that while domestic violence takes place in the family and occurs among intimates, it is in fact criminal conduct and should not be treated differently from such conduct in other contexts. In a few countries, this has led to the development of spouse-abuse statutes.

34.   Those countries that have chosen to stress the criminal nature of domestic abuse have recognized the central role of the police in the man-

agement of the issue. They have recognized, further, that the police have been traditionally reluctant to intervene in such cases and have sought to introduce strategies to encourage their intervention. The strategies have included legal measures, such as the clarification of police powers of entry, arrest and bail procedures in cases of domestic violence; legislation that compels women to give evidence against their abusive spouses; the introduction of presumptive arrest and charging policies; police training and support services.

35.   All countries, including those that have not considered the question of domestic violence in any sustained fashion, have legal measures, such as criminal and tortious sanction, which are applicable to cases of assault generally and are therefore, theoretically, available in cases of domestic assault. In general, however, crimes, torts or delicts are not defined so as to encompass emotional or psychological harms and in many countries unwanted sexual acts by a husband on his wife do not amount to crimes. Further, few countries draw a distinction between violence against women and men in their criminal and civil codes, and very few have established specific offences relating to violence which occurs in the family or between family members. The sex of the victim and the relationship between the victim and the offender sometimes do allow for the introduction of certain defences, such as the "honour defence", which, to a certain extent, may excuse crimes which occur between intimates or affect sentence

36.   All countries, as reflected in their period reports to the Committee on the Elimination of Discrimination against Women, provide matrimonial relief, such as divorce or judicial separation, for those who are treated with violence by their spouses. These remedies have proven, in general terms, to be inadequate in the context of domestic violence. In most countries, general criminal remedies are not applied unless the violence suffered is particularly severe, and even where they are applied, the criminal law, in its usual form, does not cater for the particular issues that arise in the case of domestic assault. Matrimonial relief, although providing a remedy for some, is clearly available only to those who are married and even in such cases may not be desired by the victim, who, in general terms, wishes the violence, rather than the relationship, to be brought to an end.

37.   Some countries have introduced special legal approaches to confront domestic violence. Some have introduced special criminal sanctions which apply in the domestic context. In general, however, special legal approaches to domestic violence have been in the context of the civil, rather than the criminal, law and have developed from two existing legal remedies: the breach of the peace procedure, and the injunction.

38.   In most countries, there is a procedure whereby complaints can be made to a magistrate or justice that violence has taken place or has been threatened, and the violent party is then requested to enter into an undertaking, with or without a pledge of money, to keep the peace or be of good behaviour. If the undertaking is breached, the offender forfeits a specified sum of money or is imprisoned. The process is criminal, but the standard of proof is lower. In its general form, this remedy has some potential for the victim of domestic assault, but it does present some problems, not the least of which is the fact that enforcement of the remedy depends on a further court appearance, initiated by the victim or the police.

39.   Some countries have modified and strengthened this procedure so that it is more useful in the context of domestic violence, while others have used it as the inspiration for remedies, usually known as "protection orders", which apply specifically to such violence. In general terms, the remedy developed from the procedure allows for a court order, obtained on the balance of probabilities, which can protect the victim from further attacks or harassment.

40.   A number of countries have chosen to concentrate on the civil, rather than the criminal, law to provide victims of domestic assault with remedy. In general terms, these countries have developed existing injunction or interdict proceedings. Usually an injunction or interdict is available only as a remedy incidental to a principal cause of action - for example, divorce, nullity or judicial separation - and, although seeking to provide a victim of domestic violence with relief, some countries continue to limit access to the remedy in this way. In others, however, a victim of domestic violence is able to apply for injunctive relief independently of any other legal action. Usually, the relief available is of two varieties: an order prohibiting the offender from molesting or harassing the victim, and an order excluding or evicting the offender from a part or all of the matrimonial home or the area in which the

home is situated. The orders are usually supported by a provision entitling the police to arrest the offender, without warrant, if he breaches the order.

41.   In most countries, criminal and civil laws, although of various levels of sophistication, to protect women who are the victims of domestic violence are technically in place. This is important because such laws not only provide individual victims with remedies, should they choose to take advantage of them, but also indicate clearly that a country does not tolerate domestic assault. Indeed, all Governments should be encouraged to introduce clear, accessible and well integrated legal provisions, appropriate to the particular country situation, in this context.

42.   Certainly, certain sectors have always been aware of the existence of violence, but countries have been slow to provide services for victims, offenders and their families. Although the law is usually the last resort for victims of domestic assault, reached only after others have proved to be unhelpful, Governments have chosen to concentrate on legal reform.

43.   In general terms, the response of the health and welfare sectors has been insufficient to deal with violence. Professionals in these sectors, usually uneducated in the dynamics of domestic assault, have chosen to concentrate on the victim, rather than the offender, as the key to their response. In general, both sectors have looked at such violence as an individual, rather than structural, problem and have stressed the importance of the maintenance of the family.

44.   Many national reports indicate that services for victims of domestic violence have been introduced not because of governmental initiatives but rather as a result of activity by individual women or groups of women. In general, however, once services have been put in place by the efforts of such women, Governments have stepped in and either taken over such services or

introduced services of their own, modelled on those introduced by the voluntary sector.

45.   Shelter provision has proven to be the most important service for victims of domestic violence. Shelters, which were originally conceived as advice centres for women at risk and ultimately developed to provide residential accommodation for them and their children, exist in many countries. In countries where the Government has adopted the shelter model, specific shelters are often established for different groups of women, including immigrant women, women with disabilities, aboriginal women. In general, shelter facilities usually have inadequate funding for the service requirements, so that they are inadequate in number, oversubscribed and understaffed.

46.   Other services that exist for victims of domestic assault include toll-free advice lines, counselling services and advice centres.

47.   Some Governments have chosen to implement programmes for offenders. Like shelters for battered women, many of these programmes began as community-based responses to the problem, and many were linked to shelters. In certain cases they are part of diversion schemes or a court sentence. These schemes are new, take various models, and have as yet to be analysed for effectiveness. As such, they should be approached cautiously.

48.   Government-funded and -sponsored research into the various aspects of violence against women in the family is well developed in some countries, some going so far as to have information clearing-houses on the subject. In most, however, research has not progressed beyond the rudimentary.

49.   A number of countries have initiated training programmes for those involved in domestic violence. Most of the programmes focus on the police, regarded as the front line of response. The programmes vary in duration, scope and target group, and little information about them was provided in the reports. Few countries offer the police comprehensive and in-depth training in the dynamics of domestic violence, the legal responses available and the services available for the victims. Police in most countries do not receive any training in this area.

50.   Some countries have recognized that domestic violence is the result of social norms and values that provide stereotypical roles for men and women and have concluded that these views can best be addressed by formal and informal education. Accordingly, in some countries, the subject of family violence and peaceful methods of conflict resolution form part of the primary and secondary curriculum.

51.   Many countries have relied on informal education strategies, both to inform women of their legal rights, available options and support systems and to convey to both women and men that family violence is to be deplored. Such strategies have included poster campaigns, booklets, videos, television and radio advertising and folk theatre.

(i)   Sexual harassment

52.   Few countries reported on sexual harassment. In those that did, different remedies are applied, depending upon whether it occurs in the street or in the workplace.

53.   Most countries fail to provide remedies for harassment falling short of rape, sexual assault, indecent assault or common assault which occurs outside the workplace. In exceptional cases, however, specific legislation prohibits sexually offensive behaviour, which is variously described as insulting the modesty of a woman, "eye-teasing" or "kerb-crawling".

54.   A number of countries have become aware of the importance of sexual harassment in the workplace and educational institutions and the implications that such harassment can have for the individual woman and the organization. These countries have, therefore, allowed women who have been subject to such victimization to seek remedies under legislation pertaining to employment, such as sex discrimination or equal opportunities statutes, concluding that harassment in the workplace amounts to less favourable treatment on the grounds of sex. Still others have enacted specific legislation prohibiting sexual harassment in employment, the provision of goods and services, and educational institutions, and provide remedies where such harassment occurs.

55.   Although the legislative remedies are broadly similar in approach, some statutes are more effective than others, having wider definitions of

harassment, extending coverage to contract and commission agents, allowing representative actions by unions and fixing employers with vicarious liability for the harassment of their employees.

56.   In general, governmental measures to prevent sexual harassment
have been confined to the introduction of legislation, campaigning around
and publicizing the issue being left to the initiative of trade unions, worker's
associations and private organizations. A number of Governments have,
however, produced protocols or guides indicating how sexual harassment
can be eliminated in both governmental and non-governmental institutions. A limited number of Governments, such as New Zealand, have draft-
ed standard form contracts, used when governmental contracts are
concluded, which contain clauses forbidding harassment.

57.   Some governmental bodies have increased awareness of sexual
harassment, its serious short- and long-term implications and the measures
that can be used to confront it by educational strategies. These have included the production of pamphlets, protocols and advertisements. In one country, the Human Rights and Equal Opportunity Commission conducted a
poster, magazine and advertising campaign, which included a toll-free complaint line, aimed at young women in vulnerable occupations. The campaign and its effects are continuing.

(ii) Sexual assault

58.   All countries criminally sanction sexual offenses against women.
Although there has been significant focus on the reform of the substantive
law of sexual assault, evaluations of legislative reforms reveal that most
women place more significance on reform of evidentiary and procedural
aspects of this area of the law. Thus, modifications of the requirement of
fresh complaint, corroboration and rules allowing introduction of evidence
of the past sexual history of complainants have been welcomed as significantly ameliorating the ordeal and limiting the humiliation that a complainant endures, both in the courtroom and before. Other measures, which
have included provisions providing complainants with anonymity, court
procedures which hide their identity and deny the offender bail or at least
make the complainant aware of where the offender is, have also been enthu-
siastically received.

59.   Some countries - e.g., Denmark, France, Germany, the Netherlands and the United Kingdom - have criminal injury compensation schemes entitling victims of sexual assault to compensation by the State.

60.   Support and services for victims of sexual assault have, as in the case of domestic violence, usually been initiated by individual women and women's groups. As with domestic violence, the models used have often been adopted by government at a later stage.

61.   In many countries rape crisis services, providing toll-free advice lines, advice services and accommodation for women who are the victims of sexual assault, exist. Some are run by women's groups with no support from government, others are operated by a combination of such a group and government, and some are operated by government. Some operate independently, others cooperate with the police, and some are integrated formally with the police.

62.   In most countries the traditional sexual assault reception agencies are police stations. In general terms, little attention has been paid to the singular ordeal that a rape complainant endures, and most stations are not equipped to alleviate this. Some, however, have taken account of the particular needs of sexual assault complainants and offer a multidisciplinary approach to the complaints, often cooperating with hospitals or special clinics. In some countries, further, police have introduced special examination rooms, away from the station, to render the ordeal of the victim as inoffensive as possible.

63.   Victims of sexual assault are usually ashamed, guilty and afraid of how people will react to them. Many are humiliated, ridiculed, scorned and stigmatized by police and other workers and treated with hostility and suspicion by their family and friends.

64.   The negative response to the victim of rape stems from attitudes towards women, rape victims and rape which are the result of myth and prejudice. Women are believed to provoke sexual assault by the way they dress, where they go, the way they move and behave. They are considered to be responsible for their own protection and must ensure that they do not arouse male sexuality.

65.   Evidence from many countries suggests that the police are particularly at risk of being misinformed by these stereotypes. They are thus frequently suspicious of complainants, particularly in cases where there is no obvious sign of injury, the offender is known to the complainant, the complainant delays reporting her assault or appears calm and unemotional. If the complainant is perceived to be morally dubious - for example, if she is sexually experienced -her allegation may be doubted.

66.   Police suspicion may manifest itself in various ways: the complainant may be totally disbelieved and discouraged from pursuing her complaint; the investigation may be conducted in such a way as to test her story - insensitive, bullying interrogation may take place, for example, involving a series of officers and a medical examination in unpleasant or threatening circumstances; the complainant may be kept uninformed of the progress of the investigation.

67.   Insensitive police procedures not only add to the ordeal of the complainant but obstruct acquisition of the best evidence and militate against conviction of offenders.

68.   In most countries, police officers receive basic training in the law and practice relating to sexual assault. However, this training is usually brief and underresourced. Some countries have recognized the importance of training and education in this context and have introduced specific training and education at various levels. Most of this training has been in methods of obtaining the best evidence for conviction and has thus been technical, but some has included attitude training and sensitization. Some countries have employed kits and protocols which the investigating officer is directed to use in cases of complaints of sexual assault; they ensure that officers are meticulous in their collection of evidence and also direct their inquiries sensitively.

69.   Police officers are not the only officials who need to be educated in the dynamics of sexual assault. Prosecutors, defenders and judges as well as the general public require such training. Unfortunately, although some countries do conduct specific training on sexual assault for lawyers and judges, they have not developed as much of it as in the area of domestic violence. Again, although poster and advertising campaigns around the issues

of domestic violence and sexual harassment have been conducted in many countries, sexual assault has not received the publicity it warrants.

(iii) Violence related to tradition and custom

70.   In a number of countries, women are subjected to violent or harmful treatment because of practices which are regarded as traditional, customary or prescribed by religion. Four such practices are: violence related to dowry, widowhood rites, sati and female circumcision.

71.   In all four instances legal strategies have been introduced to criminalize the practice, in the hope that this will lead to its eradication. However, here more than in other contexts where women are the subject of abuse, the law alone cannot be relied on to change practices which are rooted deeply in tradition and culture and which, to a certain extent, are defended by both women and men, despite the fact that they have patently harmful consequences.

72.   Harmful traditional and customary practices will be eradicated only when there is fundamental societal change, which will occur with attitudinal change at all levels. This sort of change can be achieved only with a combination of short-term and long-term measures aimed at the particular practice and at the cause of the practice: inequality. Such measures include formal and informal education, effective use of media and clear commitment from government, which must be prepared not only to condemn such practices legislatively but also to ensure that the legislation is implemented in good faith.

73.   In a few instances, educational campaigns sought to demonstrate the danger inherent in a practice and change both men's and women's attitudes to it. Such campaigns directed at women performing, for example, circumcision, have not been as focused as those to stop dowry-related violence, but in those countries where the practice is customary, poster campaigns and training modules for service providers have been introduced. These have aimed at the transformation of the social, religious and cultural bases of the practice. Further, in a number of these countries, high-level members of government have been prepared to make statements condemning the practice, drawing attention to the health risks to girls and women which accompanies it.

E. Effects of armed or other kinds of conflict on women

74.   The provisions of the Strategies under the theme of Peace (paras. 232-262) reflect the stage of governmental discussion on the subject in the mid-1980s, covering the climate of "cold war", the lack of clear focus on the gender difference in approaches to such matters as security, disarmament, conflict resolution, and the situation of women and children in the occupied Palestinian territories, under apartheid and in areas of armed conflict. The areas described in the Strategies and discussed during and after the Nairobi Conference by intergovernmental bodies, were often viewed as an extension of the political confrontation between East and West over such issues as disarmament, armed conflict, the problems of the Middle East and apartheid rather than an attempt to reflect thoroughly the women's perspective with regard to those issues. There were, however, some themes, such as the role of women in education for peace, in peace research, in decision-making and in non-governmental activities which had more potential for reflecting women's contributions and perspectives and which were less politicized.

75.   The same spirit was reflected in the listing of the main obstacles to peace, which affect particularly the advancement of women, which included international tension and violations of the Charter of the United Nations; the arms race, in particular, the nuclear arms race; armed conflict; external domination; foreign occupation; acquisition of land by force; aggression; imperialism; colonialism and neo-colonialism; racism; apartheid; gross violations of human rights; terrorism; repression; the disappearance of persons; and discrimination on the basis of sex. Other obstacles listed were

historically established hostile attitudes; ignorance and bigotry between countries, ethnic groups, races, sexes, and socio-economic groups and lack of tolerance for different cultures and traditions; poverty; tension in international economic and political relations; the spread of the arms race; and violation of the principle of justice.

76.   At the time of the Nairobi Conference, the different approaches of women's non-governmental organizations were articulated in feminist publications and research. Their understanding of peace, rejection of violence in all its forms, holistic approach to peace, and invisible contribution to the promotion of more conciliatory and peaceful attitudes were well established in all parts of the world (although most advanced in North America and Western Europe). The views and activities of women were, in general, in opposition to those of Governments and the "official" line of thinking. They were also very diversified, as demonstrated at the "Peace Tent" at the Non-governmental Forum, parallel to the Nairobi Conference.

77.   Although in the mid 1980s peace-related discourse and activities on the part of non-governmental organizations and of Governments remained separate, non-governmental research and literature had an impact on governmental attitudes. In the Strategies, the issue of violence against women was for the first time placed under the theme of Peace, thus affirming the feminist claim that violence in all its forms and at all levels has the same roots and that there is an obvious connection between violence against women and war-related violence. In paragraph 13 of the Strategies, the Conference adopted a broad definition of peace, reflecting the feminist view that

> "The full and effective promotion of women's rights can best occur in conditions of international peace and security where relations among States are based on the respect for the legitimate rights of all nations, great and small, and peoples to self-determination, independence, sovereignty, territorial integrity and the right to live in peace within their national borders.
>
> ...
>
> "Peace includes not only the absence of war, violence and hostilities at the national and international levels but also the enjoyment of economic and social justice, equality and the entire range of human rights and fundamental freedoms within the society.
>
> ...

"It also embraces the whole range of actions reflected in concerns for security and implicit assumptions of trust between nations, social groups and individuals. It represents goodwill towards others and promotes respect for life while protecting freedom, human rights and the dignity of peoples and of individuals. Peace cannot be realized under conditions of economic and sexual inequality, denial of basic human rights and fundamental freedoms, deliberate exploitation of large sectors of the population, unequal development of countries, and exploitative economic relations. Without peace and stability there can be no development. Peace and development are interrelated and mutually reinforcing.

...

"Peace is promoted by equality of the sexes, economic equality and the universal enjoyment of basic human rights and fundamental freedoms. Its enjoyment by all requires that women be enabled to exercise their right to participate on an equal footing with men in all spheres of the political, economic and social life of their respective countries, particularly in the decision-making process, while exercising their right to freedom of opinion, expression, information and association in the promotion of international peace and cooperation."

78.   Other themes included in the Strategies, such as the participation of women in decision-making in the areas of peace, disarmament and security; the participation of women in international activities as representatives of their countries at international meetings, including those of the United Nations and regional bodies; the participation of women in the diplomatic service of their countries; and the employment of women by international organizations, including the United Nations system have become increasingly important. With the decreasing tension between East and West and the increasing number of States Parties to the Convention on the Elimination of All Forms of Discrimination against Women, the lack of progress on the implementation of its articles 7 and 8 related to the participation of women in the political arena at the national and international level, becomes striking.

79.   The view that there could be no increase in the participation of women in peace, security, and conflict-resolution areas until the enormous gap between the de jure and the de facto situation of women in decision-making is bridged is generally recognized, and since 1990, the participation of women in decision-making has become one of the most visible issues under the theme of Peace. Although the practical progress has been very slow, there is increased interest in addressing this issue, as reflected by numerous governmental discussions, expert group meetings and publications.

80.   The 1990 review and appraisal cited certain fields, such as disarmament and multilateral diplomacy, which are crucial for the preservation of peace and yet in which women are highly underrepresented. For example, in the Talks on Mutual Reduction of Armed Forces and Associated Measures in Central Europe, which were held at Viȩnna, between 1975 and 1986, there were only 10 women in the 19 delegations. Half of them (five women out of 92 delegates, or 5 per cent) participated only at the end of the talks. In the permanent missions to the United Nations in 1989 women constituted 20 per cent of the diplomatic personnel. Thirty-six per cent (57 delegations) had no women on the staff at all. The highest percentage of women delegates were in the Latin American and the Caribbean region (39 per cent). The Western European and Others group had (26 per cent); Africa, 15 per cent; Asia and the Pacific, 12 per cent; and Eastern Europe, 4 per cent. The representation of women in the First Committee of the General Assembly, which deals with disarmament and international security in the period 1985-1988 was 7.9 per cent. The highest representation was from Latin America and the Caribbean - 16.3 per cent. These international levels reflect the situations at the national levels. The participation of women is lowest in decision-making in the area of defence.

81.   Fewer than one third of those developing countries providing national reports in 1990 indicated that specific measures had been taken for increasing women's active participation in the area of peace. Some of those countries called attention to their distribution of information on peace matters, support to women's participation in peace-related activities and conferences, and the importance of women's activities in this area. A few countries mentioned the importance of national machinery in this respect. Several developed countries mentioned their efforts to increase the participation of women in senior positions in international organizations. Theyalso mentioned valuable work by non-governmental organizations in this respect, involving support to South Africa, Central America and Palestine; disarmament; support to refugees; peace marches; support to women in developing countries; and protests against nuclear build-up.

82.   Most developing and several developed countries reported on the role of women in education for peace and the measures undertaken by the Governments to increase and support this role, by means of the dissemina-

tion of information; participation in conferences and meetings; integration of the subjects of peace, cooperation, tolerance, sexual equality, into school curricula; promotion of peace culture and art; strengthening of education for peace in the family; training in the resolution of conflicts; and strengthening of human rights and liberties. Some countries produced special material on peace issues. Peace education was considered one of the main areas of activity of women's organizations. Several countries mentioned their support to peace research through the designation of funds and cooperation with the United Nations system.

83.   In the review and appraisal, the main obstacles mentioned to the participation of women in peace-related activities were military expenditure and direction of funds for military purposes; armed conflict; low level of education; insufficient communication; economic conditions, and the large portion of the world's women affected by regional conflicts and violence against women.

84.   In resolution 1990/15, the Economic and Social Council noted, in conclusions arising from the first review and appraisal of the implementation of the Nairobi Strategies, that:

> "22.   Despite the progress made in some areas, international, regional and national conflicts persist, and women continue to number among their main victims. At the same time, women are no more prominent among those making decisions on conflicts than in the past.
>
> "**Recommendation XX**. Governments should be encouraged to increase the participation of women in the peace process at the decision-making level, including them as part of delegations to negotiate international agreements relating to peace and disarmament and establishing a target for the number of women participating in such delegations.
>
> "The United Nations and the international non-governmental organizations concerned should continue to monitor and support greater involvement of women in the peace process."

85.   Of the 63 national reports that were analysed for this document, only 34 addressed, sometimes in a very general way, the issues of women and peace. They focused on the situation of refugee women, the participation of women in the military and police force and the participation of women in non-governmental activities related to peace.

1. Women and peace in the post-cold war period

86.   With the end of the "cold war", the attempts to establish democracy, a market economy and international cooperation throughout the world have reduced the interest of some Governments in the issue of women and peace. Other Governments, however, have focused on the emerging situation and women's roles in it, pointing to the linkage between the participation of women in all spheres of life as full citizens, including the peace process, and the prospects of building new, democratic societies; women's participation in national and international decision-making related to peace; and women's participation in conflict resolution. With the concept of a new international world order, which should be formed and guarded in the future by an international peace force under the auspices of the United Nations, women's new roles came into discussion. Besides traditional peace-keeping roles, women should perform various other functions, in the international police and military, as peacemakers and negotiators of peace settlements, and as supervisors of elections, national reconciliation and democratization.

87.   Similar changes of focus and searches for new identities characterized all spheres of peace-related activities at the non-governmental level, including women's organizations, research institutions and female researchers. It seems that, at this level, increasing attention and importance is being attached to the participation of women in all aspects of peace-keeping, negotiation and peace-making, including decision-making. The fact that women have been excluded from those areas and have suffered the consequences of violent international and domestic conflicts and the destruction and waste of human and material resources is now being actively addressed by women.

88.   Women's long participation in non-governmental activities related to peace has been fruitful to them in organizing demonstrations and peace education and in offering alternatives to a militarized society. The focus has

been on avoiding or ending violence, which has been almost exclusively perpetrated by men. Women peace researchers have shown the common roots of all forms of violence, from family and personal violence to war, and have indicated that there can be no real peace without the elimination of all forms of discrimination and oppression. They have advocated participatory democracy, the preservation of a healthy environment, the elimination of instruments of war, ensuring the prevalence of values and attitudes for peace, and developing a new type of interpersonal and international relations based on partnership and tolerance.

89.   Another issue newly on the agenda, in the new context, is war-related violence and the suffering of women. Attention was given to the situation of women and children in armed conflict and the obligation of parties to observe all the rules outlined in the Hague and the Geneva Conventions and in the Additional Protocols to the Geneva Conventions. Another area under the topic of women and peace was the situation of refugee women, resulting in most cases from armed conflicts - their legal status; vulnerability to abuse, violence and all forms of discrimination; and means of assistance.

90.   In certain recent armed conflicts in different parts of the world, various forms of direct violence were used against women, including rape and forced prostitution. They were used as a "weapon", to humiliate. The most extensive gender-related violence against women was reported in the former Yugoslavia. It obliged the international community to address the issue of violence against women during armed conflicts. The focus is on the necessity of creating an international mechanism that would make possible fast and prompt international investigation and court proceedings for the perpetrators, just as in all other cases of war crimes. On the other hand, it is felt that there should be more emphasis on the empowerment of women, which would enable them to have more say in decisions related to war or peace; reconciliation or violence, which would allow them to contribute to preventing such tragedies rather than becoming their victims. There should also be more effective mechanisms for assisting women victims of war-related violence to rebuild their confidence, strengthen their self-reliance and eliminate their victims' syndrome.

91.   Thus, there was increasing understanding that women should play an equal part in the peace efforts defined in the Agenda for Peace - first, because their participation in such activities was their right as citizens of their countries; secondly, because there were reasons to believe that they would bring to those operations specific skills and abilities that otherwise would not be available.

92.   Existing research indicates that, in order to have a substantive impact on decision-making in terms of content, priorities, style and working climate, the critical mass must be at least 30-35 per cent. Such a level of participation would enable a minority to influence the culture of the group. Women have achieved a critical mass at the national decision-making level in only a few countries, particularly the Nordic countries. When women in those countries acted in solidarity, they were able to have a visible impact on political decisions and the political culture. For example, they changed peoples' attitudes to female leaders and placed on the public agendas such issues as social support service, equality, health care, protection against violence and women's reproductive rights.

93.   According to public opinion polls, surveys and other sources of information, in some countries of North America and Western Europe, women are less militaristic than men, more concerned with the preservation of peace, and more opposed to increased militarization or nuclear energy. Women more strongly support measures to protect the environment, help the economically disadvantaged, improve race relations, and regulate and control by law of various social vices. While most of the empirical studies came from developed countries, there are more and more indications that women in developing countries also made attempts to include women's issues on public agendas. For example, women's groups in Mexico have campaigned against rape and domestic violence; in India women organized the Chipko movement to secure a ban on felling trees and to replant the available land and manage it properly. In Kenya, the Green Belt Movement focused on planting trees, contributing significantly to the reduction of deforestation. Women's different political style has also been noted among female politicians at the local level. Whenever women have joined the decision-making bodies in sufficient numbers, they have created a more collaborative atmosphere, characterized by mutual respect, independent of

prevailing political differences, and have sought consensus or acceptance rather than a win-or-lose solution. They focused more on solving than discussing the problems. These approaches would be most useful with regard to peace and security matters at the national and international levels.

94.   Seven countries reported on women's non-governmental activities related to peace. Two focused on activities related to national reconciliation in war-torn areas and in the neighbouring countries. They included peace campaigns, humanitarian work, assistance to refugees, and contacts between women emigrants and the women's groups in the country in order to contribute to the peace dialogue. One country reported on women's involvement in radio programmes for dialogue and peace in the warring countries (Ethiopia, Somalia). One country emphasized that women should be trained for future positions in the process of reconstruction and that United Nations agencies should take the lead in this respect. One country reported that due to a women's campaign, one of its provinces was declared a nuclear-free zone in 1992.

95.   One country stressed the important role of national and international non-governmental organizations in increasing awareness of rural women and the important roles of women as peace makers at home, at the community level, and as teachers. Women performed those roles throughout their lifetimes participating in matrimonial, religious and governmental reconciliation.

96.   One country focused on the significant role which women's non-governmental organizations played with regard to the development of self-reliance and the leadership capabilities of women; the promotion of the ideals of disarmament and human rights through various international initiatives, friendship associations, the active participation of women in international meetings and the global peace movement; building women's networks; citizen's diplomacy; and advocating peace. Women also worked, alone and with men, in many organizations and professional associations, addressing women's concerns related to disarmament, human rights, war crimes, rape, sexual violence and conflict resolution. In this way, women have had an impact on governmental policy relating to the moratorium on nuclear weapons and preventing the deployment of cruise missiles.

97.   Reference was made to the gender gap in men's and women's atti- tudes to war and peace and to the substantial differences in view reflected by public opinion polls in relation to defence spending, social programmes and funding priorities. The tendency of women to form their own opinions and programmes on the new world order, legislation and development was noted. The issues on women's agendas included the destruction of nuclear weapons arsenals, reduction in the number other weapons world wide, rat- ification of all treaties related to the elimination of nuclear weapons and renewal of the Non-Proliferation Treaty, conversion of minds and States from military to peaceful pursuits, reallocation of resources from military to peaceful uses, peaceful conflict resolution, education for peace, reduction in violence, and protection of human rights of women.

2. Diplomacy

98.   Six countries reported on women in diplomacy, providing some fig- ures on the participation of women in the diplomatic service. It was empha- sized by a few that women's participation in the foreign service did not match their high contribution to peace at the non-governmental level. One country pointed that there was an increase in the number of women ambas- sadors, but the figures remained very low - three or two. One country point- ed to the significant increase in the number of women diplomats: 6 women out of 150 total in 1980; 23 out of 133 in 1985 and 1990; and 25 out of 106 in 1994. Reference was also made to the participation of women as members of delegations to national and international peace-related meetings, includ- ing United Nations bodies, such as the Security Council and on peace-keep- ing missions. Special reference was made to the three women out of five total, including the woman ambassador to Rwanda, participating in peace negotiations for Rwanda in 1993.

99.   One country stated that its overall goal was that 20 per cent of its exec- utive should be women by 1995, up from 11 per cent in 1994 and 7 per cent in 1985. Among ambassadors 4 per cent were women in 1985, 9 per cent in 1993. The distribution of posts was most equal within the Department for International Developmental Cooperation and the male-dominated political departments. The key missions (Washington, D.C., Tokyo, Moscow, London, Paris) were dominated by men. Women were highly represented as diplomatsin administration (42 per cent, comparing to 28 per cent in 1985).

Another country reported that among top-level executives, 6.7 per cent were women. By the end of 1991, 19.4 per cent of the foreign service employees were women, which was an improvement of 6.5 per cent over the period of a few years. In the field of development cooperation, only 11 per cent of employees in 1992 were women.

100.   Two countries reported on specific measures under consideration to accelerate the promotion of women administrative officers and women candidates for United Nations posts, plans of action to change attitudes and habits, and analyses of equality problems in the ministries of foreign affairs.

3. Women in the military, police forces and peace-keeping
101.   No systematic data exists on women in the military. The largest amount of data is held by the States members of the North Atlantic Treaty Organization (NATO) and the Western European Union. Half of those countries have legislation and policies excluding women from combat, although women's service has been encouraged for the same length of time and the same pay and including the same training and discipline as that of men. Most rules permit pregnant women to remain in the service and provide for parental leave, but limit the rank that women can achieve. Differing rules seem, however, to have limited impact on participation rates. For example, in Canada, which has an egalitarian approach, women constitute only 12 per cent of the military; in the United States which prohibits women's service in combat, the figure is 11 per cent. In 5 of the countries the participation was 2-4 per cent; in 8 of the 15, it was negligible.

4. Women in the military
102.   Research in 45 countries shows that in only 13 countries do women make up more than 10 per cent of the service members. In most countries women perform different functions. Even in countries where women can serve as regular members of a State military, there is usually a restriction on combat. Israel, where service is mandatory for women, is a case in point. In only a few countries is the combat role open - Belgium, Canada, Luxembourg, the Netherlands, Norway, Venezuela and Zambia. A majority of women are not in combat units. In Canada, which recently removed all restrictions based on gender, women constituted 12 per cent of those in active duty and 20 per cent of the reserves, but a few are in combat specialities.

The principal opening for women are in medical professions and clerical and administrative positions.

103.   The accessibility of military service to women has rarely been reported by the States parties to the Convention on the Elimination of All Forms of Discrimination against Women. Some countries - for example, Australia, Austria, Germany, New Zealand, and Thailand - have made reservations to various provisions of the Convention, including its articles 7 and 8 with regard to the participation of women in the military.

104.   The participation of women in the military has been a controversial issue. Many men and women think that it is "men's business". The historical reservation of military roles to men is largely the result of social construction, separation between men's and women's roles, and stereotypes of "the protectors" and "the protected". What is often overlooked is that the military is an integral part of any political system. All Governments have a military, and economic dependence on the military is widespread. Since the military constitutes an important element of State order, decision-making and governance, all citizens should be concerned about the kind of military they have. By being outside the military, women cannot be involved in the decision-making related to the use of military forces or changes in military institutions and overall control over their performance. The military accounts for a large proportion of public expenditure, is an important employer, and provides career opportunities and training that can lead to careers outside the military.

105.   Seventeen countries reported on the participation of women in the military. The data on the proportion of women is fragmented and not comparable. Some developing countries stated that although women were part of the military force, there were no figures available. Generally the participation of women as officers and even at the highest levels is on the increase, reaching in a few countries around 12 per cent. In one country, between September 1987 and June 1993, women's participation increased from 10.2 per cent to 11.6 per cent, despite reductions in the Department's personnel. There were three cases of top-ranking women.

106.   The same tendency was noted with regard to women graduates of military academies. In one country they constituted 9.8 per cent of the total

in June 1993, and it was noted that women were gradually promoted at rates similar to those of men. In one country, the ministry of defence established a network of women officers and cadets. In another country the scope of training for women officers and cadets was modified to suit women's requirements. In another country, the participation of women in military academies was annually determined by a decision of the Minister of National Defence. It was 10 per cent in the year 1993/94, but in reality women in all three academies constituted less than 1 per cent. A number of countries reported lifting completely or partly the restrictions on women's participation in certain units, services (for example, submarines, fighter pilots) or combat activities. In most countries women remain excluded from combat duties or are restricted in them. Women continue to be represented in medical, administrative, legal, telecommunication, logistics, transportation and teaching branches.

107.   In some countries military service is not compulsory, in others, it is compulsory for men. In most countries, the entry requirements, conditions of service and criteria for promotion for women were similar to those for men (except in areas from which women were excluded). One country, however, reported that women can be restricted to day-time duties by the commanding officer. The decision whether or not to deploy women in combat was also left to the discretion of the commander. There was a tendency to discriminate against women officers by offering them fewer educational and promotional opportunities and denying them leadership and decision-making posts because there was a "danger" of maternity and because women were "weaker". Discrimination can be also found in the rules governing marriages of personnel. They are gender neutral but, in practice, disadvantageous to women. For example, if an officer marries a fellow officer, a marriage allowance is paid to the head of the household, depending on who is senior; if a marriage takes place between officers of different ranks, the lower rank should resign; accommodation is offered to a senior spouse; marriages between women corp members and civilians are allowed, but a woman defence personnel who marries a civilian will not be given accommodation since it is expected that a husband will provide housing. Whenever the civilian husband is transferred to a town with no military barracks, the woman has to resign.

108.   A few countries stated that women started to be enlisted and recruited for the first time, as logistic support, during the liberation wars in the region. A few countries referred to the participation of women in war as rebels.

109.   A few countries referred to the participation of women in international military structures (NATO) and operations (Gulf War). One country made reference to Operation Desert Storm in Kuwait, in 1990-1991, where women represented 7 per cent of the force. They worked in all locations, including undeveloped desert areas, as clerks, mechanics, health-care providers, fuel handlers, intelligence analysts, helicopter pilots and military police. They were banned from combat but received all relevant allowances and ribbons. The perception of their performance was very high. They endured the same harsh conditions as the men; physical strength was not an issue; and gender did not determine a unit's cohesion - in fact, mixed-gender units sometimes functioned better.

5. Peace-keeping

110.   Some countries reported on the participation of women in peace-keeping. They noted that it was a positive experience. In most cases women served in support roles. In one case their participation was 32 per cent of the national force. Two Nordic countries pointed that women could sign up for a peace-keeping force after undergoing training, required for men as well. One country specified that women with military background could apply like men and be recruited, whereas women without that type of background could be recruited for administrative, support activities. Reference was made to the difficulties faced by women in the religious States. The awareness of such difficulties should become a part of the training. Although most women had non-military functions, there were three female officers. Another country noted that women performed a variety of functions, as medical and administrative personnel, in supply and logistics, as military police, and in civilian leadership positions with the Defence Department.

6. Civilian leadership positions

111.   A few countries reported on the participation of women in civilian leadership positions in the military/security sector, thus confirming that they continue to be exceptional positions for women. One country referred

to a woman serving as the chairperson of the National Unification Committee, negotiating the peace and reconciliation process in the country. Another country reported that women veterans offered comprehensive assistance to war veterans. It further pointed to the tradition of women occupying a few of the highest positions in the civilian arm of the defence forces. In order to facilitate this type of career, a variety of measures that were particularly helpful to women were taken. They included 317 family centres providing a variety of services; child care in 389 locations around the world; a special programme to address family and spousal abuse. The latter programme seemed to be particularly important since 64 per cent of the uniformed women officers and 30-40 per cent of the civilian military personnel reported being harassed. Unlike civilians, officers could not use the 1964 Civil Rights Act and had to rely on informal, ad hoc procedures. There was a high rate of unreported harassment, since officers feared dismissal or retaliation. The Department of Defence had also undertaken annual policy statements, training programmes, prompt and thorough investigations, accountability procedures for commanders and supervisors, procedures for seeking redress, sexual harassment prevention and education.

7. Police

112.   In most of these countries reporting participation of women in the police force was on the increase. Most of the increase took place in the past five years. The same tendency applied to female cadets and trainees, which in 1993 in one country reached 33 per cent of the total. Only certain countries indicated the percentage of women police officers and high-ranking officials. In one country the percentage of women police chiefs was 13 per cent, the highest of all. Most women in the police force were specifically assigned to address the issue of violence against women, including rape, and take responsibility for female prisons and women prisoners. The special contribution of women in those areas was highly recognized. It, however, limited their possibilities for promotion and career development. Most countries addressed the issue of violence against women through special awareness-raising campaigns and training for the police. One country reported on the specific cultural difficulties which police women faced with male colleagues and offenders, who did not recognize the authority of a woman. Another country reported on the creation in all police stations of special women's desks to handle the acts of violence against women. One

country reported on special equality policies procedures to address sexual harassment within the police force, and attempts to provide part-time work opportunities and re-training which might be of special interest to women. One country stated that it excluded women from the fire brigade police.

8. Obstacles and incentives to women's participation

113.   The two expert group meetings organized by the Division for the Advancement of Women in 1989 and 1991 provided some additional information on the obstacles to the participation of women in decision-making and civil service careers, including those in areas related to peace and security. In general, the obstacles include the unequal division of duties in the household and in the care of children and the elderly; the economic dependency of women; and prevailing inequality in all spheres of life, with violence against women as its extreme form. Other obstacles include women's double burden, negative attitudes to women's political participation or to women in non-traditional careers and media stereotyping.

114.   The specific obstacles to the participation of women in the civil service include lack of adequate recruitment and promotion mechanisms; the prevalence of "closed" recruitment and promotion systems, often based on patronage, without clear requirements for entry or promotion; bias in job evaluation and classification; insufficient appeal mechanisms and a general absence of women from appeal bodies and selection, appointment and promotion panels; unequal opportunities for career and training development; and the marginalization of women in some areas of the civil service traditionally considered as related to women or in positions intended to implement affirmative action policies.

115.   The factors conducive to the participation of women in political life, including participation in peace-related activities are identified in the existing documentation as level and field of education, democratic traditions of the country, public concern for women's legal rights, open attitudes to discussing women's issues, a tradition of respecting women's right to free choice in all spheres of life, a high level of literacy in the country, and knowledge of women's reproductive rights. There is also correlation between the participation of women in decision-making, including participation in peace-related decisions, and adherence to the Convention on the Elimination of All Forms of Discrimination against Women. Countries that

adhere to the Convention without religious or cultural reservations have higher percentages of women in decision-making.

116.   With regard to temporary measures aimed at the increased partici-pation of women in peace-related activities, including decision-making, not much progress can be noted. Although article 4 of the Convention provides for temporary special measures aimed at accelerating de facto equality although its provisions could be used in connection with articles 7 and 8, which state that "all appropriate measures" should be undertaken to elimi-nate discrimination related to the political participation of women at national and international levels, the introduction of quotas and targets is considered a controversial measure. Although some countries have estab-lished special measures and programmes to increase the qualitative and quantitative participation of women in decision-making and managerial posts, others consider such measures non-democratic. The most prominent example of affirmative action is provided by Nordic countries where all boards and public committees have a quota, ensuring participation by both sexes.

9. Effects of armed conflicts on women

117.   Many countries - African ones, in particular - pointed that although women were not decision makers on war and peace, the devastating results of armed conflicts made them victims of displacement, poverty, family dis-integration and loss of home and land. Armed conflicts also uprooted women from their cultural and family environment and made them refugees and single heads of households.

118.   Due to conflicts in some regions, women have suffered from increased criminality, robberies, murders and harassment by soldiers, including rape. Massacres and rapes by security forces to get information on wanted persons are cases in point. In some areas, however, women are the victims of policies of ethnic purging and ethnic cleansing.

119.   Reference was made by many to the invisible participation of women in the democratic process and decision-making. One country pointed that the reduced possibilities of women to influence political decisions on peace were due to psychological and material factors. The warfare in Europe made many to believe that it was necessary to have strong armed forces.

Although women developed a new sense of violence and an understanding of the non-use of force, very little depended on them, and the peace process in the region was thus affected negatively.

10. Women refugees

120.   Many States addressed the situation of refugees. Numerous and often violent ethnic, tribal and civil conflicts in some regions caused flows of refugees to neighbouring countries. In a few cases, also owing to military actions, there were internally displaced persons, including women. Natural disasters, such as famine, flood and drought, constituted a second reason for seeking refuge.

121.   In the majority of cases, most of the refugees were women and children. They were particularly vulnerable to abuse and violence. They had often experienced or witnessed violence in their countries of origin. They were sexually molested by men taking advantage of the chaos and the collapse of structures and by the police and the military as well. They experienced hardship in transit and in refugee camps, where in general they could not decide their own fate since they had no impact on the administration or the decision-making. There were very few cases of women involved in the administration of camps. Despite the efforts of the United Nations High Commissioner for Refugees, women and children refugees suffered disproportionately due to patterns of distribution within the camps and in the family. Refugee women had very limited work opportunities or access to credit. One country, citing the results of a study on women refugees, pointed out that among primary income earners, 35 per cent were women in villages, 32 per cent were in towns and 48 per cent were in refugee camps. Women were unaccustomed to being single heads of households, with men absent from the camps. They suffered from lack of privacy, psychological and mental health problems, broken interpersonal relations. Since men could not provide for their families, women assumed all family duties, which had negative consequences for their relationships. Women began to question the traditional role of men in the family. The study also called attention to the "invisible" displaced persons, often women, residing with relatives and not registered as refugees whose problems could not be addressed. One country reported on a special programme addressed to refugee victims of torture, which focused on women in order to teach them practical skills to service the community.

122.   Many countries pointed that an influx of refugees can interfere with the daily life, culture and economic situation of the receiving country. That may lead to the xenophobia, intolerance and the insecurity of both, the receiving and the refugee population. Receiving countries in regions of armed conflict are cases in point.

123.   Most countries reported on measures undertaken to assist refugee women. They included special educational programmes, including language courses; programmes of integration into the labour market; health care; social assistance, taking into consideration traditional barriers and child-care responsibilities; rental subsidies; education of the public through the mass media to be more tolerant to immigrants; self-help schemes, including training in tailoring and marketing; child care and family planning supported by the Government; and small enterprise programmes. One country reported on the establishment in 1994 of a special committee at the ministerial level on equal rights of men and women refugees, to examine the status of women refugees and to abolish the residence permit regulation when a woman refugee was a victim of violence or if her marriage had been dissolved. Another country referred to its refugee act, stating that women had the same opportunities as men to participate in training and instruction. Special training was provided for women as community workers. In 1989, upon assessment of the needs of refugee women, based on a special survey and contacts with women leaders and service providers, new programmes were set up focusing on special needs of women who were particularly vulnerable. They included the promotion of refugee women's initiatives, including literacy and English for homebound women; skills training; domestic violence counselling; leadership training; and assistance in establishing family business, often home-based.

124.   Many countries supported UNHCR and its programmes and worked closely with international governmental and non-governmental organizations. One country introduced a programme called "Women at Risk" focusing on the special needs of refugee women. Another country reported on special measures to help women victims of armed conflict; to combat, in cooperation with UNRWA, UNHCR and the Red Cross the bias of certain humanitarian organizations against women; to support women victims of sexual abuse in the former Yugoslavia.

125.   In some cases women played important roles in the rehabilitation of refugees and displaced persons at the family level and as community development assistants. Since in some countries, village women constituted most of the female refugees, some projects of assistance and rehabilitation included agricultural projects of non-governmental organizations with the governmental support. Some Governments created for women refugees self-help schemes, training them in tailoring, marketing, child care and family planning.

Notes

1/   Magaret Schuler, ed., Freedom From Violence: Women's Strategies from around the World (New York, UNIFEM, 1992); Violence against Women in the Family, (United Nations publication, Sales No. E.89.IV.5).

2/   Kathleen Barry, Charlotte Bunch and Shirley Castley, eds., International Feminism: Networking Against Female Sexual Slavery (New York, International Women's Tribune Centre, 1984).

3/   Universal Declaration of Human Rights, art. 16 (3); International Covenant on Civil and Political Rights, art. 23 (1); African Charter on Human and People's Rights, art. 18 (1).

4/   D. D'Monte, "Maharashtra clamps down on prenatal sex tests", People, (vol. 15, No. 3 (1998)); "Prenatal attack on women", Christian Science Monitor (10 March 1988), p. 23; V. Patel, "Sex determination and sex preselection tests: abuse of advanced technologies", in Women in Indian Society, Ghadially, ed. (London, Sage, 1988)

5/   S. Narasimhan, Sati: A Study of Widow Burning in India (New Delhi, Viking, 1990).

6/   Middle East Watch/Women's Rights Project, "Punishing the victim: rape and mistreatment of Asian maids in Kuwait", Human Rights Watch, vol. 4, No. 8 (August 1992).

7/   Asia Watch/Women's Rights Project, A Modern Form of Slavery: Trafficking of Burmese Women and Girls into Brothels in Thailand (New York, Human Rights Watch, 1993).

8/   Amnesty International, Rape and Sexual Abuse: Torture and Ill-treatment of Women in Detention. AI Index: ACT 77/11/91 (New York, Amnesty International, 1991); Women in the Front Line. AI Index: ACT 77/01/91 (New York, Amnesty International, 1991).

9/   Although rape, as well as sexual slavery and forced pregnancy, has always been a feature of war, the conflicts in the former Yugoslavia have produced the most recent evidence of women's vulnerability in conflict. See Amnesty International,

Bosnia-Herzegovina: Rape and Sexual Abuse by Armed Forces. AI Index: EUR 63/01/93 (Washington, D.C., International Human Rights Law Group, 1993); No Justice, No Peace: Accountability for Rape and Gender-Based Violence in the Former Yugoslavia (Washington, D.C., Amnesty International, 1994); Bosnia-Herzegovina: "You have no place here": Abuses in Bosnian Serb-controlled Areas. AI Index: EUR 63/11/94 (Washington, D.C., Amnesty International, 1994); "Rape and abuse of women in the territory of former Yugoslavia" (E/CN.4/1994/5). Evidence of the sexual victimization of women in the conflicts in the former Yugoslavia coincided with the revelation of systematic abduction of women, described as "comfort women", who were subsequently forced into prostitution by the Japanese army during World War II. See David E. Sanger, "Japan admits it ran army brothels during war", New York Times (8 July 1992).

10/ America's Watch and Women's Rights Project, Untold Terror: Violence against Women in Peru's Armed Conflict (New York, Human Rights Watch, 1991); Liberia: Women and Children Gravely Mistreated (Boston, Physicians for Human Rights).

11/ S. Wali, Female Victims of Sexual Violence: Rape Trauma and its Impact on Resettlement (Geneva, World Health Organization/United Nations High Commissioner for Refugees, 1990); The State of the World's Refugees: The Challenge of Protection (London: Penguin Books, 1993); "Note on certain aspects of sexual violence against refugee women" (EC/1993/SCP/CRP.2); Africa Watch and Women's Rights Project, Seeking Refuge, Finding Terror: The Widespread Rape of Somali Women Refugees in North Eastern Kenya (New York, Human Rights Watch, 1993).

12/ UNHCR, Guidelines for the Protection of Refugee Women (Geneva, 1991).

13/ "Note on certain aspects of sexual violence against refugee women" (EC/1993/SCP/CRP.2), paras. 9-12.

14/ Resolutions 1986/29 of 23 May 1986 and 1990/5 of 24 May 1990.

15/ See E/CN.6/1986/11, E/CN.6/1988/9 and E/CN.6/1992/5.

16/ Resolutions 47/96 of 16 December 1992 and 48/110 of 20 December 1993.

17/ Report of the Working Group on Slavery on its eighth session (E/CN.4/Sub.2/1982/21), chap. IV, recommendation 9.

18/ Resolution 1982/15 of 7 September 1982. The Subcommission appointed Mrs. Halima Warzazi as Special Rapporteur of the Working Group on Traditional Practices Affecting the Health of Women and Children. Her final report is to be found in document E/CN.4/Sub.2/1991/6 of 5 July 1991.

19/ Resolution 1988/57, on traditional practices affecting the health of women and children.

20/   Report of the Working Group on Traditional Practices Affecting the Health of Women and Children (E/CN.4/1986/42).

21/   Report of the Working Group on Contemporary Forms of Slavery on its sixteenth session (E/CN.4/Sub.2/1991/41). See also resolution 3/2 of the Commission on Crime Prevention and Criminal Justice, concerning international traffic in minors.

22/   Office of the United Nations High Commissioner for Refugees, Executive Committee Conclusion, No. 68 (XLIII), 1992; No. 73 (XLIV), 1993.

23/   Office of the United Nations High Commissioner for Refugees, Guidelines on the Protection of Refugee Women (Geneva, 1991).

24/   Roxanna Carillo, Battered Dreams: Violence Against Women as an Obstacle to Development (New York, UNIFEM, 1992).

25/   See art. 17 of the Convention on the Elimination of All Forms of Discrimination against Women (General Assembly resolution 34/180).

26/   Economic and Social Council resolution 1991/18. See also the report of the Expert Group Meeting on Violence against Women, Vienna, 11-15 November 1991 (EGM/VAW/1991/1).

27/   Vienna Declaration and Programme of Action of the World Conference on Human Rights, paras. 18 and 38. See also specific reference to violence against girl-children in para. 21 of the Declaration and paras. 48 and 49 of the Programme of Action.

28/   "Report of the Expert Group Meeting on Measures to Eradicate Violence against Women", 4-8 October 1993 (MAV/1993/1).

29/   Resolution 1994/45, 4 March 1994.

30/   The National Strategy on Violence Against Women (Canberra, 1992).

31/   Changing the Landscape: Ending Violence - Achieving Equality (Ottawa, Ministry of Supply and Services, 1993).

F. Inequality in women's access to and participation in the definition of economic structures and policies and the productive process itself

1.   The Nairobi Forward-looking Strategies for the Advancement of Women envisage a wide range of measures to increase women's access to and participation in the economy. They stress women's equal right to work and to receive benefits, including maternity benefits and the right to return to work. Employment was one of the three sub-themes of the United Nations Decade for Women and the Forward-looking Strategies set out a series of measures to ensure equal employment opportunities (paras. 132-147). They include the importance of enabling women to obtain "jobs involving more skills and responsibility, including those at the managerial level". They recommend changes in the structure of work that would allow women and men to reconcile productive and reproductive responsibilities. They call for the elimination of all forms of discrimination in employment, including in wages, and for breaking down gender-based occupational segregation. They call for the recognition of the contribution of older women.

2.   The Forward-looking Strategies emphasize that women's economic independence is a necessary condition for their advancement. They assert that "economic independence is a necessary precondition for self-reliance" (para. 113) and that it is necessary to seek the participation of women as equal partners with men in all fields of work, equal access to all positions of employment, equal opportunities for education and training, and the protection of women at work and to recognize the need for women to be highly productive producers and managers of political, economic and social

affairs. However, the Strategies make no direct reference to the importance of women's participation in economic decision-making. In some chapters, passing references are made to women managers and women entrepreneurs under the objectives of equality and development.

3.   Discrimination promotes an uneconomic use of women's talents and therefore wastes the valuable human resources necessary for development. Ultimately, it is recognized that society is the loser if the talents of women are underutilized as a result of discrimination. Exclusion of women from policy-making and decision-making also makes it difficult for women and women's organizations to include their preferences and interests in the largely male-dominated decisions on economic policies.

4.   In examining the progress made, the first review and appraisal concluded and recommended: 1/

> "5.   Women have always been an important part of the workforce and their role will continue to grow with development, industrialization, economic necessity and the expansion of women's access to the economy. In most countries, however, the participation of women and men in the economy continues to be unequal, characterized by job segregation, insufficient training opportunities, unequal pay for work of equal value, inadequate career prospects and lack of full participation in economic decision-making.
>
> "**Recommendation IV.** Governments, non-governmental organizations and private-sector enterprises should take special measures to increase the proportion of women involved in economic decision-making, including studies on the incidence of women in such positions in the public and private sectors, the promotion of training programmes, analysis of alternative policies to provide women with careers leading to economic decision-making, and the adjustment of national legislation.
>
> "The United Nations should study the incidence of women in economic decision-making world wide, analyse innovative national programmes to increase the proportion of women in economic decision-making positions and publicize the results, within existing resources.
>
> "**Recommendation V.** Governments and other appropriate parties should make efforts to increase the number of women in paid employment, including the adoption of measures to eliminate sex segregation in the labour market and to improve women's working conditions. Governments and other appropriate parties should collect, maintain and improve statistics showing the relative remuneration of women and men. They should renew their efforts to close the gap between women's and men's pay, possibly by 1995, and take special measures to address the principle of equal pay for work of equal value. They should also take concrete steps to mea-

sure the economic value of women's unpaid work with a view to taking it into account in national policies by 1995.

"The United Nations system should complete work on methodological aspects of measuring pay inequities between women and men, unpaid work and work in the informal sector and should publish studies of countries where such measurements have been made.

"...

"10. An economic environment of growth with equitable distribution, both at the national level and in the international economic system, is essential, as is the recognition of women's full participation. The feminization of poverty reflects the underlying structural problems faced by women in the midst of economic change. Prevailing economic policies at the national and international levels have frequently failed to take into account potential negative effects on women or women's potential contribution and have accordingly not succeeded.

"**Recommendation VII.** In order to help revitalize economic growth, international economic and social cooperation, together with sound economic policies, should be pursued. Structural adjustment and other economic reform measures should be designed and implemented so as to promote the full participation of women in the development process, while avoiding the negative economic and social effects. They should be accompanied by policies giving women equal access to credit, productive inputs, markets and decision-making and this should be incorporated fully into national economic policy and planning.

"The international development strategy for the fourth United Nations development decade should take full account of women's contribution and potential and this should be an important part of monitoring its implementation. Relevant organizations of the United Nations system should continue to examine the effects of national and international economic policies on social progress, in particular the condition of women in developing countries.

"11. The incorporation of women into the labour force has occurred on a scale unimaginable 30 years ago. Nevertheless, given unfavourable economic conditions in developing countries, the majority of women remain or are increasing in number in the informal sector of the economy.

"**Recommendation VIII.** Governmental policies, non-governmental action and international cooperation should be directed towards supporting programmes to improve the living conditions of women in the informal sector.

"These programmes should contribute, among other things, to the incorporation into the informal sector of appropriate technologies which could increase production in that sector and make domestic and international markets more accessible. Women in the informal sector should be encouraged to organize themselves so that they know their rights and are able to obtain the necessary support to exercise them.

"Appropriate organizations at the international level should gather more detailed and accurate information related to women in the informal sector in order to identify the most efficient measures to ameliorate their condition.

"...

"19. Urbanization, migration and economic changes have increased the proportion of families headed by women and the number of women entering the labour force. These women have experienced increasing difficulties in harmonizing their economic role with the demands on them to provide care for children and dependants. The double burden, rather than being reduced by greater sharing between spouses, has increased. Unless it is reduced, women will not be able to play their full and fair role in development.

"**Recommendation XVII.** Governments and other appropriate bodies should, by 1995, establish social support measures with the aim of facilitating the combination of parental and other caring responsibilities and paid employment, including policies for the provision of services and measures to increase the sharing of such responsibilities by men and women and to deal with specific problems of female-headed households that include dependants."

1. Growth in female employment

5.   During the past decade, female participation in the labour market has grown at an average of 10 per cent in all the regions of the world, twice the rate of their male counterparts. Women's representation in the economically active population increased considerably from 1970 to 1990 (see table II.F.1).

6.   In most parts of the world, women are no longer a "reserve" labour force; women are increasingly becoming the workers who remain economically active throughout their working lives. The trend towards increased female participation in the labour force is a stable one, occurring at the same time as the economic activity rates for men have been falling.

7.   In the countries belonging to the Organisation for Economic Cooperation and Development (OECD), there were 169.4 million women in the labour force in 1992, some 33 million more than in 1980. The economic participation of women grew by 2 per cent per annum, twice the rate of that of men, whose participation rate has been falling. In the United States of America, Canada, Denmark, Finland, Norway and Sweden, women make up almost half of the labour force. Female employment has grown faster than the growth of the female labour force.

Table II.F.1. Average ratio of women to men in the economically active population, 1970-1990, by region

(Number of women for each 100 men)

Region	1970	1980	1990
Africa	39	58	71
Latin America and the Caribbean	35	48	62
Western Europe and others	45	60	72
Asia and the Pacific	28	42	48
Eastern Europe	79	81	85
World	37	52	62

8.   In Central and Eastern Europe, during the process of transition, female labour force participation has remained high. In spite of the economic decline, the participation of women in the labour force, especially women between the ages of 20 and 49, has not declined more than that of men. The labour force surveys conducted by the International Labour Organization (ILO) in the Russian Federation have found that, in the first phase of employment restructuring, women's share of employment in industry actually increased because they were inclined to keep their state sector jobs longer than men. In the transition economies in Asia, the proportion of the female population that is economically active has increased. In China, for example, the increase was from 49 per cent in 1980 to 54 per cent in 1990.

9.   In the developing countries, conceptual and methodological constraints and conventional labour force definitions and statistical systems still do not adequately reflect women's productive work in the non-market economy, as producers in subsistence agriculture and in the urban and rural informal sector. However, in spite of the fact that much of the work done by women continues to be invisible, official statistics also confirm the increase in the female share of the labour force. For example, in Latin America and the Caribbean, the proportion of women in the labour force rose from 24 to 29 per cent between 1970 and 1990. In East and South-East Asia, women constitute 80 per cent of the workforce in the export-processing zones.

In Africa, unofficial research data indicate high participation rates for women, who account for most of the food producers and those engaged in small-scale trading.

10.   Gender differentials diminished between 1980 and 1990, with patterns varying between regions and countries. In spite of these differences, the number of women in the workforce increased almost continuously between 1970 and 1990. Countries that initially had the lowest rates of participation tended to experience the highest rates of increase. Women aged 15and over currently make up about 41 per cent of the world's labour force. 2/

(a)   Demographic factors
11.   Demographic factors must be taken into consideration when examining trends in productive employment. ILO predicts that the workforce will grow from 2.4 billion persons in 1990 to 3.2 billion in 2010, a 35 per cent increase. The growth will take place disproportionately in most developing regions, with very little growth in the developed countries. It is estimated that the workforce in countries like Pakistan and Mexico will grow at about 3 per cent a year in the coming years. In contrast, growth rates in the United States of America, Canada and Japan will be lower, and in most of the European countries they will perhaps decline.

12.   Predictions also indicate that women will enter the workforce in greater numbers, especially in most of the developing countries, where relatively few women have been absorbed to date. An increase is not expected in Europe, with the exception of the Mediterranean countries. Women will be responsible for maintaining rates of labour force participation in both developed and developing countries. These patterns are not only related to higher fertility rates in the developing countries but also reflect a growing trend of women leaving home for paid employment.

(b)   Changes in attitudes towards paid work
13.   The increased activity of women of reproductive age - 25 to 49 years - is another contributing factor to the higher rate of participation of women. Experience during the period 1980-1990 shows that women in this age group, as had been the case in 1970, were primarily responsible for the growth in the workforce in the European Union countries. This demonstrates a major change in social attitudes about the participation in the labour market of women of reproductive age.

14.   Between 1984 and 1991, the average rate of participation of women with children increased from 50 per cent to more than 60 per cent in the European Union countries. The rate also increased for childless women, from 71 to 75 per cent over the same period. In Spain and Portugal, activity rates for women with and without children doubled between 1987 and 1991. The same phenomenon was noted in Latin America.

15.   In the developing countries, the effect of women's changing attitudes towards work has received relatively little attention from researchers, although women are increasingly involved in economically produc-tiveactivities. Increased communication systems reaching into remote, iso-lated areas, expanded education opportunities, changing family patterns, extensive migration and explosion of urban environments have affected the labour markets. Urbanization, industrialization and migration contributed to increased numbers of women working outside the home. In these coun-tries, the percentage of women in the paid labour force increased from 28 per cent in 1950 to 41 per cent in 1993.

16.   The Human Development Report, 1993 provides indicators of females as a percentage of males in the labour force in some countries of Asia. There are high rates of participation in many countries, for example, Singapore (64 per cent), Thailand (88 per cent) and Mongolia (83 per cent).

17.   Declines in female rates of participation are anticipated in sub-Saharan Africa, while increases are expected in North Africa and in Latin America and the Caribbean. This may be related to patterns of emi-gration of the female labour force to other regions.

18.   Obstacles to increased rates of participation by women remain. Non-sharing of responsibilities in the family and the lack of social services in both developed and developing countries pose serious problems. The majority of women must combine economically productive work with the care of their children, or of disabled or elderly people. The burden of this responsibility restricts the options for women.

2. Employment structure and women

19.   There are gender differentials in rates of participation in sectors and occupations, although women's participation is increasing in those sectors that have the highest rates of growth. For the period 1970 to 1990, the rate of

participation of women approached that of men in professional and technical and administrative and management occupations. The ratio of women
to men in those occupations increased considerably in all regions, except in
Eastern Europe where, in 1970, the ratio of women to men was already high
(see table II.F.2).

*Table II.F.2. Average ratio of women to men in professional and technical and
administrative and management occupations, 1970-1990, by region*

(Number of women for each 100 men)

Region	1970	1980	1990
Africa	19	40	56
Latin America and the Caribbean	50	82	85
Western Europe and others	45	60	72
Asia and the Pacific	28	42	48
Eastern Europe	79	81	85
World	37	52	62

*Table II.F.3. Occupational category by sex, 1970, 1980, 1990,
global perspective*

(Percentage)

Occupational group	1970 F	M	1980 F	M	1990 F	M
Professional and technical	11.9	5.6	11.8	6.6	13.2	8.2
Administrative and management	0.8	2.1	0.3	2.5	1.8	3.2
Clerical	10.8	5.9	11.8	5.7	13.3	6.5
Sales	7.8	6.0	0.9	5.3	9.9	7.2
Service	18.3	5.9	13.6	6.2	14.6	6.8
Agriculture	27.0	33.5	29.1	32.7	24.7	28.0
Production	14.5	32.1	29.7	29.7	12.6	31.7
Not classified, unemployed	6.1	6.3	9.5	7.5	9.0	7.5

20.   Global trends confirm that women are entering professional and technical occupations in large numbers (see table II.F.3). Rates increased from 11.94 per cent of working women in 1970 to 13.17 per cent in 1990. The proportion of women professionals is particularly high in Latin America and Eastern and Western Europe, closing the gap between men and women.

21.   Shifts in female participation in the labour force between 1970 and 1990 should be noted. Women's employment in the traditional service sector declined during the period, corresponding to the increase in the clerical, professional and technical sectors. There was an increase in women's employment in the production sector between 1970 and 1980 and a decrease from 1980 to 1990. The decline in women's and men's participation in agriculture is also evident.

22.   In Africa, the ratio of women to men in agriculture grew from 68 to 71 per cent. In Latin America and the Caribbean, the ratio increased from 16 to 19 per cent, in Western Europe from 42 to 54 per cent and in Asia from 45 to 47 per cent. There was a decline in the ratio of women's to men's participation in agricultural employment in Eastern Europe, from 105 to 84 per cent. Eastern Europe has by far, the most equal rates of participation for women and men in agriculture (see table II.F.4).

Table II.F.4. Average ratio of women to men in agriculture, 1980-1990, by region

(Number of women for each 100 men)

Region	1980	1990
Africa	68	71
Latin America and the Caribbean	16	19
Western Europe and others	42	54
Asia and the Pacific	45	47
Eastern Europe	105	84

23.   When comparing the distribution of occupations between the female and male economically active population, a different picture arises. According to table II.F.3, the world-wide trend between 1980 and 1990 was towards a decrease in agricultural employment. Globally, 32.7 per cent of the male labour force was employed in agriculture in 1980 and 28.0 per cent

in 1990. For women, the rates were 29.1 per cent in 1980 and 24.7 per cent in 1990. Asia and Africa still have the greatest number of people employed in this sector.

24.   There were more men than women employed in the production sector in 1990, with 31.7 per cent of men against 12.6 per cent of women. A large decline in the proportion of women working in this sector occurred between 1980 and 1990, from 29.7 to 12.6 per cent (see table II.F.3). Economies in Asia and Africa tended to employ an increasing number of women in the production sector between 1970 and 1980. In Latin America, female employment in production declined between 1970 and 1990. Despite improvements, the ratio of women to men working in this sector is low in all regions (see table II.F.5).

25.   Other conclusions can be drawn from the available data. The effects of the increase in the level of education in the previous decades were reflected in the growing number of women employed in professional and technical occupations, primarily in services. Younger women and those with skills have been better received in the service sector. The increase in professional and technical positions in certain regions demonstrates this trend. Less educated women are likely to be in a disadvantageous position.

26.   In the report of Indonesia it is noted that there has been a marked increase in women's employment in the non-agricultural sectors during the 1980s. However, the increase in female non-agricultural employment has been largely confined to trade and, to a smaller extent, to manufacturing and services. In manufacturing, the number of women per 100 men actually fell slightly, from 78 to 77.

Table II.F.5. Average ratio of women to men in production,
1980-1990, by region

(Number of women for each 100 men)

Region	1980	1990
Africa	16	27
Latin America and the Caribbean	19	24
Western Europe and others	17	20
Asia and the Pacific	25	21
Eastern Europe	34	45

27.   Employment in manufacturing grew by 73 per cent between 1980 and 1990, but most of the new job opportunities were filled by younger women in urban areas. However, the growth in factory employment was even more rapid for males. This may be due to the fact that export-oriented industrialization policies have tended to favour larger-scale enterprises. By contrast, many traditional manufacturing industries, particularly those located in rural areas which are more numerous, more labour intensive and employ a larger proportion of women, especially during slack periods in the agricultural cycle, have stagnated under the pressure of increased competition. 3/ The pattern may change in the future. The establishment of the South and North Growth Triangles in the region covered by the Association of South-East Asian Nations (ASEAN), together with new export zones in other areas of Indonesia, can be expected to favour female employment. Policies to support the manufacture of handicrafts may also increase the employment of women in small-scale industries.

(a)   Segregation in employment
28.   In both developed and developing countries, gender-based segregation by occupation remains very high. Growth in the female share of the labour market has not had a significant impact on the mechanism of segregation.

29.   The 1993 Employment Report of the Commission of the European Union states that the results of the past decade are a kind of paradox. In all 12 countries, at a time when the extent of men and women's involvement in the labour market has become more similar, inequalities in employment still exist. Market segregation has persisted in the type of work done as well as in the sectors in which expansion of work undertaken predominantly by women has occurred.

30.   In Asia, where the feminization of employment is a fact and where employment has grown faster for women than for men, gender-based differentials also exist in most countries. Women's employment grew in manufacturing, services and trade, but the majority of women in the region are absorbed in subsistence agriculture as unpaid family labour and unskilled agriculture labour.

31.   The 1993 report of the Economic Commission for Europe (ECE)

network on the situation of women in the labour market demonstrates that rising female participation throughout the European Community has not reduced and is not likely to reduce occupational segregation and labour market inequality by gender. No evidence was found to suggest that higher female participation in the labour force or higher levels of economic development would reduce segregation. Over-representation of women in service and clerical work was not evident in some other countries, and the number of women in professional occupations was as high, if not higher, in some developing countries.

32.   Even the very high participation rates of women in the Eastern European countries has not led to an integrated labour market. Women in Eastern European countries were concentrated in female occupations and underrepresented in science, technology and leadership positions.

33.   Occupational segregation is likely to remain a persistent characteristic of all labour markets, and a characteristic that needs to be taken into account in all types of employment analyses. Despite the broadly similar patterns of occupational segregation, there were sufficient differences between countries to suggest that social, cultural and labour market forces within each country play an important role in shaping the form and degree of segregation.

34.   If the distribution of women's employment is considered by seven major occupation groups - professional and technical, administrative and managerial, clerical, sales, services, agriculture, and production - it can be noted that women are concentrated in clerical, services and professional and technical occupations. In Chile, where women made up 30.5 per cent of the labour force in 1991, they represented 51.3 per cent of service workers; in Canada, where women made up 45.3 per cent of the labour force, they represented 55.7 per cent of professional and technical workers, 80.7 per cent of clerical workers and 56.6 per cent of those in services.

35.   Country differences persist in the extent of feminization of many clerical and service jobs, differences associated with social and cultural organization, industrial structure, union organization, the prevalence of part-time work and labour market organization, among other factors. Women are particularly likely to remain excluded from certain service occu-

pations, where the job has retained its craft and skilled status or where men are still interested in maintaining access to service or clerical careers.

36.   The prospects for the future, without major new policy initiatives, are a continuation of the dual trend towards the greater integration of women into higher-level jobs and the increasing concentration of the remaining female labour force in lower-grade and highly feminized sectors. These trends will not remove the problem of inequalities between the sexes in the upper echelons of the labour market; they will, however, add the problem of increasing inequalities within the female workforce itself.

(b)   Service sector

37.   In the 1980s, the service sector began to attract women in many regions and countries. In the OECD countries, for example, most of the new jobs created during that period were in services and benefited women. Women's employment in the service sector world wide grew more rapidly over time than that for men. This accounts in large part for the overall increase in the growth of female employment in the past decade. Studies show that countries with the fastest growth in female employment have combined public sector activities with business and financial services.

Table II.F.6. Average ratio of women to men in services,
1980-1990, by region

(Number of women for each 100 men)

Region	1980	1990
Africa	55	75
Latin America and the Caribbean	156	184
Western Europe and others	206	200
Asia and the Pacific	49	68
Eastern Europe	32	31

(c)   Atypical and/or precarious employment

38.   Over the past decade, in both developed and developing countries, economic processes caused a situation that resulted in the limited creation of stable, full-time jobs. The majority of newly created jobs have tended to be atypical. As it turned out, these atypical employment patterns correlate with the feminization of the labour force. According to ILO studies, an increasing number of women are entering small and medium-sized enterprises in the informal sector, are taking part-time or temporary jobs or are engaged in teleworking, subcontracting or self-employment. Some women are taking such jobs because of flexible hours, which make it convenient for them to reconcile work and family responsibilities. However, for growing numbers of women, part-time or temporary work is not voluntary.

39.   Although there has been some progress in the industrialized countries, especially in the public sector, in extending social protection to part-time workers, on the whole, part-time and other non-standard forms of employment are accompanied by low pay, lack of rights, no opportunities for training and no promotion prospects. Part-time employment is concentrated in the service sector, where the majority of workers are women. Therefore, it is not surprising that the majority of part-time workers are women. In the OECD countries, women constitute between 65 and 90 per cent of part-time workers. In 1991-1992, 62 per cent of all women workers were employed on a part-time basis in the Netherlands and more than 40 per cent in Australia, Norway, Sweden and the United Kingdom. In Spain, some 38 per cent of all female workers are temporary, as compared to 29 per cent of employed men. The proportion of women among home workers range from 90-95 per cent in Germany, Greece, Ireland, Italy and the Netherlands, to 84 per cent in France, 75 per cent in Spain and 70 per cent in the United Kingdom. 4/

40.   In Africa, women tend to be concentrated in small-scale, under-capitalized, low-productivity market trade and personal service activities. In West Africa, women make up between 60 and 80 per cent of the urban labour force in trading and dominate in small-scale trading.

41.   In Latin America, there is a growing incidence of part-time employment among women. In Asia, women commonly dominate in hawking and trading activities. According to ILO studies, there has recently been an increase

in women's involvement in micro or small-scale production activities and home-based activities, as self-employed or piece-rate workers. In Indonesia, for example, more than one fifth of all women in the workforce are in trading, although this is the least lucrative of the self-employment activities.

(d)   Unemployment

42.   The growth in female employment that occurred during the past decade did not generate a corresponding drop in unemployment. The creation of jobs and steady unemployment coexisted. Though more men than women are openly unemployed because of their larger numbers in the labour force, women's unemployment rates tend to be higher than those of men. In the majority of the OECD countries, women's unemployment rates exceed those of men. In 1992, the recorded unemployment rate for women in Europe was 11.5 per cent as compared to the overall rate of 9.9 per cent. 5/ Such conclusions are based on the definition of "unemployed", which includes the following criteria: being without work, having looked actively for work in a recent period, and being available for work almost at once. This definition is restrictive, as it excludes part-time workers who want to work full-time, discouraged workers who say that job-search is fruitless, and those who need more than one or two weeks before they can start working. If all those factors were taken into account, the overall gap between female and male unemployment rates would only widen.

43.   The transition in the Central and Eastern European countries increased unemployment among women. Loss of employment by women in those countries often means more than loss of income. Women in that region have achieved a high educational level and have been in the paid labour force for a long period of time. Only Hungary reported a higher unemployment rate for men than for women. In the Russian Federation, the share of women among the unemployed has reached a particularly high level, estimated at 70-80 per cent.

44.   In Africa, the rates of open unemployment for women are often double those for men and have been rising, according to ILO observations. In Egypt, for example, the female rate of unemployment in 1991 was 27.8 per cent as compared to only 6.3 per cent for males.

45.   The same situation exists in the Asian and Pacific region. In Sri Lanka, for instance, the 1992 unemployment rate was 21.0 per cent for women as compared to 10.6 per cent for men. In Pakistan, the 1990-1991 unemployment rate was 13.8 per cent for women and 3.9 per cent for men in rural areas and 27.8 per cent for women and 5.9 per cent for men in urban areas.

46.   If absolute levels of unemployment are considered, the gender gap is rather large in some Latin American and Caribbean countries. In addition, the mean period of unemployment is longer for women than for men - 11.2 months as compared to 8 months.

47.   In most countries, the rate of unemployment has risen more for women than for men and the unemployment gender gap exists in every region. The largest increase was in Latin America. According to studies from Eastern Europe, female unemployment also rose in that region, with the exception of Hungary, where the position of women is strong in the service sector and women were not replaced by men in service activities. A lower rate of female unemployment appears in Africa and Asia. Although the ratio of unemployed women to men decreased in Asia, indicators show an increase of women listed as unclassified. 6/

(e)   Wage differentials

48.   The principle of equal remuneration is included in the Convention on the Elimination of All Forms of Discrimination against Women, as well as in various ILO conventions and recommendations. Moreover, the ILO Convention concerning Equal Remuneration for Men and Women Workers for Work of Equal Value, 1951 (No. 100) has one of the highest ratification rates of all ILO standards. However, the gap between female and male earnings represents one of the most persistent forms of discrimination against women. The pattern of unequal remuneration is universal, although the level of inequality varies from place to place.

49.   In industrialized countries, women receive 70-80 per cent of the hourly pay rates of men. In India, Japan and the Republic of Korea, women receive about half the pay of men. According to ILO data for the manufacturing sector, contained in the 1990 Yearbook of Labour Statistics, the ratio world wide ranged from 50 to 90 per cent in 1990.

50.   In Asia, the male-female gap is wider in manufacturing (64.8 per cent) and non-agricultural jobs (68.2 per cent), in Latin America and the Caribbean in non-agricultural jobs (68.7 per cent) and in Africa, in agriculture (69.2 per cent), with a large decrease in women's wages in some cases. In Asia, the ratio of women's to men's wages in the non-agricultural and manufacturing sectors decreased from 91.5 to 68.2 per cent and from 72 to 64.8 per cent, respectively, between 1970 and 1990. In Latin America and the Caribbean, the income of women declined compared to that of men between 1970 and 1990, with the largest decline in production.

51.   There were decreases in women's wages in the agricultural sector in some countries in Africa and in the manufacturing sector in Latin America and the Caribbean. These were related to the trend towards informalization in many developing economies experiencing recession and adjustment. Wages and salaries from the formal sector are no longer sufficient to cover the basic needs of households in many countries. This has implications for women in terms of the additional pressure for them to work outside the home.

52.   Increases in women's wages were noted in the non-agricultural sector in Africa, Western Europe and Eastern Europe, which demonstrate the advancement of women in the service sector. In Africa, the increase in the ratio of women's to men's wages was from 61.5 per cent in 1970 to 89.4 per cent in 1990, in Western Europe, the ratio increased from 68.8 per cent in 1970 to 78.3 per cent in 1990 and in Eastern Europe, from 69.2 per cent in 1970 to 75.4 per cent in 1990.

53.   In the manufacturing sector, over the same period of time, women's wages increased in Africa from 63.50 per cent in 1970 to 73.3 per cent in 1990, in Western Europe, from 66.0 per cent in 1970 to 74.6 per cent in 1990, and in Eastern Europe from 68.8 per cent in 1970 to 72.8 per cent in 1990.

54.   The gap between wages paid to men and wages paid to women also exists in the 12 member States of the European Community. Between 1980 and 1988, it remained constant in several countries, whereas in others, some progress has been recorded. In the industrialized world, women earn from 50 to 80 per cent the amount that men earn. Several factors contribute to this phenomenon: women work more often in sectors where salaries are lower

and where they have less access to senior positions. There are several theories to explain these factors; these theories are not mutually exclusive, but rather complement each other. Studies show that some of the discrepancies in wages between men and women can be explained by differences in training, professional experience and age. Other differences can be attributed to an unequal breakdown in sectors of activities, professions and training levels. Other differences are not explained and are the result of various forms of discrimination, direct or indirect.

3. Rural women

55.   Women play important roles in agricultural production, comprising 67 per cent of the agricultural labour force in the developing countries. In sub-Saharan Africa, almost 80 per cent of all economically active women are in the agricultural sector. In Asia, in such countries as Indonesia, Malaysia, Nepal and Pakistan, women constitute about 40 per cent of the agricultural labour force, and in Sri Lanka, Thailand and Turkey, up to 50 per cent.

56.   The most important change in the agricultural sector occurred with the introduction of cash crops, which took place in Africa and Latin America. These paid jobs were offered primarily to men, while women were left to cultivate food crops on increasingly marginal land. In addition, women are often not trained for such new activities and lack the basic resources that men have when they start to work in new areas.

57.   Women produce 50 per cent of the food grown worldwide; in Africa, they produce an estimated 70 per cent of the continent's food. In addition to crop production, rural women obtain food from many other sources. In many parts of the world, women have the primary responsibility for food gathering from communal lands and forests in order to supplement family diets and income.

58.   In most countries, livestock husbandry is also the responsibility of women. Although men often remain the owners and sellers of large livestock, the bulk of domestic labour related to animals is the responsibility of women. In Pakistan, for example, women are responsible for 60 to 80 per cent of the cleaning, feeding and milking of livestock.

59.   Rural women tend to be consistently underserved and difficult to reach with development resources. Owing to the traditional division of

labour and the persistent discrimination against women, even available scarce resources favour more men than women.

60.   Rural women constitute the group that has benefited least from industrialization and urbanization and often tend to be the worst hit by the effects of rural-urban migration. While men are leaving for the cities to seek employment, women are left on their own in rural areas, assuming increased responsibilities in subsistence food production and for their families' well-being. Rural-urban migration in Africa, Asia and the Pacific and the Middle East is dominated by men. Only in Latin America and the Caribbean do women, especially those young and single, represent the overwhelming majority in migration flows to the cities. The main reason for rural women in Latin America to migrate to the cities is the lack of access to land and the mechanization of agriculture, as well as the presence of job opportunities in the cities, especially in textiles and food-processing, and in the informal sector, in domestic services and street vending.

61.   In several countries of Asia, teenage and young women are increasingly joining the rural-urban migration. In the Philippines, for example, 7 out of 10 females employed in the service sector in urban areas are migrants.

62.   In many parts of the world, agricultural policies have been translated into increased poverty in rural areas, with farming families needing to supplement their income through diversified income-generating activities, through migration to urban areas and through attempts to expand production by cultivating marginal land, and converting food crop land into cash-crop production. The impact on women varies from the need to fit additional work into an already full and tiring day, to taking on the agricultural work of an absent husband, to additional responsibilities on a husband's enlarged plot or new production scheme, to the loss of an independent income from her personal plot which has been taken over for family production.

63.   The lack of adequate data on women's roles, both productive and reproductive, has contributed to the continuing under-estimation and undervaluing of rural women's contribution to economic production and growth. In addition, concepts and classifications commonly used for data collection do not reflect small-scale or subsistence agriculture, ignoring important parts of women's work and of overall economic production.

(a)   Access to and control of land

64.   Gender asymmetries in access to land remain one of the main obstacles to the full participation of women in rural development. Inheritance practices, whereby land traditionally passes from father to son, reinforce male control of land. Although many developing countries have passed statutes legally affirming a woman's fundamental right to own land, in practice female control of land is rare. Indeed, reform measures have not been gender neutral and women have been excluded in varying degrees either legally or by de facto measures. Bestowing rights on heads of household, as for example, on land that was formerly held communally, has overridden a variety of former land inheritance patterns in some countries and reinforced discriminatory practices against women. Moreover, in many countries, there is no legislative provision for widowed, separated or divorced women.

65.   Women typically farm small, dispersed or remote plots of fragmented land in which they have little incentive to invest or adopt new technologies. In most countries, land titles are registered in the name of the male heads of household and women do not have secure land tenure. The fact that women do not own land may mean that they cannot get access to agricultural support services, particularly credit and extension services where land ownership is a requirement or extension workers are reluctant to work with small, isolated plots.

66.   The difficulties experienced by rural women in securing access to land are even greater for women heads of household. Review of land reform programmes in various countries indicates that, regardless of whether the sex of the beneficiary is specified by law, women heads of household seldom have access to land even when their productive activities call for it. Without title to land, those women lack the collateral necessary to obtain credit and may face difficulties in obtaining extensions.

67.   The findings of the World Conference on Agrarian Reform and Rural Development (WCARRD) include the following points as issues critical to women's access to land:

(a)   High population pressure and increased commercialization of agriculture result in less equitable distribution of land rights under communal tenure; women's land rights are often eroded;

(b)   Growing population pressure has, for example, neutralized efforts to improve women's land rights in sub-Saharan Africa; women are managing smaller plots as the land quality deteriorates;

(c)   Land redistribution programmes usually target the household unit, with little attention to the distribution of land within the household and to women's special needs;

(d)   Land titling adversely affects poor rural women. Titles, usually registered in the names of male heads of household, diminish women's customary rights of land use and transfer. Consequences for women's traditional independent farming practices vary; they are often undermined, while intra-household gender disparities in income and decision-making increase. In some cases in Africa, men take advantage of their greater control over land to redesignate land formerly cultivated by women as household land. This provides the opportunity to increase male demands for female household labour on male-controlled household plots. In other cases, women receive smaller and less fertile household plots as their personal plots;

(e)   The privatization of common property resources can have a disproportionately negative impact on poor rural women since fuel and fodder gathering are primarily female tasks. The same applies to materials for handicrafts, which are an important income-generating activity for rural women.

68.   In spite of the negative prospects for rural women, national machineries have been successful in promoting innovative initiatives in some countries in the Indian subcontinent, Central and South America and West Africa. There has been a major policy change on agrarian reform in recent years, whereby women have often been defined as the beneficiaries, and granted the right to own land either jointly or with men. Legal changes are allowing a small number of women in various developing countries to take steps towards gaining access to and control over the land they farm.

69.   The improvement of women's legal access to land is a basic prerequisite for the success of rural development policies. Activities that could be considered for the improvement of women's access to and control over land include legal literacy training for both women and men on women's rights,

research on legislative reforms for rural areas, removing barriers to the effective implementation of existing laws, focusing on ways to improve women's participation in self-help and cooperative groups, enhancing productivity to create incentives for women to invest in the land they cultivate, and encouraging Governments to invest in women's labour and in meeting their needs.

(b)   Access to labour

70.   Command over labour resources is a factor that critically impacts on the real and potential productivity of women in agriculture. The amount of land they can cultivate is directly related to labour availability - their own, that of other family members and hired labour. The considerably longer labour hours of women and limited access to paid labour because of the lack of financial resources complicates the potential expansion of agricultural production even where women have traditional, and often seasonal, rights to husband's labour for such tasks as helping to clear their individual plots. Moreover, increasing rates of male out-migration imply that the availability of men, even for limited labour inputs, is reduced. The labour availability of young women is also declining as they migrate to urban areas in search of employment and improved lifestyles.

71.   Women's access to land is dependent on their willingness to provide domestic labour and to help in agricultural and off-farm activities controlled by their husbands and senior family members. Men can mobilize the labour of wives and children in male-controlled productive activities, whereas women may only have access to daughters and younger sons. The need to draw on the labour of offspring may influence children's, especially girls', rates of school attendance, and, in the longer term, impact on the perpetuation of poverty cycles.

(c)   Incorporation of sustainable development techniques into
*   productive activities*

72.   The interrelationship between women, environment and development has been increasingly recognized. In most developing countries, food production is undertaken mainly by women, and therefore, issues related to food security, land rights and environmentally sustainable land-use practices are central to their lives. Gender imbalances in access to resources impact negatively on their ability to play vital custodial roles in sustainable environment practices.

73.   Environmental deterioration has reached significant proportions over the past decade. The main causes are rapid population growth, increased pressure on land, deforestation, shifting cultivation and desertification. The depletion of forestry resources, in particular, has had a significant negative impact on women. Apart from their value as a productive resource, trees protect the quality of the soil and water and most tropical farming systems are unsustainable without trees as part of the system. Forests provide food, fodder and fibre - products that fall within women's responsibility. Small-scale enterprises dependent on forestry products are among the major employers of rural women, particularly the landless and resource poor.

74.   It is essential to learn from rural women about conservation and management of the environment and to take their indigenous knowledge into account when developing concrete policies and projects. However, their often excessive utilization of natural resources is frequently stipulated by the lack of access to appropriate technology.

75.   Rural women are in great need of labour-saving techniques, convenient and close access to water resources and the introduction of such collective facilities as community wood lots and grain mills.

(d)   Access to appropriate and affordable technology
76.   New agricultural technologies should be accessible, environmentally appropriate and preferably utilize local materials. They should maximize efficiency without threatening women's and men's jobs in the rural sector. New agricultural technologies include new crop varieties and breeds of livestock, and improved tools, cultivation methods, including consistent access to draught animals, and mechanization practices.

77.   A review of projects over the past decade reveals that technology, if not carefully evaluated before introduction and use, can have unforeseen negative effects on women. In many parts of the developing world, the mechanization of agriculture, for example the use of tractors, has resulted in the masculinization of modern agriculture and the feminization of labour in subsistence agriculture or on family farms. Another unforeseen negative impact on women results from certain types of irrigation technology: although irrigation technology can increase crop production and make

water more readily available to households and livestock, in some cases it can affect women negatively by increasing the time needed to transplant crops, weed and harvest. New technologies can also be too expensive for resource-poor rural women to buy. One way to solve this problem is to learn from the traditional practices of rural women and minimize the use of expensive technology. The upgrading of traditional food-processing techniques can be undertaken without resorting to expensive technology.

78.   Rural women have a rich traditional knowledge of the production, processing storage and nutritional characteristics of a wide range of crops and wild plants, methods of soil conservation and enrichment, and issues related to the rearing of livestock. Such stores of knowledge must be tapped.

(e)   Credit and financial services that address rural women's unique situations

79.   Among the barriers to women's access to credit and financial markets are the assumptions that women farmers do not make cropping and input decisions even when they are heads of household, that their primary involvement in subsistence production limits the time they can devote to market-oriented activities, that they pose a high credit risk and that they can absorb only small loans which carry high administrative costs for financial institutions. Comprehensive programmes of agricultural or seasonal credit which provide for group guarantees sometimes fail to extend credit to poorer women and men because of the fear that group guarantee mechanisms will be jeopardized by the risk associated with the inclusion of poor subsistence farmers. Moreover, women have limited access to cooperatives and other organizations through which credit may be channelled to farmers.

80.   Women's access to credit is often limited by their lack of proper education, as they often do not know the appropriate procedures, as well as lack of collateral and the distant location of credit facilities. In the vast majority of cases, they must rely on their husbands and male relatives, or on money-lenders who tend to charge high interest rates. On the whole, banks have tended to underestimate the productivity of women farmers and their ability to repay loans. The marketable surplus that often results from subsistence production is not taken into account nor is the fact that productivity-enhancing inputs can increase the volume of this marketable surplus.

81.   The extent of the barriers to rural women's access to credit and financial services is perhaps best exemplified by the proportion of multilateral bank loans to agriculture and rural development that reach them: in 1990, US$ 5.8 billion was allocated to agriculture and rural development in the developing countries. Of this figure, 5 per cent reached rural women even though they grow more than 50 per cent of the food in the developing world and have repayment records that are usually higher than those of men. Women's World Banking, with affiliates in 44 countries, has recorded a 97 per cent repayment rate for women in Africa.

82.   Credit is essential for women to obtain vital agricultural inputs such as seeds, fertilizers and pesticides, as well as to buy tools, procure animal draught power, hire extra labour, construct irrigation systems and take soil and water conservation measures. Credit availability is not a sufficient condition for the guarantee of sustainable improvement in women's conditions.

83.   Provision of credit must be accompanied by appropriate technological advice and training, as well as applied research, in particular in sectors in which women are involved, including traditional food crops such as cassava, cowpeas, sorghum, millet, plantain and sweet potatoes, which provide up to two thirds of family nutrition, small livestock and poultry and home vegetable gardens.

84.   Efforts to provide credit to rural women must begin with an examination of local conditions to determine the most effective mechanisms of reaching the poorest women. Provision should be made for training components, as well as strategies that replace the collateral requirements of financial institutions. Moreover, cognizance must be taken of the diversity of rural women's production activities which have seasonal components and include capital requirements for small investments as well as working capital to support market-oriented production and trading activities. Also, the mix of infrastructure, extension, training and marketing support must be carefully targeted to meet rural women's needs in subsistence and market-oriented activities. Assistance must be provided to rural women to ensure the channelling of resources to systems and subsystems for which they are responsible in order to avoid the diversion of resources to production dominated by male members of the household.

85.   Staff of financial institutions should be trained to understand both the productive and the reproductive roles of women and identify modes for matching these needs with credit availability. The special needs of women farmers must be carefully identified. This includes, for example, the need to hire help during periods of labour shortage, food processing, forestry products transformation, purchase of inputs for reforestation programmes, or the organization of fish marketing infrastructure.

86.   Policies of financial institutions can be enhanced to increase rural women's access to financial services and technical assistance through such schemes as promoting the design of plans of action for increasing women's access to financial services; encouraging documentation and exchange of experience among financial institutions on innovative credit schemes that provide easier access to rural women; development of options for financial services, technical assistance, training and resources with special attention to rural women's needs; and establishment of closer links with women bankers in those financial institutions that receive loans from international organizations. Creating and strengthening linkages between banks, government-sponsored seasonal credit programmes and village-based savings and credit groups are important means of increasing the availability of credit to poor rural women.

87.   The impact of credit availability can be dramatic, both on family well-being and on the community at large. Apart from the economic advantage of increased productivity and higher income, the increase in women's earning power has a tremendous effect on their self-confidence. Increased self-esteem has often led women to enrol in education programmes and insist on having a greater role in community activities - initiatives that previously they would never have considered.

(f)   Appropriate extension services and training
88.   The needs of women farmers have generally been overlooked in the provision of extension services. Although women represent up to 80 per cent of the food producers in some countries, they receive only 2 to 13 per cent of extension services. Only 5 per cent of extension organizations' time and resources are allocated to women world wide and only 13 per cent of extension workers world wide are women.

89.   The effective delivery of extension services to women farmers entails ensuring the availability of complete and correct information on women producers in the region, seeking ways to overcome restrictions on the inter-action and interrelationships between rural men and women, making exten-sion services useful to women as well as to men, identifying ways to provide extension advice to female producers through working with women only, as well as with mixed groups, taking extension activities to women's work sites and adapting approaches to fragmented patterns of women's time allocation.

90.   Extension services are often not effective in reaching women because information is geared to male producers' needs in cash cropping and is often not applicable to subsistence crops and livestock, which may be women's concerns. Modes of communication and organization of extension infor-mation may be inappropriate for rural women of varying and usually low levels of educational attainment and literacy, and scheduling of activities may fail to take account of women's fragmented time allocation schedules.

91.   Extension service objectives may not be realized and communities harmed when training and inputs are given to male farmers to increase cash-crop production without corresponding attention to women farmers to grow food crops. Such oversights can contribute to a decrease in food pro-duction and, by extension, increased malnutrition within communities.

92.   The link between extension services and research should be improved to ensure that gender-sensitive research findings are incorporated into extension programmes and that rural women's production-related needs are being addressed. The provision of appropriate technology that is both labour- and energy-saving should be based on research and communi-cation with targeted populations. Such technology should cover the range of activities in which women farmers, producers and processors are engaged to alleviate the constraints they face and to meet their production objectives.

93.   Research and data-collection requirements include addressing gen-der concerns in baseline surveys and questionnaires and conducting gender-disaggregated needs assessments prior to the commencement of activities. The collection of gender-disaggregated data on agricultural activities and constraints are required for use in the design, implementation and moni-toring of extension activities as are intra-household analyses and time-use studies.

94.   Extension systems should identify gender specificities in their work, pay attention to women producers and processors' extension needs and constraints, modify extension messages for their delivery, make their monitoring and evaluation system more participatory, evaluate results and problems according to gender and feed the information back to men and women. Areas of intervention should be prioritized according to the needs of women and men farmers.

95.   Strategies should be identified for the number of women extension agents. Constraints to increasing women's enrolment in lower, middle and higher agricultural educational institutions should be examined and strategies formulated for overcoming the constraints. Gender-sensitive training should be provided for male agents to enhance the understanding of the needs of women farmers. Efforts to increase the pool of women extension agents should include retraining agents in other fields in skills required to service women farmers, equalizing the status of female and male agents through equal training and employment conditions and increasing the involvement of local women as para-extension staff.

4. Participation of women in economic decision-making

(a)   Incidence and trends

96.   The increase in women's role in the economy, the growing recognition of their contribution to development and the changes that have already occurred in women's access to education in many regions of the world, as well as the progress made in diversifying their fields of study, has not been reflected in their participation in economic decision-making.

97.   The rate of participation of women managers world wide at all levels is far below their rate of participation in the labour market. There is a clear concentration in some sectors and activities; the presence of women at the senior levels is low and at the junior and middle levels of management, it is medium to high. In general, the higher the level of decision-making, the lower the level of women's participation. Even female-dominated sectors are often managed by men. However, there is some indication that changes are occurring. The number of women managers is expanding as a result of improved access to education and the longer presence of women in the labour market. This, in turn, is linked to a higher age at marriage and to low fertility. Women managers are concentrated at the junior and middle levels

of management and are trying to expand their career path. Some countries estimate that even with the influence of the above-mentioned factors (education and then longer presence in the labour market), the rate of increase is slow in comparison with other achievements in the fields of education and employment. Reports from the European region suggest that the level of women managers is higher in private enterprises than in the public sector.

98.   Almost every country reported an increase in the number of women entrepreneurs. Although in many developing and developed countries, the number of enterprises owned by women is growing faster than that owned by men, they tend to be concentrated in activities with lower rates of return, and face difficulties in expanding their activities. For example, in China, women represent one third of the 14 million persons self-employed. However, their income lags behind that of men because of the size of the enterprise and the type of business, which typically includes low-paying industries and trades. However, as women are beginning to enter into higher technical and professional industries, the income gap is narrowing.

(b)   Main obstacles identified for women managers
   (i) Access to third-level education and training
99.   One of the major obstacles to the increase in the proportion of women managers in Asia and Africa is the unequal access of girls and women to education, particularly to third-level education. In other regions, the inequality in access to third-level education has almost been eliminated. However, there are problems concerning the quality of education in certain subjects. Moreover, technical and vocational training is still male-dominated in all countries reporting. Lack of counselling and career guidance for girls and boys has also been cited as a contributing factor in maintaining traditional fields of studies for women and men.

(ii) Women's career choices
100.   Educational background has a certain impact on the choice of career. Most countries report that women are still inclined to choose careers in traditionally female occupations. Careers in the humanities, the arts, teaching, the social services and tourism are among women's "preferred" careers, while in most countries, men receive 90 per cent of the diplomas in the technical areas. A typical pattern reflected in some reports is one of women gaining entry into administrative jobs, usually having a humanities-

oriented rather than a technical background, and this leads to a lack of confidence in women's effectiveness, particularly in the manufacturing sector.

(iii) Administrative rules and recruitment procedures

101.   Examples of discrimination based on gender roles implied in administrative rules and procedures were presented by Governments when referring to recruitment techniques and selection interviews when women apply for non-traditional jobs. Some systems such as the career-tracking system, lead to different personnel management for men and women, when different task distribution is given to men and women with the same qualifications. Others referred to governmental training programmes that train women in traditional occupations. Some countries reported that the gender of the candidate was a factor in recruitment.

(iv) Factors for promotion

102.   In most countries women are concentrated in jobs with horizontal mobility. Women are perceived as less interested in upgrading their qualifications and careers and are less able to take advantage of company training. Some reports refer to the fact that men form the majority of those selecting managers and usually discriminate against women. Scoring methods used for promotion could provide a major barrier for women. Concern was expressed that as assessment techniques become more sophisticated and complex, it will be increasingly difficult to challenge potential sources of discrimination.

(v) Corporate culture

103.   Attitudinal discrimination is part of the corporate culture and this is still strongly biased against women; for example, it was reported that men as spouses do not provide the emotional back-up that a professional woman needs; that different assessments are given to women and men candidates; that few women or men wish to work for a woman; that there is a lack of solidarity among women; and that there is direct discrimination by men in denying women promotion to top posts. However, there is no specific reference to sexual harassment.

(vi) Work and family responsibilities

104.   Countries were unanimous in their position that the burden of family responsibilities fell on women and that there was an absence or insuffi-

cient sharing of family responsibilities by men and by society as well, while at the same time, women were expected to fulfil their productive and reproductive roles. The lack or inadequacy of day-care centres was the most-cited obstacle.

(c)   Main obstacles identified for women entrepreneurs
(i) Lack of equal access to economic resources, such as land
(urban and rural)

105.   In most countries, there is no legal impediment to women's equal access to land. However, in many countries, in particular those with more than one legal system, most land titles are in the name of the man, even if the property is jointly owned, and inheritance practices are often male-biased, contrary to the constitution or other provisions. An unequal distribution of land between men and women farmers is observed world wide. It is generally reported that men own more land or have greater assets than women.

(ii) Lack of equal access to credit

106.   In most countries, because women do not have collateral or knowledge about the formal financial system, they face certain constraints relating to access to credit, and have to rely on informal sources of financing with high rates of interest. A number of reports also suggest that the main problem for women owners of small and medium-sized enterprises is financial management because of their inexperience in that area. Lack of credibility by formal financial institutions is also cited as a discriminating factor against women.

(iii) Non-existence or inadequate training in management and
technical skills

107.   There are few opportunities for women to be trained in management and technical skills. The training they receive is often stereotyped by gender, as women, themselves, tend to choose training in traditional occupational areas.

(iv) Non-existence of networking and role models

108.   Most women entrepreneurs lack female role models and networking of women in the male-dominated business environment. A number of reports note that the lack of a woman's "track record", was interpreted, according to certain stereotypical criteria, as inexperience in business, par-

ticularly in the manufacturing sector. The lack of networking with other spheres of women's activities, for example in the political area was noted.

*(v) Insufficient or inadequate access to support services,
including information*

109.   Inadequate career counselling and guidance for young women, the lack of public services and the male-dominated environment of support services are reported to impact negatively on women entrepreneurs.

*(vi) Insufficient and inadequate availability of data and
information relating to women entrepreneurs*

110.   Information on women entrepreneurs and their achievements is almost non-existent. Surveys do not usually contain sex-disaggregated data on women and men entrepreneurs. Recent research activities undertaken by specialized agencies, women's and professional organizations and policy makers have begun to focus on women entrepreneurs because of their increased participation in business start-ups. However, lack of data is the main restriction.

111.   The working environment is seen as a male preserve, full of discriminatory procedures, with inadequate resources for handling both family responsibilities and productive activities.

(d)   Measures adopted to increase the number of women managers

112.   Various policies and programmes that have been adopted in a number of countries have proved to be successful in increasing the number and proportion of women managers.

(i) Affirmative action

113.   Some Governments have put into force an Equal Employment Opportunity Act for Women, requiring the public sector, and sometimes the private sector as well, to establish affirmative action programmes for women managers and to prepare annual reports thereon. In some cases, broad guidelines have been issued referring to equal partnership between men and women. In others, affirmative action has defined a percentage or quota to be reached, and merit quotas as well as regional quotas have been introduced for women candidates. Some countries have required that a certain percentage of the members of the competitive examination commission be women. One country set up a special executive service to implement public sector policies.

114.   In one country, the largest national confederation of labour unions has formulated an action programme aimed at promoting women in trade-union decision-making bodies by the year 2000 and set a target for women in the central executive committee.

(ii) Changing rules and procedures

115.   In order to introduce changes, severe penalties are being applied against private enterprises that do not comply with the Equal Employment Opportunity Act with respect to recruitment, training, promotion and in-house day-care centres. Other countries have issued special management guidelines concerning recruitment, placement and training of women civil servants. Still other countries review public sector appointment procedures on a regular basis. In other countries, private companies have to report annually to established bodies on the comparative status of women and men in relation to recruitment, promotion, qualification, training, working conditions and pay. Exemption from taxes for employers or contributions for training grants when employers employ women in traditionally male-dominated professions were among the measures taken in other countries.

116.   In some countries, the protection of women has been relaxed (for example, regarding ILO Convention No. 89 which prohibits women's night work) in order to allow women's access to managerial positions. Parental leave is allowed in some countries; in other countries, mainly in Asia and the developed countries, the network of day-care centres has been expanded dramatically. Flexible personnel policies have been introduced in some countries, including guidance on parental leave, conferences on dependant care and the issue of work and family responsibilities. In some developed countries, equal opportunity commissions comprising representatives of trade unions, women's associations and employers have been installed. In one country, it was established by law that trade unions include women in the bargaining between trade unions and employers.

(iii) Information and networking

117.   One country reported that there were regular meetings between presidents and employers of large enterprises and government officials concerning women's advancement to managerial levels across the nation.

(iv) Education

118. In some countries, actions have focused on the elementary and secondary schools, where the study of home economics courses has been established for girls and boys. In other countries, technical studies have been extended to girls. In one country, an engineering college was opened for girls only.

(e)   Measures adopted to assist women entrepreneurs

119. Several public and non-governmental organizations manage specific programmes for the development of women's entrepreneurship.

120. Many reports mentioned the creation of a loan programme for women which would guarantee loans up to a certain amount as a successful way to increase the number of loans. Some actions have included women's non-governmental and employers' organizations managing their own financial funds for their affiliates. The opening of windows specifically for women in formal banks was reported. Special funds allocated to women entrepreneurs have also been cited.

121. In some countries, a national women's council has been created in order to review issues and make recommendations to legislative bodies. It has also been reported that Governments consult with non-governmental organizations concerning national policies regarding women entrepreneurs.

122. In some countries, women entrepreneurs have established linkages with the legislative body, which facilitates bringing their interests before that body.

123. Many countries reported actions taken by governmental institutions and women's networks relating to counselling and training of women owners and potential owners, as well as the creation of long-term training centres. Training was offered in such areas as management, finance, technical and business skills, and international marking, as well as in self-confidence.

124. In some cases, a one-year voluntary mentoring programme has been established and mentors have been recruited by governmental agencies dealing with women entrepreneurs.

125.   In one country, women entrepreneurs have been secured a certain number of government contracts (procurement contracts).

126.   Efforts have been made to collect and disseminate information on women businesses. In some cases, economic censuses include specific surveys on women entrepreneurs.

127.   Research by the national machinery on women, universities and non-governmental organizations is beginning to be effected.

128.   Small cottage industry projects directed to women were implemented in the rural areas of many developing countries, with very high rates of success. In some cases, the ministry of women's affairs was the body managing the women's entrepreneurship development programme.

129.   In most developing countries, supportive actions are provided by global and women's non-governmental organizations as well as by specific non-governmental organizations.

130.   In a number of developing countries, international organizations are involved in the promotion of women entrepreneurs, with programmes and pilot projects for the self-employed, including training in management and credit.

Notes

1/   Economic and Social Council resolution 1990/15, annex.

2/   International Labour Organization, "The changing role of women in the economy: employment and social issues" (Geneva, November 1994) (GB.261/EST/2/2), p. 3.

3/   Asian Development Bank, Women in Development, Indonesia country briefing paper (Manila, ADB Programs Department East, 1991).

4/   International Labour Organization, "The changing role of women in the economy ...", p. 6.

5/   Ibid., p. 5.

6/   Ibid.

G. Inequality between men and women in the sharing of power and decision-making at all levels

1.   A number of changes have occurred since 1990 which have affected trends in the sharing of power and decision-making by women at all levels. The world-wide movement for democratization and the demise of centralized communist and socialist systems have created conditions for greater political participation but have also led to a decline in the number of top decision-making positions held by women. A related trend has been the widespread economic liberalization which has been promoted by the advanced industrialized States and multilateral lending institutions, particularly in the form of structural adjustment. The forced reduction of governmental bureaucracies and budgets has led to the elimination of ministries, programmes and resources which have been supportive of women's issues and needs. Countering these trends has been the continued rise of the global women's movement which has sustained pressure on Governments and international organizations to increase women's participation in decision-making.

2.   Global recession and international economic restructuring in the face of external debt have forced many developing nation Governments to focus on short-term economic problems, often to the neglect of longer-term development issues, and this has had a direct and negative bearing on the advancement of women. Simultaneously, pre-existing conditions of inequality in participation and in decision-making at all levels between women and men have sometimes been exacerbated by both the economic crises and the policies which Governments have adopted to cope with them.

3.   The Nairobi Forward-looking Strategies for the Advancement of Women contain numerous recommendations 1/ for ensuring equality of participation by women in all national and local legislative bodies and for achieving equity in the appointment, election and promotion of women to high-level posts in the executive, legislative and judicial branches in those bodies.

4.   At the Expert Group Meeting on Equality in Political Participation and Decision-making (Vienna, 18-22 September 1989), it was concluded that women in all countries confront a common problem: they are not full participants in the public choices that affect their lives; and they are grossly underrepresented in politics and in the civil service, especially at decision-making levels. 2/

5.   As was noted at the Expert Group Meeting, the advancement of women in other areas will be jeopardized if equality in political participation and decision-making is not achieved. Reference was also made to the close reciprocal relationship between the general advancement of women and the participation of women in politics, noting that the political participation of women was facilitated by social and economic support structures and by an absence of legal discrimination and stereotyping of women in education and in the media. Therefore, the advancement of women should be considered a priority in terms of national decision-making, and women should participate as full partners in those decisions. 3/

6.   The first review and appraisal of the implementation of the Strategies provides a baseline upon which to evaluate current trends in the progress or lack of progress made towards increased decision-making power by women.

7.   Despite the fact that most countries in 1990 used democratic methods in selecting political leaders and making policy choices and although women made up half of the electorate, it was found that relatively few women reached the top levels of political participation and even fewer reached major decision-making positions. On average, women represented only 10 per cent of legislators, and only 3.5 per cent of ministerial level decision makers in 1990. In all forums where policy decisions were proposed and made, but especially those dealing with decisions affecting women's daily

lives at the national, international and local levels, women were largely absent.

8.　　It was found in 1990 that the absence of women in the leadership of political parties and other organizations and their concomitant absence as candidates for political office were a major cause of women's underrepresentation in legislatures and decision-making. Informal barriers, or "glass ceilings", prevented women civil servants from rising through the ranks into top level administrative positions.

9.　　Notwithstanding that issues related to the advancement of women have gained greater visibility since the World Conference in 1985, it was found in 1990 that within the United Nations system women were seriously underrepresented at senior management levels. It was observed in 1990 that the issue of women's representation was receiving a lower priority in the work of many organizations. It was also noted that resource levels in real terms for activities related to the advancement of women had not increased, despite the upsurge in activities at the international level and the increasing need for resources by developing countries. During periods of retrenchment, women's programmes have been subject to the same reductions as other programmes. Therefore, much of the work related to the advancement of women continued to depend on extrabudgetary funding.

10.　　In 1990, recession and economic restructuring were already forcing Governments to neglect long-term programmes for the advancement of women. Pre-existing inequalities were exacerbated by the crisis and by the policies adopted to cope with the recession.

11.　　In 1990, there were very few women in the politics of African countries. Though democratization was giving women the right to vote in larger numbers, this did not translate into decision-making power for women. In 1990, women in Asia and the Pacific were becoming visible in political life. However, women still represented a very small percentage of public office holders. Women in Latin America participated only minimally in the executive and legislative organs of their countries in 1990. Most of the women were in lower party echelons. By contrast, the position of women in the Caribbean was most significant, with substantial numbers of female legislators, ministers and administrators in most countries.

12.   The first review and appraisal made no mention of women in decision-making in Western Asia, which was a reflection of their virtual exclusion from politics and government. Mention of cultural values which called for women to return to their reproductive and nurturing roles while relinquishing their other societal participatory roles and of the resistance of Arab States to the advancement of women indicate that the problem of women's participation in decision-making remains most acute in this region.

13.   The first review and appraisal also recommended that the number of women in decision-making positions in intergovernmental and non-governmental organizations should be increased.

14.   According to recommendation VI of the recommendations and conclusions arising from the review and appraisal, 4/ all civil service regulations should have clear statements on practices of recruitment, appointment, promotion, leave entitlement, training and development, and other conditions of service.

15.   Governments, political parties, trade unions, professional and other representative groups should each aim at targets to increase the proportion of women in leadership positions to at least 30 per cent by 1995 with a view to achieving equal representation between women and men by the year 2000 and should institute recruitment and training programmes to prepare women for those positions.

16.   Government, political parties, trade unions and women's organizations should be encouraged to establish a list of qualified women which could be used to fill vacant positions. The importance of training women in the skills necessary for political and administrative careers should also be recognized.

17.   Articles 7 and 8 of the Convention on the Elimination of All Forms of Discrimination against Women (CEDAW) 5/ also refer to the subject of political decision-making. Article 7 requires State parties to the Convention to take all appropriate measures to eliminate discrimination against women in political and public life and, in particular, to ensure to women, on equal terms with men, the right to vote in all elections and public referenda and to be eligible for election to all publicly elected bodies; to participate in the formulation of government policy and the implementation thereof and to hold

public office and perform all public functions at all levels of government; to participate in non-governmental organizations and associations concerned with political and public life.

18.   Article 8 requires State parties to the Convention to take all appropriate measures to ensure to women, on equal terms to men and without discrimination, the opportunity to represent their Governments at the international level and to participate in the work of international organizations.

1. Main trends

19.   The main trend for the foreseeable future is the continuing lack of equitable participation by women in political decision-making. It deprives women of important rights and responsibilities as citizens. Therefore, women's interests and perspectives cannot influence key decisions, which has consequences for society as a whole and for future generations - for example, on national budgets and major reforms or socio-economic models to be followed. This situation is not only discriminatory to women but is also disadvantageous to society, which is deprived of women's skills and their distinct perspectives.

20.   Existing research indicates a more encouraging trend. If women are represented in sufficiently large numbers in the decision-making arena (constituting what has been termed a "critical mass", estimated at a level of at least 30-35 per cent in decision-making bodies), they have a visible impact on the style and content of political decisions. For example, in the Nordic countries, the only region where women have achieved a critical mass at the policy-making level, owing to pressure exerted by women, issues that have long been ignored, such as equal rights, women's control over their own bodies, child care and protection against sexual violence, have gradually been incorporated into public agendas and reflected in national budgets. Evidence for this has been documented in a number of United Nations studies and reports of the Secretary-General on the priority themes. 6/

a.   Women's participation in governmental decision-making bodies

21.   Since 1987 the percentage of women in parliament has actually declined. Most of the decrease in the global average can be attributed to the

political changes in Eastern Europe, while improvements have been registered in Western Europe and Africa. In Eastern Europe the decline reflects a change in the role of parliament, from a body which merely rubber-stamped political decisions and was hand-picked by the ruling party to one which is more active in government decision-making and which is more freely selected, reflecting the unequal status of women in those societies.

22.   After the Second World War, Eastern European parliaments were supposed to reflect national demographics in terms of class, age and gender; however, they had no real political power. Since the institution of democratic reforms and economic liberalization, these parliaments have come to more accurately mirror the actual political and economic power within society, to the virtual exclusion of women.

23.   The Nordic region is an exception to the global trend of fewer women in legislatures. In 1993, the proportion of women in parliament averaged 33.7 per cent. This figure can be attributed to many factors, including a time-lagged effect of educational equality. However, it is also the result of a conscious effort by women voters to determine electoral results, at the margin, by supporting women candidates. For example, in 1993 Norway had 39.4 per cent women in parliament, representing an increase from 15 per cent in 1975. Concerned about their exclusion from power, women in one set of municipal elections systematically voted for female candidates and increased the proportion of women in municipal councils by 50 per cent.

24.   Despite the fact that women comprise, in almost all countries, a majority of the electorate, the proportion of women in parliament remains relatively low (see table II.G.1). In 1993 the average percentage of women in lower houses of parliament world wide was only 8.8 per cent. There were no women in parliament in 11 countries. In only five countries did the proportion of female parliamentarians exceed the goal of 30 per cent set by the Economic and Social Council in 1990.

Table II.G.1. Average percentage of women in parliament, 1975-1993, by region

Region	1975	1987	1993
Africa	4.6	6.7	8.0
Latin America and the Caribbean	6.0	8.0	7.6
Western Europe and others	7.0	13.4	16.4
Asia and the Pacific	5.2	7.6	5.8
Eastern Europe	19.9	21.8	6.5
World	6.8	9.7	8.8

25.   Women have the right to vote and hold office in almost every country of the world. Despite the fact that women have exercised these rights, on average, for 40 years and do vote at approximately the same rate as men, relatively few women have been elected in the democratic process to national legislatures and even fewer have reached top executive posts. Earlier United Nations studies have suggested that, to a certain extent, countries in which women have been able to stand for election for a longer period of time are somewhat more likely to have more women in parliament.

26.   There are recent indications that in some countries women are beginning to vote differently than men and, in close elections, determine the outcome. Argentina, Colombia, the Nordic countries, Austria, Germany and Poland are cases in point. In all these countries women, at least on some occasions, voted differently and expressed clear preference for those parties that put forward female candidates or candidates clearly representing women's interests and perspectives, especially with regard to reproductive rights, social support services and/or participation in decision-making.

27.   Competition for votes between political parties has forced many to promote women within their ranks and nominate them as candidates in order to gain the support and votes of the female electorate. This tactic, pursued in some parties, has forced others to join the competition and place women in visible positions. For example, the introduction of a quota system by a number of political parties in the 1980s in all five Nordic countries

induced other parties to promote women candidates. Some years later quotas were established by a number of political parties in Austria and Germany. For example, in 1986 the German Greens incorporated a provision in their constitution according to which at least half of the representation of all bodies and organs of the federal association of the party must be women. Similarly, in 1988 the German Social Democratic Party changed its organizational statutes so that at least 40 per cent of either sex must be represented in the offices and functions of the party.

28.   The principal reason why women are not elected to office is that women are not put forward as candidates. Indeed, in those countries where women do succeed in becoming candidates, they are more likely to be elected than men. One reason more female candidates are not put forward for election is the fact that they are not well represented in terms of numbers in the executive leadership of political parties. Even though women are substantially represented in the membership of parties in most countries, few women reach the top party leadership positions. There is usually a higher percentage of women in parliaments than in party decision-making bodies.

29.   In parliamentary systems of government, ministers are generally selected from members of parliament, while in presidential regimes and other types of regimes, the top levels of decision makers are recruited from a variety of sources. In parliamentary systems, the proportion of female ministers is directly related to the proportion of women in parliament and to their tenure, while the proportion of women decision makers is somewhat lower in presidential systems. Regardless, the proportion of women at the ministerial level remains very low, lower indeed than their representation in parliament. On average only 6.2 per cent of ministerial-level officials are women, and in 62 countries there are no women ministers at all. However, in the countries of Western Europe, Australia, New Zealand and other developed democracies, the proportion of women ministers is significantly higher. This differentiation can largely be attributed to the Nordic countries, where women comprise an average of 22 per cent of the ministers.

30.   In the more industrial countries, there continue to be small, but significant, increases in the number of women in decision-making positions and in legislatures. In general, there has been progress made in all regions except Eastern Europe since 1987. Of particular interest is the increase in

Western Europe. In the Nordic countries, the average percentage of women ministers increased from 16 per cent to 22 per cent; thus, the critical mass of women in political decision-making is now being approached.

31.   The data in table II.G.2 are encouraging because the 15 countries with the most women decision makers have significantly higher percentages in 1994 than in 1987. The Nordic, Caribbean and non-European developed democratic States have made impressive strides, adding approximately 10 per cent more women decision makers. By 1994, three countries had passed the 30 per cent critical mass threshold, with five other States approaching the threshold. However, these progressive countries represent less than 10 per cent of the total. Most countries have made little or no progress in promoting women decision makers.

32.   Women ministers are more likely to hold portfolios in social affairs than in other areas. On average 10.8 per cent of social affairs portfolios are held by women. Very few portfolios in the economic, political and judicial areas are held by women. However, women are beginning to be named as defence, foreign affairs and finance ministers in several regions (see table II.G.3). Women have been making breakthroughs in law and justice ministries in countries of the Western Europe and other group and in the Caribbean. In the Western Europe and other group, women have made advances in economic ministries. Only in the Nordic countries have women made significant strides in political ministries, including defence.

33.   Government decision-making occurs not only at the ministerial level. Key decision makers are also located at the subministerial level, often as permanent civil servants who have risen to their positions by career appointments. Such positions include vice-minister, permanent undersecretary, deputy secretary and director. In these categories, women are only slightly more represented, on average, than at the ministerial level (see table II.G.4). Only 7.1 per cent of these positions are held by females. In 56 countries there were no women at all in these positions at the subministerial level. In three countries (Bahamas, Dominica and Norway), over 30 per cent of subministerial officials were women. In four other countries (Antigua and Barbuda, Finland, San Marino and the United States), the proportion exceeded 25 per cent. Clearly, the proportions in any country, at any given point in time, reflect political changes. In the group of Western Europe and

other developed democracies, the proportion of women in ministerial positions is higher than that at lower levels, indicating obstacles to the career advancement of women in the civil service.

Table II.G.2. Countries with the highest proportion of women among government decision makers, 1987 and 1994

(Percentage)

	1987		1994
Dominica	25.6	Norway	45.2
Bahamas	24.0	Bahamas	32.4
Norway	20.3	Dominica	31.3
Finland	19.4	Finland	26.8
Barbados	17.9	San Marino	26.3
Trinidad and Tobago	14.9	Antigua and Barbuda	25.9
Grenada	14.7	United States of America	25.2
Seychelles	14.6	Seychelles	23.9
Romania	13.9	Australia	20.2
United Republic of Tanzania	13.6	Canada	18.9
Burkina Faso	12.9	Guyana	18.0
Senegal	12.0	Sweden	17.5
United States of America	11.7	Honduras	16.7
Cameroon	11.1	Netherlands	16.1
Philippines	11.1	Trinidad and Tobago	15.3

Table II.G.3. Average percentage of women in governmental decision-making-positions, by region and sector, 1994

	Office of President s or Prime Minister	Economic	Law and justice	Social	Political	Total
Region						
Africa	2.1	3.0	4.1	10.6	3.6	5.4
Latin America and the Caribbean	4.9	5.1	10.0	10.9	3.4	7.5
Western Europe and other developed democracies	10.8	10.7	23.2	25.0	7.5	15.2
Asia and the Pacific	1.6	2.0	0.0	6.1	2.8	2.9
Eastern Europe	3.2	1.9	0.0	5.4	0.0	2.6
World	3.7	4.1	6.0	10.8	3.6	6.2
Subregion						
Nordic countries	30.0	19.2	75.0	39.0	27.3	22.0
Caribbean	4.9	4.1	16.7	14.1	3.3	14.1
Australia, Canada, New Zealand, United States	12.5	12.0	25.0	20.2	0.0	19.8
East and South-East Asia	0.0	0.6	0.0	4.2	0.0	2.5

Source: Division for the Advancement of Women, derived from Worldwide Government Directory, 1994 (Washington, D.C., Belmont Publs.).

Table II.G.4. Average percentage of women among government decision makers by region, 1987 and 1994

Region	1987 Ministerial	1987 Subminis-terial	1987 Total	1994 Ministerial	1994 Subminis-terial	1994 Total
Africa	2.9	5.0	4.0	5.4	6.8	6.3
Latin America and the Caribbean	3.1	8.2	7.3	7.5	11.4	10.4
Western Europe and other developed democracies	7.1	7.8	9.6	15.2	12.3	13.0
Asia and the Pacific	1.8	3.1	3.0	2.9	2.6	2.9
Eastern Europe	3.0	3.9	3.5	2.6	6.1	5.0
World	3.4	5.7	5.4	6.2	7.1	6.8

b.   *Obstacles preventing women from participating in decision-making and policy-making*

34.   In order to strengthen the participation of women in political parties and, consequently, in political decision-making bodies like parliaments, specific measures such as targets, quota systems and/or reserved seats have been introduced in a number of countries. Political parties in a number of countries have adopted quota systems for women (Argentina, Austria, Belgium, Denmark, France, Germany, Greece, Iceland, Israel, Netherlands, Norway, Spain, Sweden and Venezuela). These quotas were designed to ensure that a minimum percentage of women (varying from 20 per cent to 50 per cent) were members of various political bodies, including their leadership and/or lists of candidates for elections. For example, Sweden, which was the first country to introduce such a quota system for women in 1972 has now achieved 50-50 parity. Another type of reserved seats system is found in Bangladesh.

35.   In some countries (Cameroon, Canada, Finland, Gabon, Japan, Mexico, Republic of Korea, Spain, Sri Lanka and Zimbabwe), political parties created separate women's leagues, committees or organizations within

their structures. Their main role is to provide more training opportunities for women and improved forums for the discussion and articulation of women's issues, strategies and goals. Some observers note the important role of separate women's structures within political parties but suggest that they may contribute to the alienation of women from mainstream party politics and thus detract from women's principal objective of empowerment.

36.   Some countries have centres of power based upon unbroken political traditions. Others have had more dysfunctional experiences. Other countries are struggling to cope with the tensions resulting from a shift from authoritarian rule to systems with more liberal social relations in the political arena. Different political environments influence the factors which can either promote or undermine the equal participation of women in decision-making. Some of these factors are:

(a)   An historical philosophy and experience of politics as an interaction and competition between men, along with the conscious and subconscious perception, held by both women and men, of men as the rational political actors, and of masculine characteristics of leadership;

(b)   The lack of a well-developed body of intellectual opinion and literature advocating women's participation in decision-making;

(c)   Evidence of institutionalized gender discrimination in public policy in terms of taxation, social security regulations, banking and financial law, the right to citizenship, family law and age discrimination;

(d)   Implicit discrimination within the dominant male culture of established political parties, institutions or organizations;

(e)   The absence of women's perspectives and positive contributions to society in the media;

(f)   The pervasive use of sexist language in all forms of communication;

(g)   Traditionally male-oriented assumptions regarding the nature and role of policy and decision makers in terms of the selection system, electoral system and/or size of the constituency, timing, duration and location of meetings;

    (h)   The use of networking as a patronage system;

    (i)   The perception of politics as irrelevant or divorced from daily life;

    (j)   Women's dual roles;

    (k)   Sexual harassment.

37.   Numerous obstacles, mentioned in the national reports, are discussed below, by region.

38.   In Africa, in former one-party States, the situation is similar to that in Eastern Europe. Under one-party rule, the women's affairs committee of the ruling party in one country regularly addressed women's issues. With the transition to a more pluralistic political system, the same women's affairs committee no longer has the power effectively to articulate women's issues and concerns.

39.   In a relatively developed State, featuring a multi-party system with a dominant ruling party, women's participation in national legislative bodies is largely determined by male-dominated political party structures and processes. In local elections for mayor and deputy mayor in large municipalities, women have had little chance of overcoming male-dominated structures and getting onto party tickets. Given prevailing societal attitudes, women have even less of a chance of being elected as independents. Constraints include lack of self-confidence, inhibitive party structure, lack of support by other women and husbands, negative social environment and costly campaigns.

40.   In a highly advanced Asian democracy, it was reported that societal prejudices about the abilities and aptitudes of women and gender-stereotyped roles remain deeply rooted in everyday life.

41.   In a Caribbean democracy, a 1992 study suggests that even though women are actively involved in grass-roots politics and despite the fact that all parties have a women's wing, women are not usually called upon to be leaders of the party.

42.   In a Southern European democracy, it was reported that patriarchal attitudes and structures within political parties and society as a whole were

obstacles to the advancement of women. The lack of women in parties and high-level positions was attributed to the unequal division of labour within the household and absence of adequate social structures to support family responsibilities.

43.   In a newly democratic Eastern European country, the lack of a women's lobby - a result of the former system - was mentioned as an obstacle. Various political parties and the Roman Catholic Church were said to be trying to force women to return to their traditional roles as mothers and wives. Political tensions contribute to pushing women away from politics. Women are often not elected in village-level politics due to their lower level of education.

44.   In a newly independent Eastern European State, deepening economic and political crises, the subordination of women and the paradox of their former status under the Communist system has resulted in a decline of the political participation of women compared to their active involvement earlier.

c.   Affirmative actions that have been taken to promote greater participation of women in power structures and decision-making at all levels

45.   Some of the affirmative actions cited in national reports are outlined below.

46.   In Sudan the Government established a 10 per cent minimum quota level for women's representation in all positions in local, municipal and state government. If the 10 per cent percentage cannot be attained through elections, women will be appointed.

47.   In Uganda, affirmative action has been taken by the Government deliberately to recruit more women into high-level posts.

48.   In 1992 the United Republic of Tanzania passed a law requiring that at least 15 per cent of all members of Parliament be female.

49.   The Government of Ethiopia has created technical women's departments in government agencies.

50.   An affirmative action programme exists in the civil service in

Zimbabwe. In January 1992 a government circular was issued to advance women's participation in management. Its goal is to have 33 per cent of the senior public service positions occupied by women by the year 2000.

51.   Bangladesh attributes the increase of women in the civil service - from 17 per cent of officers in the Secretariat in 1987 to 25.7 per cent in 1991 and from 7.1 per cent of officers in the Directorates in 1987 to 19.6 per cent in 1991 - to the introduction of a quota system.

52.   Since 1985 China has set up national organizations to promote the advancement of women. In 1991 a division for women's concerns was established in the Ministry of Social Affairs of the Population and Employment Bureau.

53.   The Government of the Philippines plans to ensure the appointment of women sectoral representatives in Congress and at all levels of policy-making bodies, based on a quota not lower than the United Nations quota of 30 per cent.

54.   Japan has drawn up a new national plan of action to the year 2000.

55.   Antigua/Barbuda has set itself a goal of electing a minimum of seven women to Parliament by 1999.

56.   In November 1991 under law No. 24.012 1991, Argentina established a participation quota in the list of political parties to guarantee a minimum of 30 per cent women. No party list that does not fulfil this requirement will be approved. In March 1993 the law was implemented, emphasizing that 30 per cent was a minimum figure, bearing in mind the overall goal of 50 per cent representation by women.

57.   In 1988 the Government of Sweden adopted a three-year programme to increase female representation in decision-making bodies in the public sector. It was approved by Parliament with three steps: to make the absence of women visible by presenting statistics to Parliament so it could be followed up annually; to establish concrete time-specific targets for increasing the proportion of women; and to pursue measures that help achieve these goals. The Government decided to set up the following targets: by 1992 women's representation on public administration boards and committee should be increased to 30 per cent. By 1995 the proportion of women

represented on these boards and committees should be increased further to 40 per cent. The final target is that all governmental authority boards and official committees of inquiry should have equal representation. According to the Government, this should occur within a decade - i.e., by 1998.

58.   The women's political party triggered an intense internal debate within Swedish political parties to take into account women's issues more seriously. In 1989 it was decided on a target of 20 per cent of executive positions within various ministries in Cabinet offices; in 1990, the target was reached.

59.   The Government of Finland has proposed an amendment to the Equality Act to increase women's representation in decision-making positions in state committees, advisory boards, municipal and executive bodies comprised of elected officials within governmental offices, institutions and private companies. Unfortunately, no data or statistics accompanied the report.

60.   Since the mid-1970s, existing rules have been applied pursuant to the Equal Status Act and the Local Government Act in Norway. They require that public authorities ensure 40 per cent female representation. In 1981 a provision relating to the gender-quota system for publicly appointed boards, councils and committees was incorporated into the Equal Status Act, with the requirement that there be at least two members of each sex represented on any public body. Similarly, the Norwegian diplomatic service is establishing concrete statistical goals for the year 2000, including a requirement that 40 per cent of mid-level executive positions be held by women.

61.   In the United States, in 1986 Iowa became the first state to require equal appointment of women. Since then, six other states have adopted gender-balance laws. Currently, in Iowa women comprise 47.6 per cent of all appointments to state boards and commissions.

62.   Canada has given high priority to improving the status of women in international organizations and ensuring that more women are appointed to senior decision-making positions in international bodies.

63.   In 1988 the Coordinating Committee of Women's Organizations and Women's Sections of Political Parties in Greece was established, with a

main goal of promoting equal participation of women in decision-making, especially in political positions throughout the system. In 1990 the Social Democrat Populist party introduced a 25 per cent quota system in provincial and municipal administrative structures.

64.   In October 1991, the Prime Minister of the United Kingdom announced a governmental objective to increase the percentage of women in the civil service to 25 per cent and to 50 per cent by 1996. A goal of 15 per cent was established for the most senior posts by the year 2000.

65.   The leaders of both the Radical Democratic Party and the largest agrarian party in Romania are women.

2. Increasing the participation of rural women in decision-making

66.   The establishment or strengthening of women's national machinery is an essential component of rural development strategies and of amplifying the voices of rural women so that their contributions, needs and concerns are effectively assessed and incorporated into policies, legislation, programmes and projects. This process must be coupled with the provision of sufficient human, technical and financial resources to enable national machinery to play a catalytic and strategic role in the development of country-wide networks of organizations and groups of rural women to facilitate the implementation of food and agricultural development programmes.

67.   The strategic interventions that women's national machinery can make on behalf of rural women include coordination with international organizations on measures to execute, coordinate and apply research on rural women's reproductive and productive roles and to improve the availability and quality of gender-disaggregated data on agriculture and rural development which addresses the multiple roles of women. Women's national machinery might, for example, lobby Governments to process the existing small, but significant, volume of gender-disaggregated data relating to agriculture and rural development to allow for its analysis by gender. 7/

68.   The liaison and collaborative role of women's national machinery with international organizations and both national and international non-governmental organizations cannot be understated. Women's national machinery has a potentially large role to play in collecting and disseminating information about the needs and activities of rural women at all levels.

Such machinery could channel the concerns of rural women to governmental, regional and international organizations. This role can be strengthened through technical and financial assistance by international donors which must, at one and the same time, provide assistance and play a catalytic role in the establishment of more collaborative relationships. The establishment of such linkages is particularly important in facilitating the flow of resources to targeted populations of rural women and in overcoming the traditionally low status of women's national machinery among other governmental agencies and the isolation of women's units from programmes and field activities of sectoral ministries.

69.   The facilitative role of women's national machinery is critical to the growth and development of community development organizations. Increasing the participation of rural women requires action in three main areas:

    (a)   Promotion of the establishment of women's and mixed-gender local organizations such as cooperatives, farmer's self-help associations, and credit and savings unions established for production, political, advocacy, social and economic goals;

    (b)   Promotion of training programmes for women's associations and enhancement of their capacity for dialogue and negotiation;

    (c)   Encouragement of women leaders to undertake community action and collective initiatives, particularly in agriculture, forestry and communal fish farming.

70.   Involvement in community development organizations is an effective method of increasing rural women's role in decision-making and ensuring recognition of their participation in the community. Women's integration must be reinforced by an examination of the causes of gender imbalances, incorporate the provision of technical training and address male opposition to women's involvement. Such participation increases women's visibility, enables them to learn management skills and methods for earning and saving income and enhances their bargaining power when seeking access to land, credit, agricultural services, extension courses or training.

71.   Groups offer women the benefits of pooled resources and ideas, greater access to knowledge - related, for example, to the acquisition of management skills and methods for earning and saving income - and information, and the solidarity and confidence that can develop with a like-minded group of people. Group membership can help break through the social constraints on women's access to resources. This can be of particular value in societies where women are not free to express themselves openly in public or have not developed the skill or the willingness to do so. Groups offer greater access to training and credit since the institutions supplying these resources will often choose groups as a delivery mechanism in order to raise their own cost-effectiveness of delivery.

72.   There are benefits to be derived from membership in all women's or mixed groups. The principal advantages rural women derive from all-women's groups are the openness of membership, greater freedom to participate in management and develop leadership experience, a greater comfort level for self-expression in societies where men and women do not mix easily in political structures, and the possibility to generate income and to participate in decisions regarding group expenditures. Mixed groups, on the other hand, offer greater access to the infrastructure and services of mainstream rural development. However, rural women have often found access to these groups difficult. They are often excluded from mixed farmer's groups by membership criteria which specify land ownership, illiteracy or low levels of education, or opposition from husbands (for example, to paying additional fees for a wife's membership). Women may be reluctant to join because their heavy productive and reproductive workloads leave no time for such activities or because they can derive no benefits from membership if groups do not address women's productive activities.

H. Insufficient mechanisms at all levels to promote the advancement of women

73.   The Forward-looking Strategies recommended that appropriate governmental machinery for monitoring and improving the status of women should be established where it is lacking. To be effective, this machinery should be established at a high level of government and should be ensured adequate resources, commitment and authority to advise on the impact on women of all governmental policies. Such machinery can play a vital role in enhancing the status of women, inter alia, through the dissemination of information to women on their rights and entitlements, through collaborative action with various ministries and other governmental agencies, and also with non-governmental organizations and indigenous women's societies and groups.

74.   Several reviews and appraisals of national machineries have been undertaken by the United Nations. In 1989, a directory was presented to the Commission; 8/ in the 1990 review and appraisal of the implementation of the Strategies, a chapter dealt with national machineries; 9/ and in 1991, a questionnaire was sent to the member States asking for more detailed information. Another directory was published in 1993. 10/ More qualitative information was furnished by the Seminar on National Machinery for Monitoring and Improving the Status of Women (Vienna, 28 September-2 October 1987) and the Regional Seminar on the Impact of Economic and Political Reform on the Status on Women in Eastern Europe and the USSR (Vienna, 8-12 April 1991).

75.   In the response of the Economic and Social Council to the 1990 review and appraisal, several recommendations were made regarding the

importance of national machinery for the advancement of women in promoting the integration of women's needs and concerns into government policies and programmes, in mobilizing grass-roots support and in providing information at the national and international levels. 4/

1. General trends

76.　　The process of establishing national machineries for women at the governmental level began in the late 1970s. In addition to that, efforts have been made to strengthen their policies, to create different machineries at the national, regional and local level and to redefine the functions. From 1985 member States created machineries where they did not exist. More machineries at the national, regional and local level have been created where a strong national governmental machinery existed.

77.　　The Directory presented to the Commission in 1989 8/ gave detailed information on 91 units, and the existence of another 37 was reported. In the 1991 directory, information on 127 units was presented. 10/ The 1993 directory gives information about 128 States with national machineries. 11/ In preparation for the World Conference, 106 national committees have been created.

a.　　*Governmental or non-governmental basis*

78.　　Many of the member States have national machineries located in the Government, although a large number of them still have non-governmental organizations as national machineries.

79.　　Nearly all the countries in Western Europe have governmental national machineries (excepting the United Kingdom, which is mixed). The same trend is noted in Latin America, where most are located in the Government, with the exception of Bolivia, Cuba and Panama. The same trend appears in Africa. A smaller number of machineries is located in Government in Asia, and the largest number of non-governmental organization-based machineries appears in Central and Eastern European countries.

80.　　Non-governmental organizations and national committees created for the Fourth World Conference are developing programmes and activities for women. Estimation on data from the 1992 directory and on the new machineries carrying out activities for the Conference suggests that the number of focal points for women has increased.

b.   Location

81.   Some member States have ministers of women's affairs (Australia, Austria, Bangladesh, Canada, Chile, Côte d'Ivoire, Indonesia, St. Kitts and Nevis, and Uganda). Others include women's affairs in the title of the ministers reporting to the Cabinet - for example, in ministries of youth, social affairs, employment, culture, education or law (Belgium, Cameroon, Chad, Côte d'Ivoire, Germany, Lesotho, Mauritius, the Netherlands and Niger).

82.   Another group of member States has agencies on women's issues located in a shared portfolio (Antigua and Barbuda, Argentina, Barbados, Philippines and Spain), the Minister in charge reporting to the Cabinet.

83.   A weak situation occurs when the national machinery for women is included only as a focal point in ministries with other responsibilities.

84.   The location of the national machinery has no relation to a particular region or particular political context. National machineries attached to the Cabinet can be found in every region.

c.   Other structures

85.   A trend emerging over the past decade is the creation of extra-national machineries at the national level, such as councils for equality, ombuds for women, advisory groups on women's issues and parliamentary commissions. Many developed countries have other structures located in the ministry of labour.

86.   Nordic countries have councils for equality and ombuds for women, and many Western European countries develop their activities along with equality structures created in other ministries or at other governmental or political levels, such as parliamentary commissions for women's rights. Canada and Australia have advisory councils. Many Asian and African countries have focal points in other ministries with a very different degree of responsibility.

87.   Focal points have been also created at the local level, but the degree of support and responsibility varies.

d.   Mandates

88.   Mandates drawn from law or legal rules give clear signals to civil servants, political parties and other agents and make public the commitment of the Government to women's issues.

89.   Extra machineries at the national, regional and local levels are most successful when they are backed by law and legal rules. At the regional level, between 1985 and 1994, certain countries set up equality bodies under laws or resolutions adopted by regional governments. Their duties are expressly indicated in the instrument creating them, and they are all created along the lines of the national machinery.

90.   Many countries have developed national ministerial plans of actions for improving the situation of women. This kind of commitment by the Government and by other ministries has been very useful.

91.   When mainstreaming is used, the clear responsibilities of the different ministries or agents is crucial for the success of the public policies for women.

92.   The Canadian report cites three elements of the national machinery: the Minister Responsible for the Status of Women, the Office of the Status of Women and the Canadian Advisory Council on the Status of Women. Canada's experience demonstrates that other factors are essential for developing a strong national machinery: expressed political commitment at the highest level to improve women's social, economic, legal and cultural situation; recognition of the role and contribution of women's groups; policy research and an assessment of the impact of policies on women; sex-desegregated data and information on the situation of women and research on issues of concern to women.

e.   Staff and internal structures

93.   Very few countries provided information on staff, internal structures or financial resources (Canada, Indonesia, the Netherlands and Uganda). Most, however, reported problems in these areas.

94.   Indonesia's report shows that, although many institutions have been created for the advancement of women, their effectiveness remains limited. The State Ministry for the Role of Women, which is responsible for representing the interests and concerns of women, is comparatively small. It lacks both staff and funds adequately to monitor and evaluate the implementation of programmes on women in development. Practical commitment in the form of resources has also been limited. The Ministry has no separate budget, because special projects for women are funded through sectoral departments.

95.　　The lack of statistical indicators on women partly accounts for the lack of recognition of the need to incorporate women into specific development activities and provides a practical obstacle to efforts. Future efforts will be directed towards the integration of women into mainstream sectoral programmes. Funding for special projects for women, which do reflect women's interests and concerns, comprises only a very small proportion of the total departmental budgets.

f.　　Relations with other ministries

96.　　Many member States report that national machineries have formal links across the Government. In some cases there are focal points, mainly in other ministries or interministerial committees. The status can vary considerably, between high-level executive committees and intermediate-level or advisory committees.

97.　　The effectiveness of the interministerial committees depends on the level of the officials and the monitoring and assessment of the activities reporting to the Cabinet.

98.　　In developing regions where the goal is development programmes, some interministerial committees include ministries of agriculture, food, planning and trade, development and food.

99.　　For effectiveness, the machinery should involve the Presidency and the finance ministry. The Uganda reports show that, although interdepartmental collaboration among ministries is one of the success factors, a major constraint to the implementation of the women's programmes is the lack of their own budgets.

2. Regional perspectives

100.　　The Nordic countries - Denmark, Finland, Iceland, Norway and Sweden -developed steps to promote equal opportunity policies long ago. The main areas are employment, social welfare and the family, education, housing and social planning, and participation in politics at all levels.

101.　　In many countries action plans have been adopted. The measures to be implemented concentrate on themes like women's role in the economy, combining family life with a job outside the home, violence and political participation. Developing countries have focused their programmes on development, education and health.

102.   Nearly all of the Latin American countries have national machineries for women. Their structures, budgets and the government support for them vary. The establishment of agencies like Chile's Servicio National de la Mujer, the National Council for Women in Argentina, or Instituto de la Mujer in Uruguay have instituted broad kinds of programmes. The agency in Chile is attached directly to the Presidency, with a minister in charge of women's affairs. The equal opportunity plan coordinates with different ministries and different levels of government. It also cooperates with non-governmental organizations.

103.   Although national machineries existed in Latin America before 1985, the new organs have strengthened the oldest structures or redefined objectives in accord with public policies on equal opportunity for women (Argentina, Chile, Colombia, Uruguay, Venezuela). Recently some of them were established by law.

104.   In Africa, most of the national machineries existed before 1985. After the Nairobi Conference, the region saw an increase in the number of organs at the governmental level. Most of the African States report that their national machineries develop activities related to women and development. In some African countries, the national machineries are headed by a government minister coordinating other structures. The national machinery is linked to the Cabinet within the organizational structure of government, and it coordinates policies and activities on the advancement of women.

105.   Several Governments in Africa are committed to the establishment of viable national machineries for women, as institutional frameworks that coordinate and enhance the participation of women at the national level. Governments declare that national machineries are necessary for the positive integration of women into the mainstream linked to development processes.

106.   As in many developing countries, the major constraint facing the governmental machineries in Africa is the minimal funding. For example, in Uganda, between 1988 and 1990, the average development budget for the Department of Women in Development was only 0.09 per cent of the total government development budget. That percentage recently rose to 2.3 per cent.

107.   Very few national reports updated the information on national machineries in Asia and the Pacific.

108.   Indonesia was one of the first countries in the region to establish a special ministry for women in government. A wide range of special organizations and groups are actively involved in promoting the advancement of women in various fields of development and at all levels of government. The major institutions of government also include provisions to promote the advancement of women by increasing women's participation in development. The State Minister for the Role of Women has responsibility for policy formulation, coordination and advocacy, and her mandate is to make policy recommendations to the Government and coordinate development projects for women, implemented by sectorial agencies. Other structures at the governmental level are also involved in the advancement of women, with functions including evaluation and monitoring of public policies on the situation of women. The structures for the advancement of women also include provincial and district management teams.

109.   Institutional arrangements for policy formulation, implementation, monitoring, review and appraisal or initiatives to incorporate women into development have been established to enable the State Minister to function effectively. As a member of the Cabinet, the State Minister interacts with other ministers and members of the Cabinet. Monthly consultative meetings are held with governmental agencies.

110.   In 1992 the Bureau of Planning in each department was designated as the focal point for women in development activities. This marked both recognition of the need to incorporate a gender dimension in the total work programme of departments and an increase in the priority given to women in development issues.

111.   The Indonesian report indicates that, in spite of the institutional development for the promotion of the advancement of women, much still needs to be done, by modifying the broader institutional context.

112.   During the period of transition of Eastern and Central European countries to market economies, old national mechanisms for the status of women have disintegrated. After the establishment of new Governments, non-governmental agencies have been set up to take responsibility for the

status of women. But the old structures have not yet been dismantled in many countries.

113.   Women's organizations have taken action without official support. Although they are achieving results in many countries, no national machinery exists to deal with issues relating to the status of women.

114.   The national committees set up in preparation of the World Conference might be transformed into national machineries.

115.   During the period of socio-economic and political restructuring, all of the Central and Eastern European countries have changed their policy on women. State policies on women and the family have been formulated in the Czech Republic, Hungary, the Russian Federation and Slovakia.

116.   According to the national reports, new Governments focus on policies concerning the reproductive role of women (health, child-care facilities and maternity leave). Public policies on women should also deal with equal rights, employment, decision-making and cooperation, and support to women's organizations.

117.   In some of the countries in transition, the governmental equal rights agencies have been replaced by women's caucuses in parliaments and women's organizations. There is a lack of financial support for these activities. In Poland the office of the government plenipotentiary for women's affairs, established in 1986 by the Council of Ministers in implementation of the Nairobi Forward-looking Strategies, is the only national machinery for the advancement of women in Central and Eastern Europe. It adopted a plan of action to be implemented in the period 1987-1990, with central and local organs of the administration responsible for its implementation. The national report notes that in Poland the women's movement and the Parliamentary Caucus of Women are leading the process.

118.   The 1994 national report from Bulgaria explains that, in view of the economic and financial situation, the priorities of the Government since 1989 have been structural reform of the economy and the alleviation of its negative effects on the population, especially socially vulnerable groups (old people and invalids). There is no special policy with respect to safeguarding the rights of women, owing to financial constraints. It is not realistic to

finance programmes entirely devoted to the problems of women, although there is an understanding of the need for such programmes, especially with respect to the most vulnerable categories of women, such as the elderly, rural women and young women. The report notes the need for support from international governmental and non-governmental organizations.

3. Conclusions

119.   The following conclusions can be drawn from the national reports on the success of national machinery:

(a)   The mechanisms should have a clear identity and a well-formulated mandate which defines the independent role of the mechanism in policy development and implementation as well as in monitoring and influencing policy-making in the administration from a gender perspective;

(b)   The mechanism should have political support from the highest level and a place in the hierarchy of the organization;

(c)   The national machinery should be able to mobilize and maintain adequate financial and human resources;

(d)   It should be in the position to collect relevant information on policy-making processes and it should have this information at an early stage in order to have an impact on policy development;

(e)   The staff should be recruited on the basis of their expertise on women's issues and in applying gender-impact analyses to any policy;

(f)   The machinery should cooperate with non-governmental organizations and women's groups, taking into account the independent role of non-governmental organizations vis-à-vis government responsibilities.

If the machineries for advancement of women are a complex of different bodies, the respective functions and responsibilities should be clearly defined and their mutual cooperation ensured. The national machinery should liaise with focal points in all relevant government departments and agencies.

Notes

1/   Report of the World Conference to Review and Appraise the Achievements of the United Nations Decade for Women: Equality, Development and Peace, Nairobi, 15-26 July 1985 (United Nations publication, Sales No. E.85.IV.10), chap. I, sect. A, paras. 15, 78-79, 86-92, 107, 116, 126, 313, 315, 356, 358 and 365.

2/   EGM/EPPDM/1989/1, para. 5.

3/   Ibid., para. 6.

4/   Economic and Social Council resolution 1990/15, annex, para. 7.

5/   General Assembly resolution 34/180, annex.

6/   "Equality: Equality in political participation and decision-making" (E/CN.6/1990/2); "Peace: Equal participation in all efforts to promote international cooperation, peace and disarmament" (E.CN.6/1992/10); Women in Politics and Decision-making in the Late Twentieth Century (United Nations publication, Sales No. E.91.IV.3).

7/   FAO, Report of the Inter-agency Consultation on Statistics and Data Bases on Gender in Agriculture and Rural Development, Rome, 24-26 September 1991, pp. 12-13.

8/   Directory on National Machineries for Monitoring and Improving the Status of Women (United Nations, Vienna, 1989).

9/   United Nations, Vienna, 1990.

10/   Directory of National Machineries for the Advancement of Women (United Nations, Vienna, 1991).

11/   Ibid. (United Nations, Vienna, 1993).

I. Lack of awareness of and commitment to internationally and nationally recognized women's human rights

1.   The Charter of the United Nations includes, among its basic objectives and principles, the achievement of international cooperation in promoting and encouraging respect for human rights and fundamental freedoms for all without distinction as to sex (Article 1, paragraph 3, and Article 55 (c)). The Preamble to the Charter stresses the determination to reaffirm faith in the equal rights of men and women. In the Universal Declaration of Human Rights, 1/ from which most nations derive guiding principles on rights and fundamental freedoms, the United Nations emphatically condemns discrimination on the basis of sex and clearly states that "All are equal before the law and are entitled without any discrimination to equal protection of the law. All are entitled to equal protection against any discrimination in violation of this Declaration and against any incitement to such discrimination" (article 7).

2.   These principles were applied in the International Covenant on Civil and Political Rights and its Optional Protocol 2/ and provide a legal basis for communications from individuals claiming to be victims of violations of any of the rights set forth in the Covenant as well as in the Covenant on Economic, Social and Cultural Rights, both adopted in 1966.

3.   Of all the human rights conventions, the Convention on the Elimination of All Forms of Discrimination against Women 3/ constitutes the most explicit statement of women's human rights. The Convention was the culmination of more than 30 years of work by the Commission on the Status of Women. In addition to constituting an international bill of rights

for women, codifying those rights that already existed in international law, it sets an agenda for action to provide for full enjoyment of those rights. It obliges the States parties to "pursue by all appropriate means and without delay a policy of eliminating discrimination against women" (article 2). It reaffirms the equality of human rights for women and men in all spheres of life (society and the family), obliges a State party to take action against the social causes of women's inequality, and calls for the removal of laws, stereotypes, practices and prejudices that impair women's well-being and their right to equality.

4.   A good indicator of the extent to which *de jure* discrimination has been addressed is the number of States that have accepted the Convention as a binding obligation. Just prior to the World Conference to Review and Appraise the Achievements of the United Nations Decade for Women, which was held in Nairobi in 1985, there were only 39 States parties to the Convention. As of June 1990, the time of the first review and appraisal of the Nairobi Forward-looking Strategies for the Advancement of Women, the number had increased to 102. As of January 1995, the Convention had 139 States parties. Most of these States have accepted their obligations unconditionally, although 29 States have entered substantive reservations, some based on religious law and cultural tradition.

5.   The Economic and Social Council adopted the following conclusions and recommendations arising from the first review and appraisal of the Nairobi Forward-looking Strategies for the Advancement of Women (Council resolution 1990/15):

> "3.   The interdependence of the different political and social sectors on the one hand, and the legal and social situation on the other, needs to be recognized. However, *de jure* equality constitutes only the first step towards *de facto* equality. Most countries have enacted legal measures to ensure that women have equal opportunities before the law, that is *de jure* equality. But *de facto* as well as *de jure* discrimination continues and visible political and economic commitment by Governments and non-governmental organizations will be required to eliminate it. One obstacle to eliminating *de facto* discrimination is that most women and men are not aware of women's legal rights or do not fully understand the legal and administrative systems through which they must be implemented. Some affirmative action mea sures require legal bases which still need to be created.
>
> "**Recommendation I.** Governments, in association with women's organizations and other non-governmental organizations, should take steps on a priority

basis to inform women and men of women's rights under international conventions and national law and to prepare or continue campaigns for women's 'legal literacy' using formal and non-formal education at all levels, the mass media and other means; efforts to this end should have been undertaken by 1994.

"The work of the Committee on the Elimination of Discrimination against Women should be widely publicized through forms of communication that are accessible to women in order to make them aware of their rights. National reports to the Committee should be widely disseminated within the respective countries and discussed by governmental and non-governmental organizations. Organizations of the United Nations system, particularly the International Labour Organization and the United Nations Educational, Scientific and Cultural Organization, should be requested to examine national experience in promoting legal literacy with a view to assisting Governments, non-governmental organizations and women's movements in mounting successful campaigns.

"**Recommendation II**. Governments should take steps to put legal equality into practice, including measures to provide a link between individual women and official machinery such as the establishment of offices of ombudsmen or similar systems. Where possible, access to legal redress by collective and individual legal action by national machinery and non-governmental organizations should be facilitated in order to assist women in ensuring the implementation of their rights."

6.   The World Conference on Human Rights (1993) explicitly recognized that "the human rights of women and of the girl-child are an inalienable, integral and indivisible part of universal human rights" and that "gender-based violence and all forms of sexual harassment and exploitation, including those resulting from cultural prejudice and international trafficking, are incompatible with the dignity and worth of the human person and must be eliminated". 4/ Thus, the Conference rejected any limitation of international standards of human rights for women on the grounds of conflict with culture, tradition or religion.

7.   The Conference also took a position against violations of the human rights of women in armed conflicts and considered, *inter alia*, that systematic rape, sexual slavery or forced pregnancy are violations of the fundamental principles of international human rights and humanitarian law.

8.   Other achievements of the Conference included the following:

(a)   A call for universal ratification of the Convention on the Elimination of All Forms of Discrimination against Women by the year 2000 and the withdrawal of reservations that are incompatible with the object and purpose of the Convention;

(b)   The establishment of a focal point for women in the Centre for Human Rights and a request for strengthening the structures and activities of the United Nations related to the human rights of women;

(c)   A suggestion to appoint a special rapporteur on violence against women;

(d)   A suggestion to elaborate an optional protocol to the Convention providing for individual complaints.

9.   National reports and other information suggest that there is continuing progress towards achieving de jure equality. However, the extent to which this translates into de facto enjoyment of this right is related to the seriousness and commitment with which States adhere to the provisions of laws and the attitudes of the judiciary, law enforcement officials and society at large, compounded in many instances by a lack of well-established mechanisms for monitoring implementation. Other sections of the review and appraisal examine the extent to which de facto enjoyment of equal rights has been achieved. This section concentrates on de jure equality.

1. Progress towards *de jure* equality

10.   Many countries report that they have taken steps to provide legal equality and the machinery necessary to implement it. The enactment of equal opportunity laws, for example, is reported by many countries. In addition, most States report that equality between women and men is guaranteed by their constitutions or basic laws even where it is not specifically stated. A number of countries report that they have further reinforced the constitutional guarantees by enacting separate equality laws or amending civil, penal and family codes to ensure that women are accorded equal rights, protection, equal access and opportunities in education, employment, health and matrimonial and family matters under statutory laws. These countries report that the reforms have enabled many women to assert their rights.

11.   Many countries indicate that they have made efforts to adjust and incorporate the provisions of the Convention on the Elimination of All Forms of Discrimination against Women into their laws. However, one country reports that "many United Nations conventions are yet to be thoroughly perused by the average person in any home in any country and the

essence of their intentions absorbed ... The reality is that it is important for women to know why the Convention was formulated and how it is supposed to assist in improving their situation. It is also important for women to know how the Convention links with the laws of the country and the implications of the Convention for local legislation so that they can lobby". A problem, however, remains when women lack interest, knowledge and awareness or lack motivation and the means to use laws effectively.

12.   Several reports suggest an unwillingness on the part of women to assert their claims and rights. In Asia and Africa in particular, some reports indicate that women are still fearful, reluctant, not willing or not comfortable in seeking to exercise their rights through litigation, especially in family disagreements.

13.   Moreover, even when anti-discrimination laws exist, their application may be clouded by dual legal systems that recognize the applicability of discriminatory traditional law. For example, some multi-ethnic, multi-religion countries have dualistic legal systems that permit sex discrimination, especially in areas of personal and family law. In many countries, the values of society are still strongly influenced by customary or religious practices and regulations that are sometimes in direct conflict with international human rights standards, as well as with national statutory laws where civil law differs from the customary or religious practices.

14.   Some countries with multiple legal systems report that they have embarked on a review of their statutes in order to harmonize their civil codes with the traditional values that are the basis of customary practices. Other countries report on ongoing steps to repeal or amend discriminatory laws and practices against indigenous people, ethnic minorities or particular groups or classes of the population that have been found to subject women in these groups to double discrimination.

15.   Several countries report having made commitments to achieve uniform penal and civil codes applicable to all, regardless of sex, and to ensure the full development and achievement of citizenship for all women so that women may exercise and enjoy all other forms of human rights and fundamental freedoms on a basis of equality with men.

16.   However, many countries, particularly in Africa, Asia and the Pacific,

report that their domestic laws, policies and practices have not yet incorporated or do not reflect all international norms and standards. The reasons for this vary and include a lack of political commitment; an unresponsive legal system; attitudinal obstacles to the incorporation of international standards when these are believed to be in conflict with religious, cultural or customary practices; the absence of effective domestic groups that can lobby for change effectively and without fear of intimidation; and an absence of effective enforcement mechanisms even where legislation exists.

17.   A number of countries report collective action by women to obtain their rights, including individual and class action suits through the courts in order to establish legal precedents through court decisions, often using advocates who take on cases so that the courts can quickly establish constitutional guarantees. Several countries report the use of this type of collective action at national levels, especially in the area of domestic violence and such crimes as trafficking for prostitution.

18.   A number of countries in Africa and Asia report that there has been collaboration with non-governmental organizations and donor countries in education for legal literacy. The approaches differ from country to country. Some indicated that they focused on the need to educate the general population. Many countries stated that general literacy in the overall population is, as one country put it, a "major catalyst in developing legal literacy; whereas, formal proclamation of rights by itself does not amount to a force that can change the basic power relations of the society".

19.   Nevertheless, several countries state that in order to have a more sustainable impact, legal literacy should include developing an awareness of rights in general and of existing national statutory rights in particular, since penal and civil codes protect everyone. One country recommends mobilization for a change in attitudes to encourage people to have faith in their legal rights and the process for ensuring those rights. Some countries report that they are focusing on raising women's consciousness and awareness of laws but are silent about the situation of the general public. However, others report on the establishment of legal aid centres, para-legal facilities or similar mechanisms where both women and men, as one country put it, "with minimal filing fee or without obstruction or cost to themselves, can seek assistance to obtain justice and redress under the laws in general".

20.   The reasons why women do not always exercise their rights effectively vary. Reports indicate that in some regions women are able to relate more easily to their basic problems, such as poverty, a lack of health services, a lack of child and family services and economic weaknesses, rather than to their legal rights as such.

21.   The broad concerns regarding family and matrimonial laws appear to be generally the same from region to region, although different reports emphasize the specific issues that are the most problematic and important in their particular context. For example, payment of alimony and child support and sharing of family domestic chores and responsibility feature prominently in the reports of some countries, while others emphasize economic and political rights and ownership rights to land and property. Paid labour rights, health services, social security and credit rights for all women are major concerns everywhere. Several countries also state that the achievement of certain basic human rights, such as the right to economic development and equality in education, which are lacking in their countries, will automatically lead to the achievement of other basic human rights by women as well as men.

2. Enforcement mechanisms

22.   In the implementation of human rights instruments, it is the obligation of States parties not only to respect individual freedoms and rights but also to ensure access to those rights. States are expected to create the conditions that will enable their people to exercise their rights freely in all aspects of life.

23.   While only a few countries report that they have established offices of ombudsmen or similar mechanisms for access to rights, other countries report the establishment of councils or tribunals that deal with disputes of all types. Still others report that they have created law reform commissions, task forces or similar bodies to study existing laws and practices with the aim of enacting new laws, harmonizing conflicting concepts or repealing discriminatory sections of existing laws and policies.

24.   The judicial system of any country is an important enforcement mechanism. By providing fair interpretation of the laws they can help to achieve the intent of those laws. In order to demonstrate commitment to the

principles of equality and gender neutrality, States should allow both women and men with legal capacity to sit in judgement of the laws of the land in which they live.

25.   The number of women in the legal profession and judiciary system has increased in many countries. The appointment of women to serve as magistrates or judges has increased steadily, although progress has been slow in many regions and different trends are apparent. Africa and the Caribbean show higher numbers of female judges and magistrates than do other regions of the world. States whose legal system is based on Islamic law have fewer female judges and magistrates.

3. Problematic areas

26.   Women's enjoyment of their human rights is particularly problematic in certain areas. One of these is the general area of violence, which has been   described   in   detail   in   another   section   this   report (E/CN.3/1995/7/Add.4). Others include political rights, reproductive rights, economic rights and rights within the family.

Political rights and nationality

27.   Political rights and the right to nationality have been secured by United Nations conventions that predate the Convention on the Elimination of All Forms of Discrimination against Women. However, their enjoyment still remains a problem in some countries.

28.   The question of nationality or citizenship combines with the issue of legal capacity in terms of women's rights to participate equally with men in public and civic activities and family relations. Legal capacity affects the right to enter into contracts, and without such capacity women are deprived of many opportunities.

29.   In some countries women's rights as citizens are legally limited by restrictions on their right to vote or their right to be elected to public office. Women are sometimes denied the right to pass their citizenship on to their children because a child's nationality is assumed to be that of the father. While several countries report that women are now being allowed to acquire and retain or change their nationality, some countries report that, in practice, nationality is still frequently dictated by the husband's nationality and

domicile. A woman who chooses to maintain or acquire a nationality different from that of her husband may find that her rights within the family, and in particular over her children, are restricted.

30.   The right of a woman to choose her nationality has become particularly important for women in view of the increase in international migration and in single parenthood. The report of the Economic Commission for Latin America and the Caribbean (ECLAC), in particular, emphasizes the growing importance of full citizenship for women as independent individuals. Non-sexist education and equality between women and men are considered important prerequisites for exercising full citizenship in a free society. However, some countries report that the issue of nationality or citizenship does not feature prominently because of the rural nature of the population.

Reproductive rights

31.   The issue of women's reproductive rights figured prominently at the International Conference on Population and Development. It is an area that remains problematic. At its centre is the norm set out in the Convention on the Elimination of All Forms of Discrimination against Women that women and men have the right to freely choose the number and spacing of their children.

32.   Evidence shows that a combination of factors is necessary for women to exercise their reproductive rights: appropriate legal provisions, self-reliance, literacy, reasonable economic independence and the availability of health and family planning services, means and information. These factors give a woman the ability to assert her independence in any relationship and in making decisions about whether to have children and on their number and spacing. A Government that respects and wishes to promote these rights needs to take steps to establish the conditions that allow women to exercise their reproductive rights.

Economic rights

33.   The Nairobi Forward-looking Strategies called for reforms to guarantee women's constitutional and legal rights in terms of access to land and other means of production and to ensure that women can control the products of their labour and income and enjoy the benefits of agricultural inputs,

research, training, credits and other infrastructural facilities.

34.   Article 15 of the Convention on the Elimination of All Forms of Discrimination against Women accords women equality with men before the law and generally in civil codes. The assumption was that in matters of legal capacity women would achieve identical rights to those of men and the same opportunities to exercise that capacity. However, in reality, even among States parties to the Convention, it is reported that women are yet to enjoy or exercise such equal rights without any trace of discrimination. There are exceptions - in Europe, studies show that more women than men own land. In entering into contracts or administering their ownership or property rights, many women from all parts of the world still face a variety of hidden obstacles, even where equal rights exist. As one country explained in its report, in "customary patrilineal societies, a woman does not have rights to land for fear that she could pass it to her husband's family". Some countries report that although customary laws gave women usufructuary rights that could not be tampered with by the husband, when land registration acts were introduced to cover clan lands, men took legal possession by registering only themselves as the owners in the title deeds to family land.

35.   There is a basic difference in the situation of women in the countries that recognize de jure equality between women and men in their statutory laws, even if they are not implemented in practice, and those countries that deny this principle in their legislation. Some countries report that in the majority of cases, women do not have the opportunity to exercise legal capacity on the same basis as men, even where the laws exist, because of cultural and customary practices. In practice, many women find it difficult to enter into a contract or receive credit from banks without a guarantee from husbands or male relatives. In some countries where legal capacity is not an obstacle, banks nevertheless charge women higher interest rates, thus discouraging them from applying for loans.

36.   Several national reports indicate that for many women the legal autonomy envisaged in the Nairobi Forward-looking Strategies has not been achieved in every aspect of life. In some States, although laws exist to protect rights to credit, in practice policies contradict the intent of the law. However, many reports indicate that more women are now self-employed or are entrepreneurs and thus play an important role in their countries' economies, and

that the success of women is at least comparable to that of men. Nevertheless, despite efforts to ensure equal access to credit, many women are still unable to obtain loans or credit from either government facilities or commercial banks because they lack the security or collateral required. In some cases, women are required to put up more collateral and pay higher rates of interest than men.

Basic rights within the family

37.   While specific legal provisions and policies that influence family matters vary from country to country, family law and civil law relating to such issues as rights to marriage, divorce, custody, guardianship and maintenance, as well as those matters related to inheritance and to control and ownership of property, remain problematic. Several countries report that they invoke family law before labour, criminal and commercial laws in cases involving women. One country reported that although laws in most areas have been made equal on the basis of sex, this has not been the case in family law.

38.   Other countries report that progress in changing discriminatory structures remains slowest in the area of family law. One country reports that the collective matrilineal and patrilineal family norms not only characterize the typical family structure but also dictate societal conduct. Non-conformity with traditional socio-cultural expectations, beliefs and norms is discouraged and is punished through social ostracism.

39.   Several countries report the enactment of new family codes or marriage and divorce laws that provide for equal treatment of men and women under statutory laws as they enter into marriage or seek divorce. However, many countries, particularly those governed by the Islamic Sharia and others that choose to follow non-secular laws, still report that the grounds for divorce for men can be different from the grounds for divorce for women. In some countries, in an effort to discourage polygamy and to safeguard young people from forced and early marriages, all marriage must now be registered, regardless of the system under which they were contracted. Many countries have also revised their minimum-age laws for marriages, although the age for girls tends to be lower than that for boys, averaging between 15 and 18 years of age in many countries. Freedom in the choice of a marriage partner is also reportedly a growing trend in many countries.

40.　　Several countries that originally had discriminatory laws have enacted progressive family codes. However, family law in many countries in Africa, Asia and the Pacific and Western Asia, in particular, still reflects the complex legal history of these countries.

41.　　As stated in one report, "it should not be forgotten that the new family code is intended as a compromise between traditional values, religious liberties and principles of secularism. This delicate compromise position clearly explains why the code, which in some ways liberates women, still contains many discriminatory measures against them and even appears in certain of its provisions to strengthen patriarchal power. Thus, although it introduces consent to marriage, abrogates (forced) reproduction and banishes levirate (the practice of wife inheritance), it has not abolished polygamy, the bride price, the unequal apportionment of inheritance, the choice of men as head of family and the predominance of paternal authority."

42.　　In terms of inheritance and property ownership, many countries report that women are considered secondary in the application of the law. This situation is especially apparent among countries where customary laws and religious dictates concerning inheritance and property rights have the same weight as statutory succession acts. In most traditions and cultures, excepting matrilineal societies, inheritance rights have favoured male heirs. Inheritance for widows in many cultures does not even reflect the principle of equal ownership of property acquired during marriage, "especially so in cases where the contribution was of a non-financial kind by the wife, although enabling the husband to earn an income and increase the assets". Under certain legal systems, however, family property acquired during the course of a marriage is divided equally.

43.　　Some countries report that they have specifically enacted new family codes that have led to the recognition of the economic value of domestic work. Several others, particularly from the African region, report that an illustration of customs influencing discrimination against women can be found in the laws concerning marriage, divorce, property rights and inheritance.

44.　　Women have always had a limited right to property ownership in many parts of the world, albeit to property held before or after marriage. It is reported that there are instances where a woman can receive property either by gift or inheritance but still not have the right to pass it on. In some societies or among orthodox religious groups, despite secular governance, property owned by males preferably devolves onto the male lineal descendants, while property owned by females is shared equally by widowers, sons and daughters. In other countries, inheritance depends on which law is invoked first and whether it is contested; the first procedure chosen prevails, unless contested. The courts must then decide on the conflicting claims according to the individual case.

Notes

1/   General Assembly resolution 217 A (III).

2/   General Assembly resolution 2200 A (XXI).

3/   General Assembly resolution 34/180.

4/   A/CONF.157/24 (Part I), chap. III, para. 18.

J. Insufficient use of mass media to promote women's positive contributions to society

1.   The many and complex issues that are raised in the phrase "women, media and development" are finally being recognized as central elements of local, national and international agendas of research, policy-making, funding and other action. This recognition reflects the immense burgeoning of women's own media-related activities world wide, the impact of feminist theory and research in gender and communications, and recognition of gender by international movements. The Nairobi Forward-Looking Strategies for the Advancement of Women said very little about media and communication. In resolution 1990/15, regarding the review and appraisal of the Strategies, the Economic and Social Council mentioned media only in the context of elimination of violence against women, including the recommendation, in paragraph 23, that:

> "The United Nations system, Governments and non-governmental organizations should study the relationship between the portrayal of violence against women in the media and violence against women in the family and society, including possible effects of new transnational transmission technologies."

In the mid 1990s, it is clear that the broad issues inherent in the concept of women, media and development demand and require serious analytic attention and policy support.

2.   Media have been established in different parts of the world at different times, in different order, and are used differently within various social and cultural milieux. Commercial television delivery to the audience in the United States of America, familiar with the form since the 1950s and now

watching an average of six hours a day, cannot be seen as the same phenom-enon as the satellite-based television delivery now reaching some rural Asian populations, as yet unused to the form and just beginning to integrate it into their lives. Video use, which implies mainly time-shifting and ease of access for Europeans and North Americans, may have political overtones in more regulated cultural environments where video recorders and satellite dishes have been banned. Different political contexts and cultural milieux, the structures of media ownership and control, including tendencies towards concentration and globalization, differing legal and regulatory environ-ments, and the availability of foreign cultural products all affect the nature of media provision. For women particularly, the impact and patterns of use around various media differ depending on the pre-existing cultural pat-terns, especially women's access to public space and participation in the public sphere. Thus, many crucial contextual differences require detailed investigation.

3.   Media effects are also a contentious issue. Scholars debate how media texts circulate, with arguments ranging from the powerful hypoder-mic needle image of direct effect - what the media shows is what the audi-ence absorbs - to a cultural studies approach which suggests that audiences are active and "read" media products differently, depending on their social and cultural locations. These arguments about cultural politics have impli-cations for our understanding of women's media involvement and the nature of our concerns.

4.   While globally, not everyone yet has access to mass media, everyone does have forms of cultural expression. There are oral traditions of story-telling, poetry and recitation; performance traditions of drama, dance, puppetry, melas (fairs), jatras (cultural walks) and cultural rituals; traditions of music and song etc. These forms can be used with great effec-tiveness, particularly by women to tell their own stories and histories, and should be taken on board in development-oriented campaigns by Governments, non-governmental organizations and others.

5.   A focus on women and empowerment through communication leads to broader issues of women's participation in the development process; 1/ of access to economic resources 2/ and of political influence. 3/ As Heyzer says, 4/ it is increasingly recognized that "the women/media relation-

ship can only be analyzed, and successful strategies for changing it can only be developed, if we take into account the entire cultural, political and ideological spectrum and study the economic context in which this particular relationship (between women and the media) is created and takes shape."

6.   It must be acknowledged that women are the cornerstone of development and that the involvement of women in the planning and process of development has immense ripple effects. Women do not live alone but rather in families, tribes and communities, connected to many social networks and participants in civil society. Women's knowledge and achievements help everyone. Women are concerned with the basic needs of society, with the creation of life and the preservation of the environment. While the most urgent issues of poverty, illiteracy and malnutrition continue to confront developing countries, a broader framework suggests that much remains to be done in the economic, political and cultural spheres everywhere. Women are redefining development.

1. Measures of equity and empowerment: two kinds of representation

7.   The nexus women/media/development is of immense complexity. A large body of literature documents the many different kinds of involvement women have with the media. Unlike the provision of formal education, it is harder to see media provision as a simple, self-evident good. Given the hugely varying contexts of women's involvement with the media and the many issues involved, the criteria for judging good practice need to be examined. Two useful approaches to the situation of women have been labelled the "equity" and the "empowerment" approaches. The former argues a human rights position and supports a 50 per cent solution to certain areas of women's social practice - for example, women's access to media employment. This may be of greatest significance in industrialized societies with comparatively open political cultures and a history of women's rights, although this kind of argument is increasing world wide. The latter approach tends to suggest that women's self-defining activities - the development of alternative media, women's networks, for example - are a good thing in themselves and that simple equity may be a thin victory. This may be of greater significance in contexts of developing economies, of continuing cultural barriers to the

promotion of women's status and of political environments in which human rights are problematic.

8.   These two approaches reflect huge debates within global feminist movements, and each has its pitfalls. Mattelart 5/ has suggested that the media spectacle of egalitarianism, women in high visibility in mass media, actually invokes women as the "strongest redeemers of patriarchy". The tack towards difference supports arguments about women's unique contributions, women's voices and their perspectives on all issues. Yet concerns have been raised about the marginalization of women's voices and, consequently, of their real social and political impact. Perhaps the more quantitative orientation towards equity needs to be supplemented by the more qualitative orientation of empowerment, mutually necessary and supportive.

9.   These two approaches also reflect the double meaning of representation. 6/ On the one hand, there is the notion of speaking out in political and social representation. On the other hand, there are the discourses and images of gender - how women are represented in mediated texts and cultural products. In both kinds of representation, the concern is that women represent themselves and be appropriately represented.

2. Kinds of systems and levels of analysis

10.   An analysis of women, media and development has to take into consideration the different "levels" at which media can function, of which the three most significant are the local, the national and the global.

11.   The cultural and regulatory framework for most media activity and development planning is most often dictated by government policy and, mainly, political considerations. The State's role as constructor of development priorities and allocator of resources needs to be interrogated in terms of gender-friendliness; definitions of national identity and development priorities have often neglected to include women's needs. Commercial, State and public-service broadcasting, none the less, may have different impacts on gender. A commercial media system may support certain kinds of freedoms, but the market does not necessarily reflect national developmental or women's needs.

12.   The local, or community or grass-roots, level is where most alternative or participatory media projects occur. Here questions need to be raised concerning their influence in wider social and political arenas, the numbers involved and the range of impact.

13.   At the global level, the ever more complex flows of media products and the diffusion of communications technologies are equally cause for concern, but they also offer promise for women. This is where issues about the role of the global international organizations, non-governmental organizations, regulatory frameworks, structural adjustment programmes and the General Agreement on Tariffs and Trade (GATT) and their impact on development, media and women need to be raised.

3. Positive contributions of the media to women and development
14.   The significance of media for women and development are multiple:

(a)   Media are increasingly important social institutions, act as definers of meaning and play a role in determining and maintaining cultural definitions of gender and sex roles. In a global media environment, there are concerns about conglomerization, monopolization and disempowerment as well as about the impact of foreign definitions of sex and gender systems on differing cultural milieux;

(b)   Media can help to set the social and political agendas of the crucial issues of the day, define the salience of social and political issues, focus attention on issues of significance to women, and include women's voices and perspectives - or not do so. Media can foster debates on development and on human rights, including women's rights, and the position of women in society -or not;

(c)   Media could provide a broad range of representations of women, reflecting the broad range of activities women actually perform in every society, including positive role-models: women experts, professionals, careers in both rural and urban settings;

(d)   Media can provide information and understanding about the world, key resources and aids to empowerment. That information and understanding must be gender-sensitive and gender-inclusive;

(e)   Media are in themselves potential sources of wealth-creation and employment opportunities. Women-owned and women-managed media structures could provide employment opportunities for women, as well as producing different content;

(f)   Media can provide information and strategies towards wealth-creation and the elimination of poverty; media can raise the level of public discussion about women's roles and contributions to development;

(g)   Media can be used in informal and non-formal education, health and other development campaigns, involving women and targeted towards them;

(h)   Media are a resource for women to disseminate alternative kinds of information, imagery and analysis, and to build networks.

15.   In this view, media are ends in themselves, influential sites of representation where gender sensitivity and new imagery, women's creativity and women's voices can be presented. Media are also means to other ends, vehicles to facilitate public debate about broader social issues and concerns - the eradication of poverty, sustaining the environment, health, peace - about which women have a great deal to say.

4. Change over the past two decades: mainstream and alternative media
16.   One of the key things that needs to be said is that there has been great change, much of it positive, in the condition of women and media over the past 20 years, since the beginning of International Women's Decade (1975-1985). Women are active in every cultural and media practice, from the most local and indigenous of musical and theatrical forms (community theatre, video and film collectives) to radio and television broadcasting, magazine and journal publishing, news-gathering and networking at national, regional and international levels. "Most regions have seen a steady growth in the domain of women's alternative media, as well as in that of women's associations and networks. Almost everywhere an increase in the number of women working in mainstream media has been recorded. But the power to develop media policy, and to determine the nature and shape of media content, continue to elude women". 7/

a.   *Mainstream media*

17.   In regard to mainstream media, research has had two major foci: one analyses the relative position of women within media organizations and other relevant organizations to examine the career paths and access opportunities for women. The other examines the images and manner of representation of gender in mediated content.

18.   There is an acute lack of empirical data, even from Western industrial societies, concerning the situation of women in the media. Information on gender trends in employment within the media is equally patchy, data are seldom comparable, and definitions concerning categories of employment are not constant. Figures or tables contain estimations, compiled from several national and regional reports, and are merely indicative, rather than substantive.

19.   Notwithstanding these caveats, there nonetheless appears to be a growing disjunction between the number of women in media training compared with the actual number employed in the media. Broad data on women and men from the UNESCO Communication Division databases on selected communication training institutions suggests that in four regions (Africa, Europe, North America, South America), in the institutions surveyed, women constitute half or more of those in media training. Even in Asia, which showed the lowest rate, the female figure is around 30 per cent.

20.   Yet when that figure is compared with the figures for gender distribution in media employment (broadcast organizations only), the highest figure for female employment as a percentage of the total number of employed persons, without taking into account the type of function or level of position, is just over 30 per cent in North America (the highest figure), dropping to less than 10 per cent in Asia.

21.   Even in developed countries and socio-political contexts where legislation for gender equality is more developed and women's movements are long-standing, evidence shows large gender differences in the kind of work undertaken and the levels reached. Thus, evidence from the European Commission, the United States 8/ and Australia shows female clustering in administrative jobs (secretariat, advertising, accountancy), low female presence in technical sectors, and an even lower presence in the top-ranking

managerial positions. Across Asia, the number of women joining media organizations has increased, yet they still constitute a low percentage of active journalists, often with the unexciting desk-bound beats; rarely have they progressed to managerial levels. Similarly women represent less than 20 per cent of the workers in African media industries. 9/ There appears to be some indication that women progress faster in broadcasting organizations than in print, an issue that would be worth systematic research.

22.   Equality between men and women in employment can be a useful goal, 10/ but one which needs to be put into effect at every level and in every area of media employment.

23.   However, it is by no means clear that increased numbers of women employed leads to improved representation. There is considerable evidence that an increasing number of women employed in the media does not of itself translate into qualitative differences in programming (as in the Republic of Korea) or a radically altered news agenda of priorities (Australia). For most of Asia, the growing numbers of women journalists "has not made a significant change in the content, style or presentation of information. News decisions are still made by men; even if news is increasingly reported and edited by women, the employment of women has not radically altered news agendas or priorities." 11/ In Asia, most of the "soft sections" - the weekend supplements, the health, culture and education beats - are now "almost exclusively the beats of women; defence, commerce and foreign affairs are still largely male strongholds, as are the editorships of most general and specialized publications". 12/ Although statistics for training programmes "reveal that women are increasingly opting for careers in communications, the past experience shows that this is rarely converted into a restructuring of the media agenda". 13/

24.   Mainstream media content does change, but slowly. Much of the concern is about stereotypes - that is, the narrowness of the range of representations of women in the media. For example, a broad critique of media representation in the Middle East is that it veers towards two narrow image-sets: "the conservative-traditional native woman, or the seductive foreign woman" and thus "the reality, complexity and multicultural dimension of gender roles is not addressed directly". 14/ Yet similar concerns are still raised about the skewed nature of women's representation in British

media after many years of the women's movement and growing gender consciousness. 15/ An essential concern is that media should reflect a range of realistic and diverse representations of the complexities and variations in women's lives.

25.   Another set of concerns in regard to popular culture is the sexually objectifying or violent gender imagery - women as objects of the male gaze, male sexuality, male violence. This is one of the most controversial areas of media content, even in the West where the debates about pornography and about the relationship between the effects of media representation of violence and real violence in society still rage. MediaWatch Canada is most explicit at arguing that such concerns are not about censorship but about human rights, including the right to be represented appropriately.

26.   In regard to information genres, such as news, there is another set of concerns, which is essentially "where are the women?" The answer does not reveal significant North/South differences. For example, Adagala 16/ argues that in African media, news is urban-centric and stories of women are rarely treated as newsworthy. Recent reports from both the United States 17/ and Britain 18/ suggest that women are still sidelined into stereotyped roles, with far fewer women than men presenting or appearing in factual programming.

27.   Some writers talk as though there are definable women's issues, while others ask whether media should try to reflect women's perspectives on all issues. The former position risks ghettoizing women's concerns and further devaluing the public saliency of many social issues. The latter reinforces the obvious but often-forgotten point that women are everywhere and that women's perspectives in regard to issues - political, economic and all others - must be heard.

28.   Thus in many regions, women still suffer both horizontal segregation, clustering in the lower-paying and lower-status jobs, and vertical segregation, clustering in women's assignments and "interests", not the "hard," socially significant, political and economic stories. 19/ This might partly be explained historically; having fewer women in the media has meant fewer opportunities to affect the organizational culture, management style, and actual media output. As more women gain access, the sheer weight of numbers

may begin to change things. However, we should not underestimate the lethargy inside organizations, the dynamics of socialization and conformity within them, and the sheer desire to maintain the status quo. Active policies of equal opportunity, gender equity at each and every level of media organization, the identification of "glass ceilings" and the reasons for them are needed. Since it is often the "invisible barriers" 20/ of attitudes, biases and presumptions that hinder women, assertiveness-training and support groups within organizations can help women feel less isolated and alienated and empower them to try to behave differently. Women's professional organizations, such as the International Association of Women in Radio and Television also provide international solidarity and support.

b.   Global communications

29.   Current writing stresses the need to examine the relation of women to the media in a global context - specifically, the increasing presence and potential impact of "transnational materials" on women. 21/ Transnational media conglomerates can undermine attempts to develop national cultural and media policies; national broadcast norms concerning nudity or the advertising of liquor on television are flaunted through satellite broadcasting even in some countries that forbid this kind of imaging.

30.   More problematic is that transnational media content works to further disempower the powerless. Groups - minorities, indigenous peoples and women -that have struggled for space to voice concerns, find that "with media structures changing and more sophisticated messaging entering even the hinterlands, the spaces constructed within mainstream and alternative media appear to be shrinking. The protection of constructed spaces will need the formulation of new strategies which can keep pace with technology." 22/ Advertising is problematic for the consumerist dynamics and sexualized imagery it promotes. Marketing managers are trying to mould all Asian markets into a single mass entity, using images of luxury supported by made-over European faces, a return to the conventional idea that sex sells.

31.   The spread of media transnationals has raised considerable international concern for some time, including issues of cultural imperialism and the threat to diversity through a homogenizing global media culture; it is only recently that women are being written into the international debate. Yet there are also counter-arguments about heterogenizing tendencies, new

sources of cultural and media production, and multiple flows, as well as the importance of creative "readings" and uses of media products. For example, anthropologists Abu Lughod 23/ and Davies 24/ show how Western videos are used playfully by women in some traditional societies to open up their private spheres to new images and ideas which patriarchal cultures still seek to control.

32.   Recent studies on women and new communication technologies stress similar central dynamics - notably, problems of unequal development which creates technology and information gaps between peoples and the transnationalization and increasing concentration of media processes. 25/ At the same time, women are very effective networkers. The development and the spread of new technologies allow women to build networks as never before, creating a new kind of global alternative public sphere.

c.   *Alternative media*

33.   One phenomenon that very strikingly reveals the changes that have occurred over the past decade is the immense increase in the number of alternative media run by women which are neither part of the State or public-service broadcasting systems nor part of mainstream commercial production. This increase can be documented in all regions of the world and for all forms of media. The initiatives cited below are indicative of the range of activities that exist but are by no means exhaustive. 26/

34.   The print media - newspapers, journals, magazines, newsletters, occasional monographs and leaflets - are perhaps the most established of the alternative media. Those with the widest circulation are in the United States and Europe, but there is significant development in the South. In 1990 the directory Third World Women's Publications listed over 300 titles. Some of the newer publications are Sister (Namibia), Speak (South Africa), Tamania Mars (Morocco) 27/ and Asmita (Nepal).

35.   Print activity raises questions about the appropriateness of a medium -print in a context of massive female illiteracy? - and thus about intended audiences. The experiences of the Tamania Mars collective, for example, raise concern about the potential for dialogue among women across class and urban/rural divides and bring to light the problems that exist in obtaining financial support, both national and international, for women's projects.

Tamania Mars demonstrates the many struggles involved in women's right to speak, argue, occupy public space and open up public debate, but also shows how much can be done and shared with others.

36.   Services supportive of a feminist press have emerged around the world -such as DepthNews in Asia; the Women's Feature Service, based in New Delhi; the Women's International News Gathering Service (WINGS), in the United States; and FEMPRESS, in Chile.

37.   One of the main questions surrounding these alternative news services is how much of their material actually circulates internationally and whether it ultimately makes its way into the mainstream press. Indeed, it can be asked whether their stories might become useful sources for broader discussion of the situation of women. Monitoring research on these issues would be useful.

38.   Although electronic media have been utilized by women in North and America and Europe for some time, they are increasingly available in other regions and put to many different uses. In local contexts - as with the use of video by the Self Employed Women's Association (SEWA) in India or the use of video and radio by indigenous women in Bolivia and other parts of Latin America - they help women define their roles, develop skills and dispel fears, remember, and build for the future. 28/ There is Radio Tierra in Chile and Feminist International Radio Endeavour (FIRE) in Costa Rica, which aims to give voice to those who never had one. The FIRE collective conceives of radio as a process of meeting, dialogue, and participation with other women and puts great store in the transformational power of women's personal testimonies. Other radio projects are oriented towards more specific development needs and empowering women to play a role in development planning.

39.   Radio remains one of the cheapest and most widespread forms of electronic media in the South, accessible to women and enjoyed by them. The Development through Radio project in Zimbabwe has created a unique way of communicating horizontally among communities, vertically up to responsible officials, and back down and out to the rural areas, yet its very success and its desire for expansion threaten to overburden the system in terms of demands on resources and personnel. As a model, it shows how to

foster participation of women within their communities and how to link media to development efforts, one of the few precise examples of the women/media/development nexus.

40.   Women are active in many other media also. Latin America is home to Cine Mujer, a collective of women film-makers, film being well-established and popular in many regions and all too often omitted from media analysis. Satellite EVE, based in Buenos Aires, has a national focus and aims specifically to stimulate women's creativity and ability to organize and use the power of the media for the construction of a more pluralistic and equitable society, using video, photography and investigative journalism as its main vehicles. WETV, being developed in Canada, intends to provide an alternative, global television service available on every continent through international satellite services, providing the first global access television service; it has a particular concern for women. The World Association of Community Radio Broadcasters (AMARC), in Montreal, is a network of new communicators who identify themselves with the construction of a new world order in communication and in society, and also support initiatives to support women's voices on the global airwaves.

41.   Women have shown themselves to be excellent networkers, living locally but thinking and acting globally, expressing solidarity across boundaries. Some of the networks with a focus specifically on women are the Caribbean Association for Feminist Research and Action (CAFRA), Trinidad and Tobago; the Women and Development Unit (WAND), Barbados; SISTERLINK, Australia; the Institute for Women's Studies in the Arab World (IWSAW), Lebanon; and FEMNET, Kenya.

42.   An organization such as the International Women's Tribune Center, New York, acts as a clearinghouse of information about women's activities globally. It also publishes The Tribune and manages Women, Ink., a marketing and distribution service funded by UNIFEM, which subsidizes distribution to the South by sale of publications in the North. Isis International, operating out of Santiago, Chile, and Manila, Philippines, was established as an non-governmental organization in 1974, as a women's information and communication service supporting the empowerment and full participation of women in development processes through the formation of networks and channels of communication and information. Isis has over

50,000 contacts in 150 countries, and it publishes Third World Women's Publications and Powerful Images (1986), which lists over 600 films, videos and slide shows by third-world women.

43.   There are regional networks like the Asia Network of Women in Communication (ANWIC), New Delhi, which publishes Impact and aims to mobilize Asian women, through communication, to achieve a more equitable and just social order, recognizing the diversity present in the region. There are networks operating within a religio-cultural milieu, like Women Living Under Muslim Law (WLUML), which publishes a quarterly news sheet as well as monographs on varied topics, including violence against women, reproductive rights and disenfranchisement. They have strong links with women's groups in the North (Women Against Fundamentalism in the United Kingdom) whose focus is often on the dilemmas of women in minority ethnic groups whose voices are often not heard by the dominant culture.

44.   Networking is facilitated by the use of the INTERNET and e-mail, with, for example, the Women and Environment Network (WEDNET) forging links between its Canadian base and African researchers, and Mujer a Mujer, a Mexican-based women's collective concerned with free trade and structural adjustment, coordinating projects in Mexico, Canada, the United States and Nicaragua. There are a variety of electronic bulletins: Women Envision, by Isis; the South East Asian Women's Information Project (SEA-WIN), in the Philippines; feminist list-servers and discussion groups, many under the aegis of the Association for Progressive Communication. Electronic mail can be cheaper than the telephone, faster than "snail mail", and many women's groups are providing training for women activists and organizations on computers and e-mail.

d.   Media monitoring

45.   Another key activity that has increased in the past decade is media monitoring. One example is MediaWatch, Canada, whose goal is to transform the media environment from one in which women are either invisible or stereotyped to one in which women are realistically portrayed and equitably represented in their physical, economic, racial and cultural diversity. Monitoring bodies focus on specific areas for media change, such as the use of non-sexist and "parallel" language, depicting women as experts, depicting

women realistically, depicting contemporary families, and seeking an end to the portrayal of women as sexual objects. They provide media-literacy training so as to empower audiences. Indeed, their materials could be used as the basis of clearly focused international activities to improve the media representation of women. Other organizations such as the World Association of Christian Communication (WACC), London, are also involved with media awareness training.

e.   Indigenous culture and performance

46.   One other area of alternative communicative activity that often gets overlooked but may be of special relevance for women is the use of and support for folk cultures and oral traditions in development-oriented and participatory communication projects - among them, dance in the United Republic of Tanzania 29/ and story-telling by African-American women. 30/ These are no-cost or low-cost, low-technology practices. They have the potential to ensure that one builds on the past and develops existing female knowledge and skills, creating dialogue and equal relations, and not separating media makers from media consumers. 31/ Indigenous modes of performance can also be used as a bulwark against cultural imperialism, encouraging women to take pride in their own authentic forms of expression.

47.   One women's collective set out to weave performative narratives out of ordinary women's lives. Their experience raised many issues about self-management; internal democracy - in particular, the emergent class distinctions among women; the financing of women's groups - in this case, from external sources; and the need to become self-sufficient.

f.   Blurring boundary between mainstream and
      alternative media

48.   With the rise of so much activity, discussion increasingly revolves around the distinction between mainstream versus alternative media. The once clear, even radical, distinction seems increasingly blurred. A feminist publishing house that struggled at one time to survive financially, build a reputation and an audience and find manuscripts may at another become so successful that the main factor that distinguishes it from any other publishing house is that it is run by women (albeit an achievement in itself). The firm Kali for Women, in New Delhi, started in 1984 to support writing by and about women in the third world, had to raise funds for each publishing

venture; by 1994, it was financially solvent. The Women's Press, Virago, and Sheba in the United Kingdom were created expressly to publish women's writing; now many mainstream publishers and booksellers do so as well. Recently, one of the first feminist book shops in London, SisterWrite, and one of the first feminist magazines, Spare Rib, ceased their activities, eclipsed by mainstream economics. The development of new commercially run cable channels for women in North America and Europe fit into mainstream patterns of organization and finance yet produce mainly for female audiences - an alternative in the mainstream?

g.   *Researching alternative media*

49.   One problem with the research done on alternative media is that much of it describes rather than analyses and can be too easily celebratory, without asking the difficult questions: who constitutes the audience for such media - that is, are they used only by women? are they internally democratic? do they represent the concerns of all subgroups (class, race, sexual preference) of women? do they aim to become redundant as the mainstream changes? do they remain marginal and serve to further marginalize the concerns of women? are they and the cultural practices in any one location translatable to others? do they really "empower" and, if so, what are the indicators of that empowerment? do they help women participate more fully in other areas of socio-economic, political and cultural life?

50.   Critical and analytic studies are needed to answer these questions. The International Association for Mass Communication Research (IAMCR) has a network of researchers interested in gender issues, and a new network of feminist researchers in media was formed at the Bangkok Conference in February 1994. More and better trained researchers can play a significant role in asking important questions and producing new evidence.

5. Women as audience and cultural consumers

51.   In the debate about women and the media, the lack of studies and information about women as audiences, women's cultural tastes and media habits, and what women like and want from the media is glaring. While audience studies and reception analysis have slowly become a more central part of the North American and European research landscape, "there are no documented data or literature on the topic of women or men in the audience of the media in the Arab World" 32/ and the same is true for other regions.

52.   It cannot simply be suggested that all images of women are negative or disliked by audiences. Nor can it be suggested that women always read media content "critically" or "resistively". It is generally agreed that women hold views both at variance with the media and in conformity with them. This indicates that further and more profound research is needed on what women do like and how media are used and fitted into daily routines and family lives.

6. What still impedes women's media empowerment?

53.   Many of the world's people have access to broadcast messages today, since radio and television, spurred by new systems of delivery such as satellites and cable, diffuse globally. But access to electronic media is by no means universal. Radio signals are globally available, and transistors have overcome any lack of infrastructure; nationally based television services have been established in all but the poorest and smallest of countries of the South. Yet actual audience access to television remains poor. For example, while the average number of television sets per 1,000 people is 783 in North America, the equivalent figure is only 13 in Africa, and 39 in developing countries as a whole. 33/ The provision of telecommunications, cinema seats and other kinds of media services are even more skewed globally in favour of the industrialized world.

54.   Access may be inhibited in various ways - by, for example, a lack of national infrastructure (transportation and electricity) or a lack of the financial resources to purchase receivers. Access to print media (books, newspapers, magazines) and electronic print (computer technologies, e-mail, INTERNET) is denied to many because of the on-going problem of illiteracy, where women have an unequal share of the burden. Literacy is increasingly seen as the key to development. While "the extensive primary education of the past few decades has boosted literacy rates, particularly among young people, there are still far more illiterate women than men in every part of the world. Moreover, illiteracy rates have fallen faster for men, so the literacy gap between men and women is still growing". 34/ UNESCO confirms this view: "Female literacy is a problem in most regions, and especially so in the least developed countries ... one out of every three adult females in the world today is illiterate, compared to only one out of five adult males". 35/ Access to and development of the media - and social develop-

ment as a whole - is predicated on far better access for girls and women to basic education, literacy programmes and other forms of technical training.

55.   Access to different forms of cultural consumption (cinema, theatre, opera, dance) is often denied through cost, difficulty of physical access, control over women's use of public space, and class-bound cultural habits. Access to media use is also denied through the sheer exigencies of time-consuming work, and lack of "leisure" time. Women often do an undue share of work.

56.   Access to resources is also gender-skewed. Resources means funds to buy equipment, pay for travel, pay for salaries (is too much of women's activity volunteer?). Women often lack the political and social clout or the well-oiled networks needed to raise funds. Lack of funds then impedes access to other resources, such as information. The potential use of INTERNET to build global movements of solidarity breaks down when the actual grass-roots groups cannot afford the equipment or the sign-up costs.

57.   Women's media activities are also determined by broader contexts, such as the scope of political democracy. Globally, many nations have embarked on difficult transitions to democracy. For many this has been the occasion to rethink their legal frameworks and structures and to formulate broader media laws, including the right of expression, as in article XIX of the Universal Declaration of Human Rights. In that work, it is vital for gender equity and the rights of women to be recognized from the beginning. As the Fiji Women's Rights Movement proclaims, democracy without women's human rights is not democracy.

58.   A major concern must also be that, if a tyranny of political elites is overthrown, it must not be replaced by the more anonymous but all-pervasive tyranny of the global market. Bahsin, 36/ among others, warns about the trends toward centralization, monopolization, globalization, and the dispersal of power from, for example, national radio/television organizations to global media moguls. Here women should make common cause with other international organizations and movements concerned with national media policy-making and cultural heritage, and develop inventive strategies of audience response.

59.   In parts of Africa, the Middle East and Central Asia, as elsewhere, it is sometimes traditional culture and traditional concepts of patriarchy that inhibit the free movement and self-expression of women. Across Asia, for example, "the portrayal of women and the representation of feminine values and attitudes towards women in media is governed by indigenous social norms ... cultural and religious traditions have governed the imaging of women by mass media in the region. The traditions have also influenced the participation of women in the industry as well as patterns of their social behaviour". 37/ Tamania Mars, the networks of Women Living Under Muslim Laws, and Women Against Fundamentalism are all involved in ongoing struggles to gain recognition for broad human rights movements and specifically to secure for women the right to speak and participate in the public sphere.

60.   Feminist theory has long argued that the public and the private are not separate spheres and that, thus all attempts at regulating the public spaces of politics, employment, and media representation in a society will be meaningless if the private spaces of family and community life remain under traditional patriarchal control. Indeed, even in the "modern" West, public discourses about family life, moral values and sexual violence remain strongly patriarchal - personal struggles continue over the kitchen sink and the remote control.

61.   Economic inequality and rural poverty have a major impact upon women and media. Current funding mechanisms and structural adjustment policies employed by the World Bank and International Monetary Fund (IMF), often formulated to support human rights, appear to have quite the opposite results. Prices of subsidized materials rise so that paper becomes too costly or media projects have to be run at a profit in order to survive, and consequently, voices supporting democracy cease to be heard. Careful analyses of the impact of structural adjustment programmes on women and media and a rethinking of the conditions imposed for receiving aid are necessary. As Bam points out, "Elimination of discrimination against women cannot be fully realized when there is inequality among members within a society, which in turn is partly the cause of unequal relations among nations". 38/

62.   In certain countries legislation and media guidelines or codes of ethics have been developed to improve women's representation; some of them may be applicable elsewhere. The Fair Exposure guidelines issued by the Status of Women office in the Australian Prime Minister's Secretariat or the Indecent Representation of Women (Prohibition) Act passed in India in 1986 or the Canadian court's agreement that obscenity is to be defined by the harm it does to women's pursuit of equality are worthy of analysis as to their effectiveness, replicability and limitations. Similarly, citizen initiatives such as the Tokyo-based Forum for Citizens Television need to be studied.

7. Conclusions

63.   The struggle for increased and enhanced access of women to relevant media work and decisions in media operations and to equity in all forms of freedom of expression is not finished but is a continuing endeavour. The vast number of women's media projects, movements, organizations and networks the world over have produced some significant successes, but it must be recognized that they are but a few steps in a long march towards women's equality and empowerment. However, perhaps now more so than a decade ago, political and economic contexts and new technologies are emerging which can be appropriately harnessed for women's needs. Based on the research and experience of the past two decades, the points outlined below may be considered for an eventual platform, a foundation for future strategies.

(a)   Since functional literacy is key to social and economic development, programmes and projects which seek to strengthen the basic education and the training of girls and women to fulfil more dynamic roles in development and media production should be given priority. There is also need for teaching women media literacy and basic research skills as tools of empowerment;

(b)   Women should have equal access to further training and higher educational opportunities as well as equal access to employment opportunities in the media, as elsewhere, at all levels and types of employment: technical, budgetary, managerial, administrative, creative, performative. Competence and quality, not gender, should be the operant criteria for employment or budgetary decisions;

(c)   Women have the right to see the range of their values and perspectives and their varied lives adequately and appropriately represented in the mass media, with due respect for their ethnic and social backgrounds and their cultural, religious and ethical mores;

(d)   Women's perspectives, views, experiences and expert opinions concerning any news issue should be actively sought and given equal importance to those of men; confining women to the role of dealing only with "women's issues" is an inadequate and impoverished solution;

(e)   Women's work in alternative media has shown remarkable progress over the past 15 years and should be further strengthened in terms of financial, moral and intellectual support; where feasible and appropriate, these efforts should be more concretely integrated into development plans. As the distinction between mainstream and alternative media continues to blur, further support should be given to initiatives that encourage a full range of women's expression and creativity in all kinds of media operations, at national, regional or global levels;

(f)   Development organizations and technical agencies should support positively those projects that seek to strengthen and secure positive and public roles for women in media and development. Conversely, they should be alert to the potentially negative effects of projects and programmes that isolate women and confine them solely to household roles, and should even abstain from supporting such projects;

(g)   Research itself is a mode of empowerment, since enhanced knowledge of a problem can lead to more comprehensive and effective solutions. Basic research is still needed to monitor media employment patterns and media output for gender bias in every region. Concomitant with this is a need to develop more appropriate, feminist modes of research, with possibilities for issues to be defined by local peoples, and for the research findings to be fed back to the subjects of study. Research strategies need a more focused, comparative and analytic approach, particularly on the role of women as readers, audiences and consumers of cultural products, and in relation to the multiple flows of global media products. Given the too facile misinterpretations of data, quantitative research should be supported by qualitative studies. Research training programmes involving women trainers and trainees from all regions would greatly enhance this work;

(h)   Although published research on women and the media has increased in volume, much of it is inaccessible, particularly to women in the South. There is need for further development of regional documentation centres and libraries, the publication of bibliographies of international research work on gender, media and communication, and better dissemination of research findings;

(i)   The significant gains made by grass-roots activists, media researchers, non-governmental organizations, advocacy groups and policy makers show the need for ways to interlink them. Similarly, stronger links are needed across disciplinary and sectoral divides (media workers, development workers, health workers). If media can play useful functions in specific campaigns and if women are active in producing media content, existing positive activities could be directed to new issues and concerns, thus eliminating the need of putting up new structures;

(j)   It is important to acknowledge the initiatives taken by major international and regional organizations in support of women's media and development activities. Given scarce resources, however, consolidation, partnership and twinning of efforts would result in more economic use of funds and more dynamic and solid cooperation. In view of the trickle-up effects evidenced by a number of women's media programmes and projects, it might also be considered whether a certain proportion of development funds should be earmarked a priori to favour those activities.

Notes

1/   Caroline Moser, Gender Planning for Development (London, Routledge, 1993); Julia Cleve Mosse, Half the World, Half a Chance (Boston, Oxfam, 1993).

2/   Jocelyn Massiah, ed., Women in Developing Economies: Making Visible the Invisible (Paris, Berg/UNESCO, 1993).

3/   Anne Phillips, Engendering Democracy (Oxford, Polity Press, 1991).

4/   Noeleen Heyzer, "Women, communication and development: changing dominant structures", Media Development, vol. XLI, No. 2 (1994), p. 13.

5/   Michele Mattelart, "Women, media and power: a time of crisis", Media Development, vol. XLI, No. 2 (1994), p. 11.

6/   Gayatri Chakravorty Spivak, "Can the subaltern speak?" in Marxism and the Interpretation of Culture, Cary Nelson and Lawrence Grossberg, eds. (New York, Macmillan Education, 1988).

7/   Margaret Gallagher and Lilia Quindoza-Santiago, eds., Women Empowering Communication (Bangkok, WACC/IWTC, 1994), p. 7.

8/   George Gerbner, "Women and minorities in TV: a study in casting and fate", Media Development, vol. XLI, No. 2 (1994).

9/   Esther Adagala and Wambul Kiai, "Folk, interpersonal and mass media: the experience of women in Africa", in Gallagher and Quindoza-Santiago, op. cit.

10/   Vijayalakshmi Balakrishnan, "Indigenous social norms and women in Asian media", in Gallagher and Quindoza-Santiago, op. cit., p. 45.

11/   Ibid., p. 42.

12/   Ibid., p. 43.

13/   Ibid., p. 55.

14/   Julinda Abu-Nasr and Randa Abul-Husn, "Among veils and walls: women and media in the Middle East", in Gallagher and Quindoza-Santiago, op. cit., p. 154.

15/   Broadcasting Standards Council, Perspectives of Women in Television, Research Working Paper IX (London: Broadcasting Standards Council, 1994).

16/   Agadala and Kiai, op. cit.

17/   Gerbner, op. cit.

18/   Broadcasting Standards Council, op. cit.

19/   Margaret Gallagher, ed., Women and Media Decision-making: The Invisible Barriers (Paris, UNESCO, 1987).

20/   Ibid.

21/   Adagala and Kiai, op. cit. Balakrishnan, op. cit.; Khamla Bhasin, "Women and communication alternatives: hope for the next century", Media Development, vol. XLI, No. 2 (1994); Teresita Hermans, "Women and the media: a global perspective", Mass Media Awareness Seminar: Media and Women in the 90s (Bangkok, WACC, 1990).

22/   Balakrishnan, op. cit., p. 57.

23/   Lila Abu-Lughod, "Bedouins, cassettes and technologies of public culture", Middle East Reports, vol. 159 (1991).

24/   Hannah Davies, "American Magic in a Moroccan Town", Middle East Reports, vol. 159 (1991).

25/   Silvia Perez-Vitoria, "Women and new communications technologies", Reports and Papers on Mass Communication, No. 108 (Paris, UNESCO, 1993).

26/   See also World Communication Report (Paris, UNESCO, 1989).

27/   Peter Lewis, "Alternative media: linking global and local", Reports and Papers in Mass Communication, No. 107 (Paris, UNESCO, 1993).

28/   Carmen Ruiz, "Losing fear: video and radio production of native Aymara women in Bolivia", in Women in Grassroots Communication, Pilar Riano, ed. (Newbury Park, CA, Sage, 1994); Clemencia Rodriguez, "A process of identity construction: Latin American women producing video stories", in Riano, op. cit.

29/   Penina Mlama, "Reinforcing existing indigenous communication skills: the use of dance in Tanzania", in Riano, op. cit.

30/   Susan Dyer-Bennem, "Cultural distinctions in communication patterns of African-American women: a sampler", in Riano, op. cit.

31/   Bhasin, op. cit.

32/   Abu Nasr and Abul-Husn, op. cit., p. 155.

33/   World Communication Report, 1989 (Paris, UNESCO, 1989).

34/   The World's Women: Trends and Statistics, 1970-1990 (United Nations publication, Sales No. E.91.

35/   UNESCO, World Education Report 1991 (Paris, UNESCO, 1991), p. 27.

36/   Bhasin, op. cit.

37/   Balakrishnan, op. cit., p. 37.

38/   Brigalia Bam, "Women, communication and socio-cultural identity: creating a common vision", Media Development, vol. XLI, No. 2 (1994), p. 15.

K. Lack of adequate recognition
and support for women's contribution to
managing natural resources
and safeguarding the environment

1.   In the Nairobi Forward-looking Strategies for the Advancement of Women, 1/ the theme of environment is dealt with in a specific chapter under the objective "Development". Attention was focused on natural and man-made disasters and the environmental degradation that results. There was concern that such degradation deprived a growing number of poor women, in rural and urban areas, of their traditional means of livelihood and pushed them into marginal environments, leaving them in critical circumstances.

2.   The theme of environment was also implicitly touched upon under the objectives "Equality" and "Peace". Women were recognized as intermediaries between the natural environment and society in areas such as agro-systems, the provision of water, energy and sanitation, and in relation to demographic pressure. However, the lack of statistics specific to the environment and disaggregated by sex was considered an obstacle to the assessment of women's contribution and needs, as reflected by the example of the Green Revolution and many agrarian reforms which failed to understand the environmental impact and the key role played by women producers.

3.   In order to reduce the negative impact of environmental degradation on women and, at the same time, increase and improve women's real and potential impact on the environment, actions were suggested for the

creation of alternative means of livelihood for affected women and the inclusion of women as beneficiaries in and contributors to all programmes and projects dealing with environmental degradation and ecosystem management. The main actions were related to the promotion of women's control of resources such as land, capital and technology, the control of the product of their labour and the rights to benefits from agricultural research, training and credit.

4.   Governments were also requested to include women at all levels of decision-making in the planning and implementation process. Sanitary conditions needed to be improved, including drinking water supplies. The environmental impact of policies, programmes and projects on women's health and activities should be assessed and any mismanagement corrected, if negative effects are detected.

5.   In the first review and appraisal of the Nairobi Forward-looking Strategies, it was noticed that the theme of the environment was one of those least often referred to in the answers from Governments. However, related areas such as agriculture, rural development, water and energy supply received considerable coverage. In this case, many developing countries saw a direct link between macro models of development and environmental degradation, with its detrimental effects on women's lives. In this context, deforestation was mostly associated with large-scale lumbering, agricultural expansion and over-use of existing agricultural land than with micro survival practices.

6.   Adding to the intermediary role between the natural environment and society suggested by the Forward-looking Strategies, most countries recognized that women are active, key actors in conservation and the safeguarding of natural resources, acting as managers, producers and users. Many countries expressed the view that traditions, inheritance laws and practices and lack of funding for women's programmes resulted in a lack of resources for women, jeopardizing the possibilities and opportunities of increasing and strengthening women's impact on the environment.

7.   Another suggested factor was that the majority of programmes were still oriented towards developing small-scale and non-sustainable projects, often separated from main development projects and, moreover, in answer to the need for alternative but also sustained means of livelihood.

8.   On the other hand, in 1990, there was concern about the lack of national machinery to deal specifically with environmental issues and with special concerns to women's involvement as planners, contributors and decision makers in the field of environment.

9.   In some developing countries, in order to increase the supply of energy for rural and poor households, education on energy conservation and alternative sources of energy has been made available to women at demonstration centres.

1. General considerations

10.   The environment is referred in many reports presented for the 1994 review and appraisal of the Nairobi Forward-looking Strategies for the Advancement of Women as an important new area of concern, recognizing the role of the United Nations Conference on Environment and Development (UNCED) in such awareness. Many national reports from all regions reported specifically on this issue, while other reports made reference to it. This reflects the growth of the awareness about the importance of women in environmental considerations.

11.   Some countries noted that they have specific national machinery on the environment, usually inaugurated in the past five years, in preparation for and fulfilment of Agenda 21, 2/ while others mentioned their concern with this international document.

12.   A common statement is the recognition that women are affected in specific ways by environmental degradation and that, on the other hand, women's practice and knowledge in dealing with environmental issues should be better assessed.

13.   Some countries declared that the women's movement has had a great impact on discussions about sustainable development, before and after UNCED, and that thanks to women's associations and non-governmental organizations, the environment is gaining higher priority on society's agenda. Emphasis is also given to the role of women's associations and women non-governmental organizations, but more as pressure groups than partners in the national machinery.

14.   The association between the social roles of women and men and the environment is considered complex by the majority of countries that dealt

with the subject and generally was approached without support of desegregated data by sex, making it difficult to monitor achievements in women's conditions of life and status in relation to men.

15.   Very little information is provided in relation to global programmes and mechanisms established since the Rio Conference and their impact on women on the linkages between environmental degradation, women's quality of life and, for example, big business practices. National reports presented a broad list of issues when considering environment as a specific field of action. However, in addition to women's roles in areas such as water and energy and the effects on women's health, for example, not all the countries follow the same guide, indicating a flexibility of interpretation of what is an environmental theme. These variations also suggest the need for more systematic international efforts from the United Nations system to introduce and diffuse a set of standards, areas of concern, perspectives, and suggestions for indicators.

16.   Despite recognition of the growth, visibility and importance of women's non-governmental organizations and women's associations to run and monitor environmental programmes, in general there is an institutional weakness between women's organizations and the governmental environmental machinery.

17.   The importance of women's practices in health care, farming systems, crop production, food processing, the use of forest resources and energy, water and sanitation supplies is increasingly being recognized world wide. Nevertheless, few efforts have been made to reverse women's underrepresentation in formal governmental institutions that deal with those issues. Women's presence in the national machinery that deals directly with environmental issues is said to be growing in some countries. However, women are far less well represented at the top managerial levels of departments and ministries in fields such as environment, ecology, fishery, forestry, rural development, agriculture, water, energy, sanitation and habitat. The slight progress made in some countries and areas is considered insufficient for facing the long-term inequalities in the sharing of power and decision-making between women and men. Some Governments mentioned that women's domestic burden and traditional values that support the male status jeopardized women's real power-sharing.

18.   Women's health and the environment were addressed, highlighting damage caused by chemicals and pollution to the reproductive systems of women and by radioactive elements to mothers' milk. Epidemiologic studies indicate a possible link between breast cancer and organocholorine pesticides such as DDT. Exposure to toxic substances such as pesticides, lead, and radiation are also thought to cause male infertility and female sterility.

2. Regional trends

a)   Developing countries

19.   Most developing countries expressed their concern with the environment, indicating that awareness of its importance and the centrality of women's roles is a recent but growing trend which has been stimulated by the active involvement of women's associations, non-governmental organizations, international agencies and the Agenda 21 process.

20.   Most national reports gave a clear indication of the gravity of the environmental situation and its impact on women. For example, testimonies on how African women are more affected than men by the precarious balance between fragile natural resources and population density were common.

21.   In developing countries, where natural resources are central and in the absence of alternative means of livelihood and services, some countries suggested that poverty is strongly linked to the mismanagement of natural resources, resulting in environmental degradation. For women, environmental degradation means an increase in their workload of domestic chores and other reproductive activities. In these countries, adult women and girls are more likely to be charged to get water for the family's needs, walking about 30 km daily in some rural areas, as stated by a government report from a Sahelian country. Water and wood-gathering are also tasks commonly performed by adult women and girls. The quality of the environment - of its soil, water and energy sources - affects women's daily routines. Time and energy are spent every day trekking back and forth to the river or other water source.

22.   According to other national reports, the elimination of traditional means of livelihood, such as wood collection, is not so acutely related to the survival strategies of the poor. Rather, environmental degradation is exacerbated

through the use of unfriendly technology and fertilizers by business corporations and rural-based industries. Water contamination, desertification and deforestation, caused by the type of land use and land control of large private corporations, are affecting the quality of life of rural families, compelling rural to urban migration in different areas. It is recognized that laws and regulations to control such practices by Governments are needed. In Asia, many national reports stressed that, due to loss of croplands, erosion, land conversion, deforestation and other natural and man-made environmental calamities, millions of families suffer, and women, in particular, pay the social cost of displacement and increasing out-migration. They also expressed the need for laws dealing with environmental protection, training about environmental protection; bio-gas and solar energy; campaigns for planting trees, grass and flowers; investments on energy conservation and environmentally friendly technology; and programmes to deal with population pressure on the land. Poverty and consumerism are extreme processes highlighted as basic causes of environmental degradation. Some Governments also stressed the need for a new paradigm of development.

23.   Women as conservers of the natural environment, especially indigenous women in the Latin American and Caribbean region, are praised for their environmentally sound technical knowledge. The need to stimulate and use such knowledge by formal researchers is recognized.

24.   In many African countries, where more than 70 per cent of the population live in rural areas, the rural population is characterized by a high level of male absenteeism which leads to increased women's responsibilities for livestock and crop cultivation, including the work traditionally done by women as mothers, food providers, home makers, traders, health-care givers and water and fuel suppliers.

25.   In urban areas, the major specific environmental problem referred in many national reports is linked to poor or non-existent sanitation systems. These services, to the extent that they exist, are actually provided by women, supplying water and fuel.

26.   Despite women's active role in the management and creation of the urban and rural environment, women do not have the authority to decide on land use in order to create alternative means of livelihood and contribute

to environmental development. They are still discriminated against with respect to their access to and control over land and property in general, despite fundamental changes in the law. In many countries, land is not accessible to female heads of household or to single women. In some countries land is routinely allocated to the male of the household. In some African countries, in the case of a female head of household, the closest senior male relative is requested to make the application on behalf, not of the woman, but of the male heir.

27.   In some reports, food security is also a basic part of the debate on the environment. Women are recognized to be the basic producers of food for local consumption, but they haven't the power to decide on the use of the land or the means to improve its productivity. The majority of Governments recognized that, in addition to de jure restrictions in land ownership by women, de facto obstacles existed and poverty associated with legal illiteracy on rights and traditional values were mentioned as two such obstacles. One country mentioned that just 15 per cent of rural women owned the land they worked. Studies presented in several national reports found that the agrarian reforms adopted by some countries did not benefit women, since special national machinery and instruments to deal with inequalities were not adopted. In one developing country women had an opportunity to gain access to and ownership of land through agrarian reform programmes, but, 90.2 per cent of the land was still controlled by men.

28.   Along with the lack of access to property, the lack of access to credit is considered one of the basic obstacles to the economic advancement of women in rural areas in most developing countries. The reasons suggested were the absence of financial institutions in rural areas, lack of collateral, lack of information about credit sources and cultural inhibition and prejudice. It is estimated by one African country that rural women represented no more than 10 per cent of all borrowers. Even in the case of special programmes to provide credit to women, the number of women producers with access to credit is very small in the rural areas. Many developing countries commented that local village usurers have been the main leading source for people in dire need of money. Women and men who have to use such credit sources are facing the burden of high interest rates.

29.   It is observed that a sexual division in relation to natural resources isthe norm, and that women are more likely to be relegated to less produc-

tive areas, more hurt by environmental hardship. The division of power between men and women is reflected in the unequal distribution of land. Women tend to work the most endangered and unproductive land. According to one national report, when an agrarian reform was introduced at the end of the 1980s, men obtained 73 per cent of the dry land and 83 per cent of the irrigated land.

30.   According to several Governments, environmentally sound technical knowledge depended on credit facilities not at the disposal of rural women. One Government from the Latin American and Caribbean region mentioned, in regard to this obstacle, its efforts to design credit programmes related to technology for women. The results were said to be poor, and less than 15 per cent of women benefited from the programme.

31.   In Asia, developmental strategies for agricultural improvement are slowly beginning to have some effect on the traditional divisions of gender roles in rural areas. Farm manure, which was traditionally carried by women or transported by ponies, is now beginning to be delivered by machine power. Weeding tools have greatly reduced the drudgery of weeding in water-logged paddies, which is mostly a woman's task. For some countries modernization has tended to reduce women's paid employment in rural areas while increasing their unpaid labour on family farms. For example, one Government wrote that current agricultural practices, especially the increasing use of herbicides, are displacing large numbers of women and reducing labour per hectare.

32.   Women's participation in agricultural activities still lacks visibility in official statistics. Several Governments, while recognizing the important role of women in rural areas for family survival, did not recognize their economic contribution to the national economy. This was attributed to the lack of gender sensitivity in formal economic indicators.

33.   Agricultural extension services usually target men who are in cash-crop production. In many countries few women obtain access to extension services, even though they grow much of the food consumed in the household. In some countries extension education is oriented to home economics tasks, with no emphasis to production or trade skills. Programmes seem to assume that women are not involved in agricultural production and do not

require technical information. The majority of extension workers are men. Cultural constraints limit the extent to which extension agents can work with women farmers. Literacy training for women has concentrated on issues such as home economics, nutrition, and food-preparation. In rural extension work, a common assumption is that women are primarily house-makers who do not need training and information about agricultural work. Training institutes related to agricultural activities have a very limited number of women agents trained in agricultural subjects.

34.   Many reports noted that at the beginning of the 1990s more women were found in decision-making positions in departments related to the environment and/or agriculture or in ministries of community development or agriculture. Nevertheless, in many countries ministries such as those responsible for sanitation, water and energy do not have a mechanism for specifically addressing women's roles in those areas. Similarly the housing ministry in several countries cannot easily address the shelter needs of female-headed households, given women's legal disadvantages in land ownership and their limited incomes. Most Governments recognized that, despite the traditional responsibilities shouldered by women in rural and urban poor areas and their knowledge of environmental issues, women lack representation in decision-making positions in the national machinery. They also recognized the low awareness of the role women play in caring for the habitat in urban and rural settlements. The importance of women's knowledge of food security is not yet integrated into development planning or project implementation.

35.   The existence of a women's office in the Ministry of Agriculture is not uncommon. In Africa, in countries where women's organizations are strong at the national level, the national machinery on women included a focal point in the Ministry of Agriculture.

36.   A large gap between women and men in the choice of careers has also been noted. A relatively low proportion of college students enrolled in agriculture were women. However, one African Government reported that at the university level, in medicine and food sciences, women's enrolment had grown from 20 per cent and 13 per cent in 1988 to 28 per cent and 40 per cent in 1991, respectively. In most developing countries women's educational levels

have improved over the decade. Still, women are underrepresented in the sciences related to the environment, such as agronomy, veterinary medicine, biology, ecology and health.

37.   Many international and national non-governmental organizations and women's associations direct their efforts towards environmental issues. In many countries they cooperate directly with the Government. Non-governmental organizations are engaged in environmental protection, raising awareness of the environment, and developing and informing the public on energy-saving devices, water and sanitation systems and tree-planting. One obstacle to the effectiveness of non-governmental organization work in Africa is that the organizations can offer services only so long as they have resources.

38.   Forests are basic survival resources for many women in developing countries. Although women obtain food, fruits and leaves from forests for consumption and commercialization, they are usually underrepresented in projects of forestry conservation. An increasing awareness of women's role in soil forestry management and alternative energy is remarked upon by some Governments. Women's roles in the management of forestry resources, especially in dealing with edible and medicinal herbs, is emphasized by some Governments, and traditional women's knowledge in this field, especially that of indigenous people, is considered an area that deserves more attention in national development programmes.

(b)   Developed countries
39.   Few developed countries reported on the issue of the environment per se. However, some related areas were mentioned under other concerns, and the majority of the reports mentioned some degree of concern on the issue of sustainable development.

40.   In the developed countries of Europe and North America, an increase in the educational level of women is highlighted as an improvement of the past decade. However, educational involvement in some areas that are strategic to the environment, such as technology and the sciences, is still commonly lower among women than men. A strategy to encourage greater participation of girls and women in mathematics, the sciences and technology is cited as a positive action just beginning to be taken by Governments.

41.   Unequal power relations are found when governmental departments related to the environment are studied, although important steps towards women's representation at decision-making levels have been taken recently. A few countries said that women were found in strategic environmental decision-making positions, such as in the ministry of agriculture and fisheries, and positive results from these appointments were mentioned. Illustrative is the example of a country that appointed a woman to a high position in a related ministry related to the environment. It subsequently launched campaigns, projects and financial support schemes, such as grants for establishing new agricultural enterprises and training programmes, which have proved very effective in recruiting young women to the agricultural sector. However, a disappointing picture still prevails regarding the access of women to top decision-making in the field of the environment.

42.   In the economies in transition, the same concern is expressed - i.e., that women are not fairly participating in the new decision-making processes. In some countries, in areas related to agriculture and the environment, high-ranking women can be found. They include a minister of health, a minister of environment and urban planning, and officers in charge of environmental issues and in the ministry of science and technology. Women's factions and women's groups within political parties are mentioned as dealing with environmental issues.

43.   Governments of the region recognized the specific problems of rural women and mentioned that they were addressing their concerns. One country indicated that, besides services, such as day care centres and transport, steps were being taken to enable women from rural areas to take advantage of the opportunities offered by the introduction of new technology - for example, in homeworking. Nevertheless, it was recognized, by different countries, that more had to be done to meet women's needs in rural settlements.

44.   The food sector plays a significant role in many economies in transition. In one country, about two thirds of workers in the state agricultural sector are women. Some countries indicated that in the 1990s there was a growth of women's emigration from the rural areas, accelerating the ageing of the rural population. It is also stated that women managing farms were in general less educated than men and that older women were more dependent

on the rural infrastructure. Moreover, equipment was out of date, and the work was physically difficult. They also noticed that female-headed farms were smaller than those run by men.

45.   Inadequately developed rural trade networks, in spite of favourable changes which have taken place since 1989, coupled with inadequate health care, educational and cultural deprivations, and poor public transportation, telephone and energy services are basic reasons for the hardship of rural life cited by women in economies in transition.

46.   However, women are said to have equal access to credit in the economies in transition, and in one of them, unmarried mothers are being given credit under favourable conditions. However, despite the fact that there are no legal obstacles to the ownership of land, capital or other means of production by women, it is recognized that the de facto situation may be different. Disaggregated data on the ownership of land, real estate and other means of production are not available.

47.   Food production is still a basic source of living for many women in some developed countries; however, as mentioned in the report of one country, the majority of women in the agricultural sector are unpaid family workers.

48.   In the developed countries, women and men usually have equal rights to inheritance. However, according to one country report, there is discrimination against women in agricultural enterprises. The agricultural property of the deceased is first allocated to the sons. Although this provision has been included in the law in order to prevent the fragmentation of agricultural land, it contradicts other legal provisions, as was noted by women's groups that participated in the elaboration of the national report of that country. In the same country it is said that women workers in the agricultural sector have been neglected. The social security law provides a voluntary social security system for independent and self-employed agricultural workers, but it excludes from social security benefits women agricultural workers who are not heads of households and those who usually work as unpaid family labourers.

49.   In terms of urbanization and environmental security, services that have an impact on the quality of life in the use of the urban public space,

such as those related to air pollution, drinking water, sanitation, transport, crime control, space and public vehicle design, the needs of disabled persons and those with toddlers or infants, and women's safety, health and workloads are addressed in some of the reports from the developed European and North American countries.

50.   Some national reports focused on housing conditions. One country reported that single parents had worse housing than the population as a whole and were less likely to own their own dwelling. They often lived in cramped and/or poor houses despite the recognition of improvements in the housing conditions of the population in the decade. It was noted in one report that, in general, governmental housing policies did not treat women and men differently; where women had particular needs, they were taken into account at the national and local levels. Women heads of household were typically better represented in local authorities or housing associations in metropolitan areas.

51.   Water quality standards and the need for safe drinking water are commonly referred to in reports that deal with environmental issues. Poor women in both urban areas and rural areas were pointed out as the groups most affected.

52.   One coastal European country indicated a concern with the absence of research, institutional measures or programmes for women in the fishery sector.

53.   In some countries women's presence in the national machinery dealing directly with environmental issues was said to have increased during the past three years. However, in others, the usual inequality of power existed - i.e., the pyramidal structure, with women underrepresented in the top managerial positions, despite the constant rhetoric praising women as natural conservationists, more connected than men to an ethics of caring for the earth and more affected by unfriendly environmental actions.

3. Actions taken
(a)   Developing countries
54.   National reports listed a variety of projects that were considered successful in the regions of Africa, Asia and the Pacific, and Latin America and the Caribbean. Generally, Governments stated their recognition of the

importance of international cooperation and environmentally sound projects for women's advancement.

55.   Three types of models have been set up in different countries to deal with women and the environment: integrated programmes and projects, taking into consideration women and men as beneficiaries; women's components in development programmes and projects; and projects for women only.

56.   Some countries mentioned plans on environment and sustainable development with specific reference to women. Commonly, agriculture, water, energy, natural disasters and food security are the basic areas of concern of these plans. More and more projects, especially in relation to food production, fisheries and alternative energy supply, and drinking water facilities, mentioned women as beneficiaries or partners.

57.   It is recognized by many African countries that the current institutional involvement of women in water and sanitation services is still low at the community level. In a recently adopted national water policy, one African Government stipulated that all village water committees should be made up of six people, half of whom should be women.

58.   Some national reports stated that in the 1980s international cooperation followed a pattern by which women were considered more as the beneficiaries of development than as partners in it. Others reported that in some cases women were considered only in their role as mothers and caretakers. It is observed that in the 1990s a change had been registered in that pattern and that a new perspective was introduced in programmes and projects. Donor agencies were incorporating gender and environmental concerns into project formulation and implementation and were providing technical assistance for the development of gender sensitivity in macroeconomic policies at the national level. But, on the other hand, some reports also stated that a clear definition of what is understood by gender and how gender should be dealt with in development plans, specifically environmental plans, is still missing.

59.   In Africa, where the principal source of energy is wood, grass-roots women's associations and non-governmental organizations have been engaged in many initiatives to save wood. The 1991 energy policy of one

African country, which counted on the collaboration of women's non-governmental organizations and cooperation from international agencies, put emphasis on the use of renewable energy sources, such as solar and wind energy, biogas and natural gas. However, it had little success.

60.   Women's role as environmental managers, through knowledge of appropriate and environmentally sound energy sources, such as in the selection of wood, was seen as basic. One Government is investing in the diffusion of alternative kitchens, reforestry programmes and organic fertilizers in order to introduce alternative styles in the relationship between population and natural resources. Awareness by women of soil forestry management and alternative sources of energy is being promoted by certain African Governments. However, programmes on the environment usually do not mention women in relation to conservation. Programmes for improved kitchens to stem the demand for energy have been initiated in a number of countries, with the participation of women's non-governmental organizations and international agencies. According to one national report, improved kitchens can save up to 50 per cent of the wood consumed. Women participated actively in the planning and implementation of the programme, with the support of a communication project to promote social awareness of women's role in the programme.

61.   The Sahel was a target area for action in the Nairobi Forward-looking Strategies. The region continued to deserve special attention at the national and international levels.

62.   Several African countries mentioned the establishment of rural child-care services, run by women's grass-roots organizations, with the support of the Government and international agencies. They were, however, few in number and in great need of continued support.

63.   Several Governments mentioned that, in rural areas, non-governmental organizations ran successful programmes to provide water for productive activities. Others provided easily accessible sources of potable water for rural and urban areas. According to one Government, thanks to its water programme, 45 per cent of the rural population and 75 per cent of the urban population would have benefited by the end of the decade.

64.   A self-help programme for home improvement to teach women basic skills, with emphasis on environmental issues, was mentioned as a success story in one national report. The popular programme reached 2,000 women, who then formed groups of their own to sustain their activities, by, for example, establishing community gardens. Household food security programmes, set up with the assistance of an international agency, were mentioned by different African Governments as very beneficial to rural women.

65.   Several projects were mentioned in the national reports as important contributions to the advancement of women's status. Many of them are oriented towards the creation of alternative means of livelihood, such as income generation and survival strategies, taking into consideration poverty and the extreme needs of certain groups of women, while others are oriented specifically towards environment conservation. They are complemented by education and training. The majority of the projects counted on international cooperation.

66.   In some countries, projects launched at the end of the 1980s included self-sufficient fish-breeding units run by men and women and designed to regenerate hydrographic basins; credit and land legalization with special attention to women in agricultural activities; and skills-training courses on crafts and food preservation.

67.   Some Governments are implementing, with international cooperation, national programmes and policies related to sustainable development, with special emphasis on organic agriculture, and community health, with popular participation and a gender perspective. One programme is designed for the integrated development of a mountain region, with special concern for coffee production and the exploitation of forests. It hopes to discourage migration. It is said to have benefited women by providing water services and electricity and access to social services. Another country has a nationalenvironmental policy for rural women, and another one mentioned that women are integrated into the national programme for water and sanitation services. Research on environmental issues and on gender in agricultural activities is being conducted by several countries. One country referred to a programme of research on the working and living conditions of women

in the flower industry, with special attention to health effects and the problems of indigenous women.

68.   Indigenous women's knowledge of herbs, forestry and environment protection is mentioned by some Governments as a traditional source that is coming to be recognized and supported by specific development projects. On the other hand, it is recognized that much is to be done in this field.

69.   One African island country mentioned the importance of a fishery production project run by women, with the support of an international agency. An African regional network of women in agriculture, with the support of a European country, has been working on several local projects, such as the construction of collective and individual sanitation services. Forestry programmes, with women tending nurseries and planting trees, have been implemented by many Governments.

70.   The importance of international cooperation and environmentally sound projects for advancement of women was highlighted in many national reports. However, caution was expressed that, in the area of environment, most of the donor support to women has been directed to microprojects in the form of supply, training and credit facilities. Some countries mentioned that much of the international support for programmes for the advancement of women came in the form of initial fund, or seed, money. After the money is spent, these programmes have great difficulty surviving or spreading into other areas of the country.

71.   Certain African national reports highlighted programmes of development to mitigate the social costs of structural adjustment policies, giving responsibility to the rural population, chiefly women, in the management of natural resources.

72.   One African Government stated that, in its development plan, priority is given to educating and demonstrating to farmers how to expand

their farm yields and how to construct simple on-farm storage facilities. Specific attention is to be given to women small-holder farmers.

73.   Some national reports mentioned the participation of grass-roots groups in projects about forestry, energy, water management, and pollution control in urban areas.

74.   One national report mentioned a project on alternative technologies to encourage village women to improve the environmental health in their villages by improving local water and sanitation and making smoke-free fuel-efficient stoves available.

75.   Another national report mentioned the organization of a cooperative production system to develop an alternative cultivation process which protects the soil from erosion and nutrient depletion.

76.   Another Government mentioned a project that provided assistance to small-holder and marginal farmers to increase their productivity. The project also included an alleviation programme and provided agricultural credit, especially to women.

77.   In another country, an environmental impact management agency was created to assist in the formulation of policies on environment pollution control, implement hazardous waste management, and monitor and control activities that have an important environmental impact.

78.   In another, there is an ongoing project oriented towards tree-planting, terracing and the rehabilitation of degraded land. One project, involving women farmers, converted an arid area to available land by processing human waste into fertilizer.

79.   Among other development projects to benefit women and the environment in the near future, some Governments mentioned the production and marketing of green charcoal as an alternative source of energy, organic fertilizers, and bio-pesticides; the promotion of recycling; the inclusion of gender-sensitive advocacy on the environment in the curricula at all levels of education; housing for the rural poor, with special emphasis on female heads of households, women in urban areas, and migrant working women; and the construction of adequate shelter, with clean drinking water, meeting the needs for culturally appropriate and practical space for cooking and child care.

80.   Some Governments had decided to use a gamut of strategies, including training and gender-sensitization, in formal and informal educational systems, through community groups and non-governmental organizations.

81.   Other actions were mentioned, such as the promulgation of a series of laws to promote environmental protection and prevent air pollution. Efforts were being made to train people in colleges and universities about environmental protection; half of the trainees were women. One Government mentioned that it supported different types of research institutes with a full range of subjects on environmental science and technology. Women were mentioned as the natural beneficiaries of the country's environmental protection efforts. In one country, in order to reduce the pollution by toxic gas and cinders resulting from burning coal - so important for household use - women had started to use coal briquettes and new stoves. Biogas and solar energy systems had been used to reduce air pollution and reduce the intensity of women's labour.

(b)   Developed countries

82. Regarding housing policies, the national reports from the developed countries mentioned the rule of considering the particular needs of disad-vantaged groups of women. In housing legislation, a safety net for pregnant women and families was devised. The institution specifically concerned with women's rights in one national machinery had been demanding that the public and private providers of housing recognize the needs of young women leaving care, low-income women, older women, single parents, ex-service wives and others.

83.   In the legal realm, one country referred to a "right to manage", recognizing the strong role of women in tenant management organizations. Air pollution, air quality and clean water are also subject to regulation in developed countries. A national report on the situation of women in a North American country observed that guidelines were recently released to help health agencies develop fish consumption limits, designed specifically to protect women, especially those of child-bearing age, and children against exposure to chemical contaminants in non-commercial freshwater and estuarine fish and shellfish.

84.   Some Governments had incorporated into policies the proposals of women's groups for improving the quality of life, the habitat and the envi-

ronment in urban settlements. Women's knowledge is mainstreamed into governmental planning in a few cases. One European Government mentioned as a successful experience the adoption of "a women's perspective" in public planning since 1985. Such a perspective aims at providing a basis for decisions concerning the use and protection of resources and seeks the participation of all affected parties. A municipal master plan was developed to go beyond traditional physical and economic planning, to encompass culture, school and the environment, taking into consideration issues that affect women's daily lives. Different types of municipal plans, with similar participatory methodology, were adopted in the fishery and agricultural sectors. According to one report, a shift towards more "feminine" values was achieved: a more caring and integrated approach, with more concern for environmental protection and ecology, and the practicalities of everyday life and diversity of ideas. The women's perspective began to be integrated into new businesses. Despite the recognized success of that type of participatory planning, sensitive to gender and the environment, such experience was limited to specific small municipalities, benefiting a small number of persons.

85.   Another country reported on the implementation of a scheme, launched in 1993, which consists of the identification of those products that do the least harm to the environment in order to help women as consumers make informed decisions. The Government is also working with regional electrical companies to produce a voluntary scheme of information on energy efficiency for domestic appliances. Another country mentioned legislation on pesticides and food safety, recognizing that, although federal legislation is not targeted towards women, several rules have a significant impact on women and children, due to persistent sexual divisions of labour and power, with women in charge of food shopping, preparation, and in the rural areas, production too.

86.   Only one Government noted that information is made available on the environmental safety aspects of biotechnology and on genetically modified organisms. Besides campaigns, projects and programmes run by women's non-governmental organizations, some Governments reported on the following activities of the women's movement: the organization of a "green" university, research and dissemination of knowledge on the environment, and the organization of a year of the environment in Europe.

87.   Women's organizations are thought to have played an active role in a national referendum in which the nuclear option of one country was abolished. The scope of the women's movement against environmental disasters was broadened to protest and prevent such disasters as they relate to economic power: the use by corporations and Governments of toxic chemicals and hazardous waste, for example. One referendum closed down a factory that manufactured pesticides. The success of similar campaigns was listed by a few countries.

Notes

1/   Report of the World Conference to Review and Appraise the Achievements of the United Nations Decade for Women: Equality, Development and Peace, Nairobi, 15-26 July 1985 (United Nations publication, Sales No. E.85.IV.10), chap. I, sect. A.

2/   Report of the United Nations Conference on Environment and Development, Rio de Janeiro, 3-14 June 1992 (A/CONF.151/26/Rev.1 (Vol. I, Vol. I/Corr.1, Vol. II, Vol. III and Vol. III/Corr.1) (United Nations publication, Sales No. E.93.I.8 and corrigenda), Vol. I: Resolutions adopted by the Conference.

III.
International Action

1.   International action to implement the Nairobi Forward-looking Strategies has taken place at various levels and through different means, as specified in the Strategies themselves. At the intergovernmental level, there has been a shift in policy development away from considering women as a self-contained "group" that can be dealt with in isolation, to a realization that consideration of gender is central to policy development and successful programme implementation. Evidence of the shift can be found in intergovernmental bodies that are concerned with women as well as in intergovernmental bodies dealing with other issues.

2.   This shift has also been reflected at the level of the organizations of the United Nations system, from the United Nations Secretariat through the programmes and funds under the authority of the Economic and Social Council and the General Assembly, to the specialized agencies. It is reflected in research and policy analysis, technical cooperation and financial assistance, in staff administration and in coordination activities.

3.   The shift in terms of policy is perhaps greater than in its application to operations. Here, as is documented in the study on technical assistance and women: from mainstreaming towards institutional accountability (E/CN.6/1995/6), the process of mainstreaming has often been characterized by difficulties. That study recommends an increasing reliance on institutional accountability to improve the prospects of successful mainstreaming.

4.   In addition to changes in the practices of individual organizations, prospects for coordinated action can be further enhanced by using more effectively existing coordination tools, such as the focal point network, the inter-agency machinery and the system-wide medium-term plan.

5.   The following review and appraisal is based largely on contributions provided by organizations of the United Nations system. It does not include all of them, since many have reported regularly through reports on the preparations for the Fourth World Conference on Women. It seeks to illustrate many of the main features of international action to implement the Nairobi Forward-looking Strategies which can also be relevant for the implementation of the platform for action.

A. Intergovernmental level

6.   Many of the major intergovernmental bodies concerned with advancement of women or of related issues have evolved procedures and adopted policies that have helped mobilize international action. The description which follows highlights some of these, for the main intergovernmental and expert bodies dealing with women, and a selection of other bodies, especially of the specialized agencies.

1. Commission on the Status of Women

7.   Following the World Conference to Review and Appraise the Achievements of the United Nations Decade for Women, held in Nairobi in 1985, the Commission on the Status of Women undertook, at its session in 1987, to reform its method of work in order to play its role in implementing the Nairobi Forward-looking Strategies more effectively. Its sessions were annualized through the year 2000, its membership was expanded to reflect more accurately the composition of the United Nations, and its agenda was restructured to focus on its coordination, monitoring and policy formulation functions.

8.   Its substantive work was organized around three priority themes per year, one each for the objectives of equality, development and peace. The themes were selected in terms of their importance for accelerating the implementation of the Nairobi Forward-looking Strategies. Starting in 1988, the Commission has considered 21 priority themes. On most, the Commission agreed on a resolution containing recommendations on standards and policies to address the underlying problems in each theme. When the Commission did not act, as in the case of the themes of elimination of de jure and de facto discrimination (with an emphasis on positive action) or women in the peace process (with an emphasis on women in the military),

it was because an international consensus on the issue was not yet formed. The Commission's consideration of the themes has formed the background for the current identification of issues to be addressed as a matter of priority in the Platform for Action.

9.   In the area of women's human rights, the Commission undertook to prepare the Declaration on the Elimination of Violence against Women, which placed the issue in a rights context, and undertook a review of its communications procedure with a view to making it more effective.

10.   The Commission has also begun a practice of making recommendations on issues with a significant gender content but which are being considered mainly in other subsidiary bodies of the Economic and Social Council. Thus, for example, the Commission made recommendations regarding the approach to celebrating the International Year of the Family to the Commission for Social Development. It also made recommendations on substantive matters to the preparatory bodies for the World Conference on Human Rights and the International Conference on Population and Development.

11.   In the coordination area, the Commission had reviewed in detail the draft of the system-wide medium-term plan for women and development for the period 1990-1995 at its 1987 session and undertook a similar review of the proposed system-wide medium-term plan on the advancement of women for the period 1996-2001 at its thirty-seventh session.

2. Other functional commissions of the Economic and Social Council
(a)   Population Commission (future Commission on Population and Development)
12.   Following the International Conference on Population and Development (ICPD) in 1994, the General Assembly has determined that a revitalized Population Commission, which will be renamed the Commission on Population and Development, will monitor, review and assess the implementation of the Programme of Action that was adopted at the ICPD. The Commission is to meet on an annual basis, beginning in 1996.

13.   The Programme of Action strongly endorses the importance of gender issues for all aspects of population and development programmes and policies. Among its 243 proposed actions, nearly one third make explicit ref-

erence to women, the girl child, or gender, and many more deal with issues that clearly have a gender dimension. Recommended actions include, among others, establishing mechanisms for women's equal participation and equitable representation at all levels of the political process and public life; promoting women's education, skill development and employment; and taking positive steps to eliminate all practices that discriminate against women, adolescents and girls. In addition, the recommendations note that development interventions should take better account of the multiple demands on women's time, with greater investments made in measures to lessen the burden of domestic responsibilities, and with attention to laws, programmes and policies which will enable employees of both sexes to harmonize their family and work responsibilities.

14.   Another important area concerns the new comprehensive concept of reproductive health, including family planning and sexual health, as defined in the Programme of Action. The Programme also recognizes men's key role in bringing about gender equality. Recommendations deal with actions to promote equal participation of women and men in all areas of family and household responsibilities including, among others, responsible parenthood, sexual and reproductive behaviour, prevention of sexually transmitted diseases, and shared control and contribution to family income and children's welfare. The Programme proposes a range of actions aimed at eliminating discrimination against the girl child and eliminating the root causes of son preference. Countries are also urged to take full measures to eliminate all forms of exploitation, abuse and violence against women and girls, including rape in the context of war and "ethnic cleansing", to prohibit female genital mutilation, and to prevent infanticide and prenatal sex selection, among other things.

(b)   Commission on Human Rights

15.   In compliance with the provisions of resolution 1993/46 of the Commission on Human Rights, in which it requests all special rapporteurs and working groups of the Commission on Human Rights and the Subcommission on Prevention of Discrimination and Protection of Minorities, in the discharge of their mandates, regularly and systematically to include in their reports available information on human rights violations affecting women, several Special Rapporteurs have devoted particular attention to this topic.

16.   In a number of resolutions, the Commission has drawn attention to the situation of women, as well as practices of discrimination against women -i.e. resolution 1994/18, on the implementation of the Declaration on the Elimination of All Forms of Intolerance and of Discrimination based on Religion or Belief; resolution 1994/51, relative to the proclamation of a decade for human rights education; resolution 1994/49, on the protection of human rights in the context of human immunodeficiency virus (HIV) and acquired immunodeficiency syndrome (AIDS); resolution 1994/334 on human rights and the administration of justice. In decision 1994/104, the Commission decided to endorse the recommendation of the Subcommission on harmful traditional practices affecting the health of women and children. At its fifty-first session, in 1995, the Commission will consider the adoption of a plan of action for the elimination of these practices.

17.   The Commission on Human Rights, in its resolution 1994/45 of 4 March 1994, on integrating the rights of women into the human rights mechanisms of the United Nations and the elimination of violence against women, decided to appoint, for a three-year period, a Special Rapporteur on Violence against Women, including its causes and its consequences. Subsequently, the Special Rapporteur has been appointed to carry out this mandate within the framework of the Universal Declaration of Human Rights and all other international human rights instruments, including the Convention on the Elimination of All Forms of Discrimination against Women and the Declaration on the Elimination of Violence against Women, and to report to the Commission on an annual basis. A preliminary report (E/CN.4/1995/42) will be considered by the Commission at its fifty-first session.

18.   In its resolution 1994/53, on human rights and thematic procedures, the Commission, noting that some human rights violations are specific to or primarily directed against women, and that the identification and reporting of these violations demand specific awareness and sensitivity, called on the thematic special rapporteurs and working groups to include in their reports gender-disaggregated data and to address the characteristics and practice of human rights violations under their mandates that are specifically or primarily directed against women, or to which women are particularly vulnerable, in order to assure the effective protection of their human rights.

19.   In August 1994, the Subcommission on Prevention of Discrimination and Protection of Minorities decided to consider the Human Rights of Women and the girl child under every relevant item of its agenda as well as in all relevant studies and requested that all reports submitted contain a gender perspective in their analysis and recommendations (Subcommission resolution 1994/43).

3. Committee on the Elimination of Discrimination against Women

20.   The Committee on the Elimination of Discrimination against Women is the monitoring body for the Convention on the Elimination of All Forms of Discrimination against Women, established in 1982. It is the only human rights treaty body that is exclusively concerned with discrimination based on sex. At the time of the Nairobi Conference, the Committee was in its early stages of work. Over the next 10 years, the Committee has seen the volume of reports it is to consider increase dramatically as the number of States parties to the Convention has increased.

21.   The Committee has also begun the practice, as in other human rights treaty bodies, of making general recommendations on articles of the Convention, as well as other issues raised by it. The Committee's recommendation 19, on violence against women, was a major contribution to the formulation of the Declaration on the Elimination of Violence against Women, for example.

22.   The Committee has undertaken its own review of its activities that are contained in a separate report to the Fourth World Conference on Women.

4. Other human rights treaty bodies

(a)   Human Rights Committee

23.   Several articles of the International Covenant on Civil and Political Rights expressly relate to gender discrimination. The Human Rights Committee has always attached great importance to the monitoring of States Parties' compliance with those provisions and, in general, to the promotion of the rights of women.

24.   The lists of issues prepared in conjunction with the consideration of States Parties' reports regularly contain questions concerning the participation of women in the political, economic, social and cultural life of the coun-

try, and the proportion of sexes in schools and universities. Similarly, in the concluding observations adopted by the Committee at the end of the consideration of reports, States are frequently urged to adopt further measures to improve respect for the rights of women under the Covenant.

25.   In its general comment relating to the principle of non-discrimination, the Human Rights Committee pointed out that States Parties should, if necessary, take affirmative action in order to diminish or eliminate conditions which cause or help to perpetuate discrimination prohibited by the Covenant. Such action may involve granting part of the population certain preferential treatment in specific matters as compared with the rest of the population and is considered to be a case of legitimate differentiation under the Covenant.

26.   The Committee has developed some jurisprudence relating to the protection and promotion of the rights of women in individual cases dealt with under the Optional Protocol to the International Covenant on Civil and Political Rights which provides for individual complaints for violations of the Covenant.

27.   On 14 October 1994, the pre-sessional working group of the Human Rights Committee took note of the various recommendations made by the World Conference on Human Rights with regard to the integration of the equal status and human rights of women into the work of the human rights treaty bodies. The working group recommended a number of measures relating to a general comment on article 3, to be adopted on the status and human rights of women, as well as to consider examining its reporting guidelines, and the lists of issues concerning the consideration of States Parties' reports so as to include concrete questions on the equal status and human rights of women.

(b)   The Committee on Economic, Social and Cultural Rights
28.   The Committee on Economic, Social and Cultural Rights, in its monitoring of States Parties' compliance with the provisions of the International Covenant on Economic, Social and Cultural Rights, in accordance with article 4 of the Covenant, pays particular attention to the measures undertaken by States Parties in order to ensure the equal rights of men and women to the enjoyment of all economic, social and cultural rights set forth in articles 6-15 of the Covenant.

29.   In its examination of States Parties' reports, the Committee takes into account information provided by States in their reports under the Convention on the Elimination of All Forms of Discrimination against Women, as well as the deliberations and findings of CEDAW with respect to them.

30.   In 1990, the Committee revised its reporting guidelines, inter alia, to bring them into line with article 3 of the Covenant and with its own practice. In its revised guidelines and written lists of issues, submitted to States Parties prior to the consideration of a report by the Committee, the Committee requests as a matter of course gender specific data from States Parties.

(c)   Committee on the Rights of the Child
31.   A number of activities carried out by the Committee on the Rights of the Child, in connection with the implementation of the Convention on the Rights of the Child, have a direct bearing on the rights of women. For instance, the Committee on the Rights of the Child, when examining reports submitted by States Parties on the implementation of the Convention, stresses the need to ensure gender equality in all matters related to the child and to effectively protect and promote the human rights of the girl child. The need for concerted efforts on problems such as discrimination against girl children, their exploitative use in child labour, early marriage, prejudicial health practices, or denial of educational opportunities, are frequently referred to in the Committee's discussion.

(d)   Committee on the Elimination of Racial Discrimination
32.   Although the Convention does not explicitly refer to discrimination on the basis of sex, the Committee considers information concerning women who suffer discrimination on the basis of sex and race. In 1993, in reviewing the report of Kuwait, the Committee referred in its closing comments to discrimination against "foreign women domestic servants".

5. Governing bodies of specialized agencies
(a)   International Labour Organization
33.   Following the Nairobi Conference, the ILO adopted the Plan of Action on Equality of Opportunity and Treatment of Men and Women in Employment, geared, inter alia, to ensuring systematic coverage of the Nairobi Forward-looking Strategies for the Advancement of Women

throughout the organization's various activities and the means of action of its technical departments. The major areas identified in the Plan are human rights and the promotion of equality; employment promotion including improving the situation of women in the labour market, women workers in the formal and informal sectors; training; working conditions and environment; social security; labour legislation, labour relations, labour administration, workers' and employers' activities; women in specific industrial sectors; and in the different regions. Equality for women in employment has continued to be a priority theme in the ILO's programme and budget. In addition to the resolution of 1985 on equal opportunities and equal treatment for men and women in employment, a resolution concerning ILO action for women workers, adopted by the International Labour Conference in 1991, gave further impetus to the ILO's work on women, including its implementation of the Nairobi Strategies.

34.   The ILO's efforts have also covered how to increase women's participation in the delegations to the International Labour Conference and other ILO meetings. The governing body, at its two hundred fifty-sixth session, recommended that concrete measures be taken by the ILO constituents and by the Director-General to increase women's participation in ILO meetings. For example, the former should appoint more women participants to ILO meetings and the latter should organize informal gatherings for women participants during such meetings and provide child-care facilities at the International Labour Conference. Accordingly, the Office organized the first and second informal meetings in honour of women participants at the International Labour Conferences on 8 June 1993 and 8 June 1994. The participants expressed appreciation of not only the panel discussions but also the opportunity the meetings afforded them to exchange views, develop ties and encourage their active participation in the International Labour Conference. The Memorandum, sent to the delegations to the Conference, currently includes a statement to the effect that the questions considered at the International Labour Conference and other meetings are of equal relevance to women and men and that efforts should be made in all member States to include women among both government, employers' and workers' delegates and advisers of national delegations. In addition, the Office has also taken steps to investigate the possibility of a child-care facility at the International Labour Conference and the modalities for organizing the

activity and to ascertain, from the conference delegates, the extent of the needs. Women at the two hundred sixty-first session of the Conference, in June 1994, constituted 14.5 per cent (17.7 per cent governmental, 9.2 per cent employers and 12.2 per cent workers) of the delegates. A review of women's participation in other ILO meetings in 1993, outside the International Labour Conference, clearly showed that some ILO departments had managed to increase the level of this participation. The percentage of women's participation in 1993 ranged from 34 to 0 per cent. The figures, however, compiled from July 1993 to June 1994 depict a slightly more favourable situation, with the percentage of women's participation ranging from a high of between 54 and 40 per cent to a low of 15 per cent. Various measures have been adopted by a number of the ILO departments to promote the participation of women in their meetings. For example, a paragraph emphasizing the need for women's participation in the seminars is often added to the invitation letters to the organizations concerned.

35.   The main constraint remains the fact that high-ranking officials are often selected for ILO meetings and that women seldom hold such positions. Furthermore, some of the ILO programmes, such as Occupational Safety and Health and certain of the industry committees, have observed that, since they cover technical fields which continue to have limited numbers of women professionals, especially in the developing world, the participants selected at the national level for their meetings often continue to be male, despite requests made to the national authorities to include women. It is also relevant to examine the positions held by women at ILO meetings. There is currently a woman chairperson of the ILO governing body and women also chair some of the committees of that governing body. A few women have also recently chaired or served as vice-chairpersons of some of the other ILO meetings.

(b)   Food and Agriculture Organization of the United Nations
36.   Following the Nairobi World Conference, the FAO Conference took measures at its twenty-fourth session (1987) to implement the provisions on rural women in the Nairobi Forward-looking Strategies by requesting a plan of action for the integration of women in development. At its twenty-fifth session (1989), the FAO Conference unanimously approved the Plan of Action, which covers the medium-term period 1989-1995, and specifically

endorsed the objectives and strategies in the first progress report on the implementation of the Plan of Action. In November 1991, the Conference, at its twenty-sixth session, approved the medium-term plan covering the period 1992-1997 and reconfirmed its commitment to the implementation of the Plan of Action by highlighting it as one of the nine organization-wide challenges and one of five thematic priorities.

37.   In 1989, the FAO Conference approved seven programmatic and five administrative priorities, as defined in the first progress report. An eighth programmatic priority dealing with sustainable development was approved by the FAO Conference in 1991. The eight programmatic priorities of the Plan of Action are: training on women in development; policy advice to member Governments; project development and monitoring; reorientation of home economics and agricultural curricula; preparation and promotion of WID guidelines and manuals; data collection, research studies, communication and public information; population education and WID; and sustainable development, natural resource management and environment. The five administrative priorities are undertaking organization-wide efforts of awareness and compliance; increasing financial resources for WID activities; increasing female staff; enhancing and strengthening internal action on WID; and strengthening external working relations.

38.   At its twenty-seventh session in 1993, the FAO Conference confirmed support for the continued implementation of the Plan of Action and called for the revision of the Plan for the period 1996-2001, to be presented to the FAO Conference at its twenty-eighth session, in November 1995. In addition, the FAO Conference, in 1993, urged the organization to intensify collaboration with other United Nations agencies, non-governmental organizations, and research institutes to promote WID issues; and expand support to member countries in policy and legal advice and institutional strengthening so as to develop the critical mass necessary for the advancement of women in all domains relating to food and agriculture. The conference further requested that FAO continue to increase the proportion of women in the organization's professional staff, especially at higher grades.

B. Organizations of the United Nations system

39.   At the international level, much of what is done centres on the organizations of the United Nations system, composed of international civil servants. Individually and collectively they have sought to implement the provisions of the Nairobi Forward-looking Strategies. Below is an illustrative review of many of these activities.

1. Structure of implementation

40.   Virtually all of the organizations of the United Nations system have activities related to the implementation of the Nairobi Forward-looking Strategies, linked by a network of focal points. As at 1 January 1995, there were 41 designated focal points in the organizations of the system.

41.   The institutional structure of implementation is highly varied, reflecting the specific mandates of the various organizations. They include organizational entities which are exclusively concerned with advancement of women such as the Division for the Advancement of Women, the Institute for Research and Training for the Advancement of Women, the United Nations Development Fund for Women, and Integration of Women in Development Service of FAO. They also include entities which, as part of larger programmes, deal with gender, such as the Gender Statistics Unit of the Statistical Division of the United Nations Secretariat. They include units or programmes set up within operational entities of the United Nations such as the Gender and Development Programme of UNDP. This structure provides a basis for implementation of most of the kinds of activities set out in the Strategies.

42.   There are no clear means of determining the amount of resources devoted to advancement of women. A cross-organizational programme analysis in 1989 estimated that the total amount of resources explicitly allocated to advancement of women during the biennium 1988-1989 was $24 million. An attempt to update these figures for the biennium 1990-1991 estimated that it was $62 million, 1/ although this was not considered either an accurate or a comparable figure.

43.   The most recent report (1992-1993) of the Administrative Committee on Coordination on expenditures by programme, 2/ which includes an estimate of resources devoted to the advancement of women from all sources of funds, shows that $138.6 million was expended during that biennium, between the United Nations Secretariat, United Nations funds and programmes and specialized agencies. The total expenditure of the system from all sources and on all programmes during the period was $20,171.8 million.

44.   Each of the organizations of the system has articulated a structure for implementing the Forward-looking Strategies. One example of how an implementation structure has been developed is provided by the Food and Agriculture Organization of the United Nations (FAO).

45.   A restructuring programme in FAO was approved by the FAO Council, at its one hundred sixth session in 1994, in an effort to better respond to the organization's priorities of promoting sustainable agriculture, rural development and food security, in which women play major roles. A key development in the restructuring is creation of a new Division on Women's and People's Participation in Development in the new Sustainable Development Department. The Division comprises the Women in Agricultural Production and Rural Development Service which has been renamed the Integration of Women in Development Service, the People's Participation Service and the new Population Programme Service. The restructuring process is ongoing during the 1994/1995 biennium.

46.   The Interdepartmental Working Group on Women in Development was established in 1976 to serve as the Organization-wide policy advisory and coordinating body on women in development. Its technical secretariat also coordinates with the women-in-development focal points in the FAO

regional offices for Africa, Asia and the Pacific, Europe, Latin America and the Caribbean, and the Near East. FAO contributes regularly to the reports of the Secretary-General, the Commission on the Status of Women, the system-wide medium-term plan and to inter-agency meetings on the implementation of the strategies. FAO is the lead agency for the ACC Subcommittee on Rural Development, which reviews the implementation of the strategies as a regular agenda item during its annual meetings.

47.   At present there is no organization-wide budgeting system that would permit a quantitative assessment of the amount of regular and field programme resources directed to female beneficiaries. The only identifiable data on financial resources for women in development relate to the coordinating Unit which has received a constant share of resource since the Plan of Action for the Integration of Women in Development was approved. In the 1990-1991 biennium the subprogramme "Women in Agriculture and Rural Development" had a budget of $3.114 million, representing 9.6 per cent of the programme "Rural development" and 1.46 per cent of major programme "Agriculture". For the 1992-1993 biennium, representing 11 per cent of the Programme "Rural development" and 1.45 per cent of major programme "Agriculture". As gender and women in development efforts are mainstreamed throughout the organization, the above budget figures do not reflect the importance of FAO's programme to promote the advancement of rural women.

48.   A similar approach has been taken in UNESCO. Taking as an overall frame of reference the Nairobi Forward-looking Strategies for the Advancement of Women, which remain valid until the year 2000, UNESCO's action has been developed through an interdisciplinary approach within each major programme area, in the form of activities of specific concern to women, both as beneficiaries and as active participants.

49.   The second medium-term plan (1984-1989) constituted an important step forward. It presented for the first time an overall analysis of the Status of Women and introduced a transverse, recapitulatory programme (major programme XIV). The organization's action was henceforth to be based on a double strategy:

(a)   The organization has continued to propose specific programmes and actions aimed at combating various manifestations of discrimination against women and at increasing the scope for their participation in the life of societies;

(b)   At the same time, however, a special effort has been made to ensure that the specifically female dimension of the general problems to which the organization's programme have been addressed was taken effectively into account in all those programmes.

50.   UNESCO's strategy of action consisted in integrating the female dimension into the whole range of programmes and activities contemplated under the second medium-term plan. It is true that, by definition, UNESCO's endeavours have always been addressed to women as much as to men. The organization considered that the persistence, however, of instances of inequality between the sexes require that, whenever necessary, the specific situation of women should be taken into consideration not only in analysing the problems identified but also in devising and applying the solutions.

51.   In the United Nations Industrial Development Organization, after the Nairobi Conference and following the conversion of UNIDO into a specialized agency in 1986, a Unit for the Integration of Women in Industrial Development was established. This Unit is currently placed within the Office of the Managing Director, Country Strategy and Programme Development Division. It is responsible for providing policy guidance and advisory services to UNIDO staff and to Governments for the development and promoting of gender-sensitive operational and research activities as well as for ensuring the integration of gender issues in the design and implementation of UNIDO services and other activities in order to enhance women's equal participation, quantitatively and qualitatively, in the mainstream of industrial development.

52.   UNIDO's policy-making organs - i.e., the Industrial Development Board and the General Conference - have since 1986 adopted a number of decisions and resolutions on the integration of women in industrial development. Most of them continuously call on UNIDO to take the appropriate measures to facilitate the issue in all UNIDO technical cooperation and

research activities. The necessity to increase the participation of women in the policy and decision-making at the national, regional and international levels is also very much emphasized. UNIDO's activities on women in industrial development are also guided by the UNIDO's medium-term plan 1990-1995 as well as 1996-2001 in which the integration of women in industrial development is one of the priority themes.

53.   In response to the above-mentioned decisions and recommendations, strategies have been outlined under the UNIDO programme and plan of action for the integration of women in industrial development 1990-1995, and four major areas of the programme have been identified: integration of women in programme/project cycle; in studies and research activities; in women-specific programmes/projects; and in support and pro-motional activities.

2. Women staff in organizations of the United Nations system

54.   The Nairobi Forward-looking Strategies place emphasis on the role of organizations of the United Nations system as models for the incorporation of women into decision-making. Implicit in all discussions of mainstreaming is the notion that if women and men were fairly represented at all levels and in all sectors, the incorporation of gender concerns into plans, policies and programmes would receive more emphasis.

55.   An examination of the position of women in the organizations of the United Nations system shows that considerable progress has been achieved since Nairobi, that overall the critical mass of 30 per cent has been reached, but that nowhere is the proportion of women at management level near that figure. While the proportion of women at senior and middle-management levels has doubled, it is still small. There are, however, positive signs. Near-equality has been achieved at entry level in organizations throughout the system. In several organizations, there has been significant progress also at management levels. The most progressive has been UNFPA, where gender balance has been achieved at all levels.

Table. Percentage of women in professional positions in organizations of the United Nations system, by level, 1987-1993

	Senior management	Middle management	Regular professional	Entry-level
Organization	**1987**			
United Nations Secretariat	5.1	10.9	29.4	35.8
United Nations Voluntary funds	3.5	11.7	27.3	40.7
Specialized agencies	2.3	4.1	18.9	36.6
Other	0.0	2.2	19.8	68.4
Subtotal	3.4	6.6	23.4	38.1
	1990			
United Nations Secretariat	7.8	15.2	34.2	43.1
United Nations Voluntary funds	7.5	16.5	31.1	48.9
Specialized agencies	3.8	7.1	26.2	48.0
Other	0.0	5.3	20.0	61.1
Subtotal	5.6	10.5	29.5	47.1
	1993			
United Nations Secretariat	12.6	16.2	32.2	47.8
United Nations Voluntary funds	12.4	20.5	33.4	49.5
Specialized agencies	4.7	9.1	28.1	43.8
Other	0.0	6.0	21.8	71.4
Subtotal	8.4	12.9	30.4	47.0

Source: Division for the Advancement of Women, based on statistics compiled by the secretariat of the Consultative Committee on Administrative Questions of the Administrative Committee on Coordination, various years as at 31 December.

56.   Since 1990 a number of organizations have undertaken positive measures to increase the proportion of women among professional categories and at decision-making levels.

(a)   United Nations Secretariat
57.   The United Nations Secretariat, under successive mandates from the General Assembly has pursued an affirmative action strategy, the contents of which have been reported regularly to the Commission on the Status of Women and the General Assembly. The results can be seen in the table above.

(b)   United Nations funds and programmes
        (i) United Nations Population Fund
58.   UNFPA involvement in the area of women, population and development (WPD) has been a hallmark of the organization since its inception. Improving the status of women is important as a human rights issue because women have the same equal rights as men in health, education, employment, law, etc. In addition, it is especially important in the context of UNFPA's mandate because women's status affects and is in turn affected by such demographic variables as fertility and maternal and infant mortality.

59.   In 1975, UNFPA became one of the first United Nations organizations to issue guidelines on women, population and development. In 1987, the Governing Council endorsed the Strategy to Strengthen the Fund's Capacity to Deal with Issues Concerning WPD for a period of four years. In 1991, the Governing Council again endorsed the Strategy with modifications. The ultimate objective of the Strategy is the total integration of women's concerns into all UNFPA's activities and the increased participation of women in all projects supported by the Fund. Women are viewed as both beneficiaries and participants.

60.   To achieve the objectives of the Strategy, UNFPA has followed two approaches. The first is to mainstream women - that is, to see that women are fully involved both as beneficiaries and participants in all programmes and projects, whatever the nature of the activity (Maternal Child Health/Family Planning (MCH/FP); Information, Education and Communication (IEC); basic data collection, etc.). The second approach is to support women specific projects - i.e. activities aimed specifically at benefiting women and

improving their status. Such projects may include education, training, skill development, and economic activities. They may also include activities seeking specifically to increase the awareness of policy makers, leaders, media and the general public to the importance of women's issues in population and development. As of mid-1994, there were 124 such projects in all regions; with a total allocation of approximately $34.28 million. However, since UNFPA policy is to mainstream gender concerns into all the activities it supports, funding devoted to the advancement of women far exceeds this amount.

61.   Regarding institutional arrangements, the Women, Population and Development Branch of the Technical and Evaluation Division is responsible for awareness creation, advocacy, and for providing guidance and technical support for operational activities. Branch advisers have been placed in country support teams in four regions and at two agency headquarters (ILO and FAO) to provide technical backstopping to UNFPA-assisted population programmes.

62.   UNFPA is continuing its efforts to reach equal representation of women and men in the professional staff. As of December 1994, women constituted 43 per cent of UNFPA's professional staff. At the field level, women make up 39 per cent of the professional staff. Women lead three of the eight country support teams (one post is vacant, under recruitment with a woman candidate and women make up 52.94 per cent of the total number of professional country support team's advisers.

(ii) United Nations Children's Fund
63.   UNICEF has already reached the mandated goal of 35 per cent women in posts subject to geographical distribution - i.e., international professional posts -and has very nearly reached its own Executive Board's target.

(iii) World Food Programme
64.   The advancement of women has been seriously addressed following the appointment of Ms. Catherine Bertini as Executive Director. There has been an increase in female staff, as reflected in the recruitment for programming and technical posts and for posts at the director level and above. Out of 53 appointments between 1 January 1992 and 30 September 1994, 24 were female. Female representation in the category of director or above increased

from none to 30 per cent. Over the same period, the Office of Personnel recruited 80 project staff, of which 17.5 per cent were female. Country directors and managers at headquarters have been reminded of their responsibility to promote an increase in qualified female personnel. Country offices have been encouraged to launch information campaigns in the local press to achieve both increased representation of women and persons from developing countries.

(c)   Specialized agencies
(i) International Labour Organization

65.   In recent years, there have been positive developments in women's representation on the staff of the ILO. There are now two women out of the three deputy director-generals. Women currently form about 25 per cent of the organization's professional staff.

(ii) Food and Agriculture Organization of the United Nations

66.   Although FAO has not set targets for female professional staff in the organization, some progress has been made in increasing the number of women in professional positions. At FAO headquarters the percentage of female professional staff was 20.2 in 1994. The number of women at the P-4 level increased from 34 in 1989 to 61 in 1993, representing 17.2 per cent of the total at this grade, and at the P-5 level the figure increased over the same period from 14 to 21, representing 7.3 per cent of the total. In 1993, there were three women at the D-1 level and one woman at the D-2 level, representing 1.5 per cent. At the lower professional grades, the number of women almost equals that of men. At the P-3 level, 44 per cent of the staff are women and at the P-2 level women constitute 46 per cent. In the regional offices and FAO representations, the percentage of women staff increased from 9.3 to 10.3 per cent for the period 1989 to 1994, while in the field it increased from 3.4 to 6.3 per cent.

67.   Notwithstanding the assistance received from member countries in encouraging qualified women from their countries to apply for posts in FAO's specialized technical fields, women represented less than 20 per cent of the applicants for such posts. Although the percentage of women in the technical units remains low, the proportion in subject areas more traditionally related to women, such as the Economic and Social Policy Department (21 per cent), the Department of General Affairs and Information (38 per

cent), and the Administration and Finance Department (31 per cent), is more in line with United Nations targets.

(iii) United Nations Educational, Scientific and Cultural Organization

68.   UNESCO has made considerable progress in the employment of women in posts which call for decision-making ever since Mr. Federico Mayor was appointed Director-General. The percentage of female professionals has been improving constantly, so that in 1994, at levels P-1/P-2/P-3, more than 50 per cent of the staff are women; two Assistant Directors-General are women, and more than 10 per cent of D-1 posts are held by women. The organization is still aiming to reach the target of 30 per cent for level P-4 and above by 1995, as requested by the General Conference.

69.   In order to increase the representation of women at all levels in the professional category and above, the Director-General has requested member States to include the name of at least one female candidate for every three male candidates submitted for vacant posts.

70.   In 1989, the Young Professionals Programme was reactivated. Since then 50 per cent of the young professionals recruited by UNESCO are women. This programme is also designed to improve geographical distribution and is open to unrepresented or underrepresented countries only.

71.   To contribute to the promotion of UNESCO's professional posts held by women, the Bureau of Personnel has elaborated a specific roster of potential women candidates with data concerning their educational background, work experience and competencies.

72.   On 8 March 1993 the Director-General issued a note concerning the equality of men and women in the Secretariat. It stressed the importance of the development of policies to prevent and combat sexual harassment in the work place. He also stated that every effort would be made to avoid assumptions based on stereotypes about the effectiveness of men or women in certain jobs and that discrimination based on stereotypes resulted in a waste of talent.

(iv) United Nations Industrial Development Organization

73.   In the resolutions of the General Conference and decisions of the

Industrial Development Board, a number of actions have been called for to improve the status of women in the Secretariat. The Director-General has been requested to report to the policy-making organs on the progress made on the implementation of the plan of action adopted in 1989. The Director-General has been urged to take every opportunity offered by any restructuring and to continue his efforts to achieve, to the extent possible, an overall representation in the professional category of 25 per cent women by 1993 and 30 per cent by 1995. He has reiterated the need to use redeployment as a means to redress the imbalance in the representation of women at the senior and decision-making levels.

C. International services and support for the advancement of women

74.   The organizations of the United Nations system provide a variety of services and support for the advancement of women at the international level, ranging from information-gathering, analysis and dissemination through operational activities. These services have both broadened and deepened since the Nairobi Conference.

1. Research and policy analysis

75.   Research and policy analysis is a central means of supporting policy dialogue at the intergovernmental level. The reports prepared by organizations of the United Nations system, individually and together, have helped change understanding of gender at the international level. Certain publications, like The World's Women: Trends and Statistics, have become major benchmarks for appraising progress.

76.   Much of the research has also been of use to the academic community.

(a)   Division for the Advancement of Women

77.   Since 1990, the Division for the Advancement of Women has continued the development of policy research for the Commission on the Status of Women. This has included preparing three reports on priority themes per year and biennial reports on the effective mobilization of women for development.

78.   Reports on priority themes were often prepared using expert groups. Since 1987, a total of 19 such expert group meetings have been organized. As a by-product of its work on priority themes, the Division produced a series of publications on women and decision-making.

79.   As part of the preparations for the Fourth World Conference on Women, the Division, in cooperation with other organizations of the United Nations system, prepared the 1994 World Survey on the Role of Women in Development and the present review and appraisal.

80.   In support of the Committee on the Elimination of Discrimination against Women, the Division prepared analysis of articles 2, 6, 7, 8, 9, 15, 16 of the Convention on the Elimination of All Forms of Discrimination against Women and the first draft of the report on progress in implementing the Convention. The Division has also organized a series of regional and subregional training seminars on the Convention. From 1987 to 1993, a total of six such seminars were organized.

(b)   Other United Nations Secretariat divisions
         (i)   Statistical Division
81.   Since 1990, the goal of the Statistical Division to compile and disseminate gender statistics in new, more user-oriented formats has advanced considerably with the preparation of the second issue of The World's Women: Trends and Statistics and version 3 of the Women's Indicators and Statistics Database (WISTAT). The Division also continues work to improve statistical concepts, methods and data collection programmes to provide a more complete and objective picture of the situation of women and of equality between the sexes.

82.   The first issue of The World's Women: Trends and Statistics, published in 1991, broke new ground in presenting and analysing gender statistics in a format that is widely used and accessible. Its success led to the request for an updated issue for the Fourth World Conference on Women. A key element in the success of the first issue was the unprecedented inter-Secretariat and inter-agency collaboration in its preparation, promotion and use. In the second issue, the original sponsors, UNFPA, UNICEF, UNIFEM and the Division for the Advancement of Women, are joined by UNDP, WFP, INSTRAW, UNESCO and the Department for Public Information of the United Nations Secretariat.

83.   The statistics underlying the two issues are in WISTAT. The database was launched in 1988 and has become the most authoritative and widely used international source of statistics and indicators available on the

advancement of women and achievement of equality between women and men. The development of WISTAT has been supported by UNFPA. In early 1995, version 3 of WISTAT was released as a CD-ROM, containing a new database and user interface and the spreadsheet format used previously. Special features of the CD-ROM database are country profiles with gender indicators and a brief set of general indicators and multi-user capacity for putting WISTAT on local networks.

84.   In cooperation with INSTRAW, the Division has made considerable progress towards achieving objectives established in the three global conferences on women for the purpose of improving the coverage of women's activities and concerns in economic statistics and the labour force, national accounts and the informal sector. The publication Methods of Measuring Women's Economic Activity was prepared on appropriate methods and data tabulation programmes for use in population censuses and household surveys, to highlight women's role in economic activity and production. The Division also cooperated with INSTRAW and the Inter-Secretariat Working Group on National Accounts to ensure that methodological issues affecting the equitable measurement of women's work in SNA were taken into account in the SNA revision issued in 1994. It also cooperates with INSTRAW in follow-up work on time-use studies and the measurement and valuation of women's unremunerated work. Results of this work are summarized in the second issue of The World's Women.

(ii) Population Division

85.   The Population Division provides gender-disaggregated statistics, conducts a variety of analytic studies that have a gender dimension, monitors population policies and organizes expert meetings that deal with gender issues. Every two years the Population Division produces population estimates and projections, by age and sex, for all countries and areas of the world. Such estimates and projections were recently published separately for rural and urban areas. Apart from their direct interest, these statistics serve as "denominators" for the gender-disaggregated estimates and projections in areas such as school enrolment and employment which are produced within and outside the United Nations system. The Division also regularly monitors fertility, contraceptive practice and mortality levels, by sex, as well as Government policies related to population concerns. Since 1990, special

studies and expert meetings have dealt with female migration, education and fertility, abortion policy, gender differences in age at marriage and living arrangements of women and children, including women-headed households. Ongoing studies deal with sex differences in infant and child mortality, among other topics. Gender-specific statistics and analytic studies from the Population Division have been employed in preparations for the Fourth World Conference on Women in various ways. Notably, the Population Division has provided a variety of statistical information and analytic studies to the Statistical Division for use in the new edition of The World's Women, and the WISTAT database also contains a variety of data series from the Population Division.

86.   The Population Division has been the substantive secretariat of the Population Commission and, in collaboration with UNFPA, provided substantive support for the International Conference on Population and Development.

(c)   Regional commissions: ESCAP

87.   Since 1986, the Women in Development Section of ESCAP has undertaken to develop indicators and statistics to monitor the situation of women within the framework of the Women's Information Network for Asia and the Pacific (WINAP) and published Statistical Compendium on Women in Asia and the Pacific in 1994.

88.   In 1989, the Section launched a project to examine existing practices regarding the integration of women's concerns into development planning, devised a set of guidelines on the means of improving on the situation in 1991 and prepared reference materials for organization of national workshops in the fields of education, energy, fisheries and water resources in 1994. Since 1989, ESCAP has undertaken a project to design, implement, analyse and evaluate legal literacy programmes, formulated guidelines on upgrading the legal status of women in 1989 and conducted national literacy campaign in nine countries.

(d)   United Nations Institute for Research and Training for the Advancement of Women

89.   Since the last review and appraisal, INSTRAW has carried out a number of interlocking research activities aimed at addressing women's

issues and including them in the mainstream development process, through an integrated, multidisciplinary approach. Its major programme areas included statistics and indicators on women, women's work in the informal sector, communications, women and credit, women and water supply and sanitation, and women and new and renewable sources of energy.

90.   It made major initiatives to remove gaps in data on gender issues. Some of the results included the publication The Situation of Elderly Women, Available Statistics and Indicators, prepared jointly by INSTRAW and the Statistical Division; Handbook on Compilation of Statistics on Women in the Informal Sector in Industry, Trade and Services in Africa; Synthesis of Pilot Studies on Compilation of Statistics on Women in the Informal Sector in Industry, Trade and Services. These were used in national training workshops in four African countries. A panel on gender statistics and the valuation of unpaid work through time use is currently being organized with the Statistical Division for the NGO Forum at Beijing in September 1995. Following up on these initiatives, INSTRAW has initiated a major research study aimed at developing cost-effective data collection methods that will capture all the activities of women and men and techniques for valuing unpaid work using time-use and other auxiliary data.

91.   INSTRAW undertook an in-depth investigation of the conceptual and methodological issues related to internal and international migration and published The Migration of Women: Methodological Issues in the Measurement and Analysis of Internal and International Migration in collaboration with the International Organization for Migration and the Population Division of the United Nations.

92.   INSTRAW sponsored research in three Latin American countries on women and communications, based on which actions have been initiated to promote a better portrayal and participation of women in the media. A research programme on the situation of women in agriculture during the transition process in Bulgaria and Hungary was also initiated in 1993. Similarly, research studies at the regional level on women's access to credit were conducted by INSTRAW in Africa, Asia and Latin America and were synthesized, together with an overview of the laws in 59 countries regarding women's access to land, in a publication entitled Women and Credit.

93.   INSTRAW, in its work, has cooperated with several organizations of the United Nations system, including the Statistical and Population Divisions, the regional commissions, UNFPA, UNDP, UNICEF, ILO and FAO.

(e)   Specialized agencies
(i) International Labour Organization

94.   Of particular significance in the ILO's efforts to implement the Strategies is the execution of a multidisciplinary and interdepartmental project on equality for women in employment, during the 1992-1993 biennium, to enhance the effectiveness of legislation, tackle obstacles to equality in the labour market, develop appropriate statistical methodologies for the measurement of job segregation and gender differences in wages, and formulate policies and concrete measures for promoting gender equality in the world of work. The project generated substantial data and insight and demonstrated the complexity and multifaceted nature of the gender-inequality problem in the world of work and the need for an integrated and comprehensive policy framework for tackling it. The project produced an information kit and a training package on women workers' rights to disseminate information about women's rights. Its other outputs included publications and seminars on women and trade unions, especially the role of trade unions in organizing women workers in the informal, home-based and other unorganized sectors; sexual harassment, collective bargaining and the promotion of gender equity; women and social security; positive action and women's employment; women's skill diversification in vocational trades; comparable worth in pay; enforcement of equality provisions in law; statistical measurement of gender wage differentials, and job segregation and occupational concentration.

95.   Other efforts by the ILO to promote equality of opportunity and treatment for women in the world of work have been undertaken through standard-setting, research, workshops, seminars and other meetings, advisory services, technical cooperation and dissemination of information. The areas covered include standards and gender equality; poverty alleviation; group mobilization and employment promotion of the disadvantaged groups of women workers; women and trade unionism; employers' organizations and the promotion of gender equality; women's entrepreneurship

and small-scale enterprises; the training of women managers; vocational training; structural adjustment, labour market flexibility and women; the reproductive and productive roles and needs of women workers; cooperatives and labour relations. The overall strategy is to mainstream, or integrate across the board, gender issues and women's concerns within the organization's programmes and objectives. This strategy is complemented by women-specific activities such as for rural women and other disadvantaged groups. The ILO's recent active Partnership Policy, which aims at bringing the organization closer to its constituents and through which multidisciplinary teams of technical advisers have been established in the various regions of the world, has provided an appropriate set-up to mainstream women and gender concerns in the ILO's technical assistance to its member States and to ensure an integrated and multidisciplinary approach to the consideration of women's concerns. A project for gender training of ILO staff is currently under implementation to enhance the capacity of the organization's staff to ensure gender sensitivity in their activities.

(ii) Food and Agriculture Organization of the United Nations

96.   One of the priority areas of the FAO Plan of Action for the Integration of Women in Development is providing gender-responsive policy advice to member countries. During the 1993-1994 biennium, FAO responded to requests in the areas of macroeconomic policies, strengthening women-in-development machineries and general policy advice in at least 40 countries. This included technical assistance to ministries of agriculture, women-in-development units and other governmental agencies; the organization of workshops at regional and country level; and the development of guidelines and training modules for policy makers. As a complement to strengthening women-in-development machineries, FAO provides assistance to rural women's groups and has, for example, sponsored the Latin American and Caribbean network of institutions and agencies in support of rural women in 19 countries.

97.   Priority areas for research and policy analysis have included: extension and the reorientation of agricultural and home economics curricula; rural women, population and environment; and women and sustainable development. FAO has organized a number of expert consultations and workshops, carried out studies, and developed guidelines in these areas.

A considerable number of case studies and publications have resulted from these efforts, including guidelines for the integration of women, population and environment in rural development policies and programmes; guidelines for integrating women and gender issues in fisheries and forestry programmes, a study on agricultural extension and farm women; and a framework on reorientation of home economics for rural development in developing countries. Gender issues have also been incorporated into many other FAO publications and guidelines.

98.   FAO recognizes that if women are to benefit from and participate in development efforts, development specialists and policy makers must be sensitized to gender issues. Therefore, gender analysis training became FAO's first priority in implementation of the Plan of Action adopted in 1989. By the end of 1992, FAO had carried out 42 two-day gender analysis workshops at headquarters and in regional offices, with 773 officers attending, representing approximately 80 per cent of all professional staff. FAO has also carried out gender analysis training with two other target groups: national-level women-in-development machineries and selected counterpart groups in member countries. A programme on gender analysis and forestry in Asia, carried out in 1991-1992 in six countries, resulted in a training package. In 1992, FAO, in collaboration with gender and development trainers and managers from UNDP and the World Bank, initiated the development of the Socio-economic and Gender Analysis Training Programme. A portfolio of training packages, including field manuals, is being developed with the assistance of ILO Turin, ILO Geneva, and the United States Agency for International Development.

99.   Improving statistics is another priority area of the FAO Plan of Action. In 1991 FAO organized an Inter-Agency Consultation on Women and Statistics and, as follow-up, is providing assistance to member countries to measure accurately the contributions of rural women to agricultural production, environmental sustainability, poverty alleviation, food security and nutrition, and a pilot programme is being implemented in eight countries of the Near East and some countries of Africa. An extensive review of the programme of the 1990 world census of agriculture, carried out in preparation for the Year 2000 Round, suggested changes to permit improved collection of gender-disaggregated data on human resources. Other efforts include:

case studies on the availability of gender-disaggregated data, collaboration with national statistical offices to review agricultural survey questionnaires, and the provision of gender-responsive agricultural databases and country profiles.

(iii) United Nations Industrial Development Organization

100.   The UNIDO strategy, concept and approach is to promote the advancement of women in the development process through "mainstreaming", by acknowledging women as actors and equal partners of the target groups of UNIDO's activities addressing the problems and needs of both men and women. However, women-specific programmes and services will remain all the more necessary in order to remove specific constraints which prevent women from participating fully in the mainstream of development. UNIDO has also developed practical tools that enable programme/project designers and implementors to give consideration to women throughout the programme/project cycle, such as a reference file on the consideration of women in project design, management and evaluation, adjusted to facilitate its application in objective-oriented project planning. With the establishment of a database on women in industry, containing both bibliographical information and country information notes on women in industry, the consideration of gender aspects has been facilitated in programme/project design. At present, the database contains information on women in industry for about 100 developing countries.

101.   By placing a women-in-development expert in the research division, the methodology for reviewing industrial employment in a UNIDO's industrial review series was revised to embrace broader issues concerning human resource development and to include gender-specific data and information. Studies on women in industry have been conducted, such as one on the changing techno-economic environment in the textile and clothing industry and its implications for the role of women in Asian developing countries.

2. Development cooperation

(a)   United Nations Secretariat
(i) Statistical Division

102.   Two developments advanced significantly the ability of the Statistical Division to undertake technical cooperation activities in gender -

statistics: the establishment, on a trial basis, of a post for a technical adviser in statistics on women in development by the Government of Norway in 1990; and a three-year project, begun in 1992, to build national capability to prepare gender-statistics publications.

103.   Working with staff of the Statistical Division, the technical adviser has assisted countries in developing and implementing programmes in gender statistics. This includes the review and assessment of existing data collection programmes as to the adequacy of available data related to gender, building ties between users and producers of these statistics and planning the tabulations and publications relating to gender. The technical adviser has also worked with UNIFEM, INSTRAW, UNFPA, UNDP, the specialized agencies and the regional commissions to provide authoritative statistical guidance in their own work on women in development.

(ii) Population Division

104.   The Population Division recognizes that there is a vital and mutually supporting interaction between research and technical cooperation. The Division produces manuals and reports that are widely used in developing country training programmes in the areas of population and development. Research on gender-related issues, as mentioned above, also contributes to the Division's ability to deliver technical support for the advancement of women. Departmental reorganization and changes in donor arrangements have recently led to changes in the provisions for technical cooperation. The Division now has a team of technical support specialists working actively to disseminate information and provide expert advice and support to developing countries.

(iii) Department of Development Support and Management Services

105.   In 1987, in keeping with the Nairobi Strategies, the Department's predecessor (Department of Technical Cooperation for Development) established guidelines for incorporating a women's component into projects. The Department's approach has focused on human resources development, through training, and on capacity-building, through the strengthening of financial and institutional arrangements.

106.   The use of training as a particularly effective vehicle for promoting the role of women in development is seen in the Department's efforts to

increase the number of women candidates for fellowship awards and training opportunities, particularly in public administration and economic planning and projections. Women were also being trained in such fields as energy, geology, mining and water resources management.

107.   Most of the Department's grass-roots projects have women's components, with emphasis on improving their socio-economic conditions. The formation of women's groups to engage in common endeavours has in many cases helped to achieve this goal and will receive increased attention. A loan guarantee scheme operated by a local bank in cooperation with the project provides women with credit, not only for fixed costs but also for working capital needed to sustain their income-generating activities.

108.   Special attention has been paid to combining technical skills training with training in basic planning, business management, marketing, group organization, and leadership in order to develop and sustain income-generating activities. Enhancing the planning and managerial capability of local institutions has also been emphasized in order to assure continuous support to women's activities after the termination of external assistance, and to foster self-reliance and sustainability.

109.   The Department conducted a series of workshops focused specifically on developing policies and approaches in order to channel more women into the public sector. Interregional workshops on the development of managerial skills for women in public management were held in Thailand, Malaysia, and the former Yugoslavia, with participants at the policy-making level from 26 countries. Guidelines were developed to help policy makers address and anticipate gender issues that actually and potentially inhibit the accelerated enhancement of the role of women in public management.

110.   In consideration of the limited resources available, and in order to maximize the impact of its efforts, the Department has stressed networking and inter-agency collaboration and coordination. In addition to collaboration from United Nations entities, the success of gender-based and other development programmes, in the Department's experience, requires support from Governments, non-governmental organizations and the private sector. The recruitment of women as experts and consultants for projects is

an active area of concern for the Department, although acceptance rates have continued to be low. The Department has been more successful in placing recent graduates as associated experts: 30 per cent of them are now women. The Department has also intensified its efforts, in collaboration with Governments, to elicit greater support in hiring women as national professionals in projects.

(iv) Economic Commission for Latin America and the Caribbean

111.   In fulfilment of its resolution 483 (XXI), ECLAC has carried out activities to implement the recommendations of the Nairobi Forward-looking Strategies in all areas of its work. The following activities were carried out under various subprogrammes: identification of women as agents of agricultural and rural development by the Agricultural Development Unit; training activities by the Latin American and Caribbean Institute for Economic and Social Planning (ILPES), especially the course on development, planning and public policies which includes a series of lectures; studies and seminars carried out by the Joint ECLAC/UNIDO Industrial and Technological Development Unit on themes such as the gender dimension of human resources training and formal education, women entrepreneurs and female employment in the industrial and tertiary sectors; a study by the International Trade, Finance and Transport Division on the impact of sectoral policies on women; research and information activities by the Latin American Demographic Centre (CELADE); meetings on information management by the Latin American Centre for Economic and Social Documentation (CLADES).

112.   Various dissemination activities were organized in collaboration with UNICEF, ILPES, the Pan American Health Organization (PAHO), the Regional Employment Programme for Latin America and the Caribbean (PREALC), the Colegio de México, CELADE, UNFPA and the Social Development Division of ECLAC, to which the Women and Development Unit belonged until November 1993.

(b)   United Nations Development Fund for Women

113.   In 1985 UNIFEM's mandate was expanded to not only provide direct technical and financial support to women's initiatives in developing countries but also to mainstream women into development planning and decision-making. To undertake this work UNIFEM became an independent

entity in autonomous association with the United Nations Development Programme. Based in New York, UNIFEM operates at the local, national, regional and international levels through its 11 UNIFEM regional offices in Asia and the Pacific, Western Asia, Africa, Latin America and the Caribbean and its representation through UNDP offices at the country level.

114.   Currently UNIFEM is working primarily in three programme areas: agriculture and food security; trade and industry; and macro-policy-making and national planning. The Fund promotes women's access to training, science and technology, credit, information and other tools for development. It also links grass-roots women to national and international policy-making bodies and into global debates on issues such as poverty alleviation, the environment and human rights.

115.   UNIFEM's regional programmes address the specific concerns of grass-roots women in each region: UNIFEM's Africa Investment Plan 1994-1995 addresses problems of special significance to African women and the role they play in development. It focuses on the following areas: agriculture and food security, trade and industry, environmental sustainability, and refugees and displaced persons. UNIFEM's Asia and the Pacific Development Plan 1994-1995 aims to strengthen the institutional mechanisms that link women at the local level to formal development-planning and decision-making structures in the following areas: agriculture and environment, trade and industry, national planning and women in politics. In Latin America and the Caribbean, UNIFEM's Participatory Action Programme for 1994-1995 focuses on poverty alleviation, environmental management, violence against women, and citizenship and democracy.

116.   At the global level UNIFEM focuses on credit and financial systems, science and technology, women's rights as human rights, and sustainable development. The Fund also networks with parliamentarians and ensures that women are on the agenda and help shape the outcome of key international conferences such as the 1992 Earth Summit in Rio, and the 1993 United Nations Human Rights Conference in Vienna. UNIFEM is currently active in preparations for the 1995 Social Development Summit in Copenhagen and the Fourth World Conference on Women in Beijing.

(c)   United Nations Development Programme

117.   In 1986, following the Nairobi Conference, UNDP upgraded its existing one-person desk on women's issues to a Division, staffed by four professionals and two secretaries. The mandate of the Division was to ensure the mainstreaming of women's concerns into all UNDP's headquarters and country office activities.

118.   A three-pronged approach was developed to act upon this mandate, reflecting relevant requirements of the Forward-looking Strategies. First, policy guidelines, a women-in-development strategy, and monitoring tools were developed and distributed, ensuring an appropriate and recognized policy framework. Secondly, an ambitious gender analysis training programme, funded by the Government of Norway, was embarked upon. Focused upon senior decision-makers and middle-level operational staff, this training programme led to a broad-based grasp within the organization of the principal issues involved and contributed to the shift by UNDP from a women-in-development approach to a gender approach during the period 1990-1992. Thirdly, a team of women-in-development focal points was established in each regional bureau, working closely with the focal points also established in each country office.

119.   Since 1990 the renamed Gender in Development Programme has worked towards putting into operation the mainstreaming approach, based upon the positive policy environment and structures established during the previous four years. The goal has been, in accordance with the strategies, to ensure that women participate in and benefit from UNDP-funded projects to the maximum possible extent. To this end close relationships have been built with the country offices. Over 3,000 staff members and government colleagues have been trained, technical backstopping has been provided in the preparation of project documents, country programmes, country strategy notes and national human development reports, and approximately $7 million of Special Programme Reserve funds have been made available to country offices specifically for gender programming purposes. As a result, over 40 projects have been approved in the area of strengthening national capacity with regard to gender. By participating in the project appraisal process, and conducting field visits to country offices, gender concerns have also been incorporated appropriately in a broad range of projects. There is

now widespread experience in the implementation of projects reflecting gender concerns, which will be reinforced during the coming programming cycle as UNDP country offices coordinate system-wide efforts in sustainable human development.

120.   This process, which is ongoing, has been reinforced by mainstreaming of gender concerns in the thematic units of UNDP, so that their back-stopping of country offices reflects full awareness of gender issues.

(d)   United Nations Population Fund

121.   In terms of programme areas, maternal and child health/family planning has been the largest single area supported by UNFPA. Approximately 50 per cent of its funding goes to such programmes. Within the area, priority has been given to improving the health of women and children as part of an integrated approach and to activities aimed at improving these services and making them more accessible to women. Emphasis is placed on women's reproductive rights, the Safe Motherhood Initiative, and quality of care, including provision of a wide range of family planning methods. Priority has also been given to education and training activities which enhance women's participation in these programmes, especially at the managerial, supervisory and policy-making levels and to creating employment opportunities for women as providers of maternal and child health/family planning care. In the field of education, UNFPA has supported formal and non-formal education programmes for women, including functional literacy and population education; specific activities to reduce school drop-out rates for girls; managerial and supervisory training which enhances women's participation in population programmes. It has also supported the development of educational materials and approaches that improve the general understanding of women's issues, especially as related to population issues. It is the policy of the Fund to ensure that data are disaggregated by gender in collection, analysis and dissemination. Priority has been given to support activities, including training, which ensure, for example, that the concepts and methods used in censuses and surveys will result in complete and unbiased data on women and men, including women's economic contributions. UNFPA collaborates closely with other United Nations organizations.

122.   UNFPA has supported research in the area of women, population, development and environment. Thus, a project is under way which examines

the linkages between women, population and the environment in Kenya, Mexico and Malaysia. It also collaborates with other agencies in the United Nations system on women, environment and development. It supported, with UNICEF, a symposium on environment, women and children prior to the United Nations Conference on Environment and Development (UNCED). In other regions, UNFPA has supported special projects or components of projects which are specifically designed to assist women. A broad range of activities is included under this category -e.g., support to women's economic activities; research and awareness creation of women's contributions to development in their many roles - reproductive, productive and environmental; and strengthening of women's organizations.

123.   UNFPA has always worked very closely with women's non-governmental organizations. It has supported the participation of representatives of many women's non-governmental organizations from developing countries in major international conferences such as UNCED, and in preparations for the International Conference on Population and Development and the Fourth World Conference on Women. Special efforts are made to include women's perspectives in policy and research related to family planning and reproductive health.

(e)   United Nations Children's Fund
124.   Since 1985, UNICEF has made concrete efforts to integrate women's issues into its programmes through articulation of policy objectives in 1985 and an implementation strategy for mainstreaming women's issues in 1987. In 1994, the Executive Board endorsed a policy paper on gender equality and the empowerment of women and girls and urged the follow-up of its recommendations in country programmes of cooperation. The paper reflected the shift from women in development to gender and development and stressed the need for actions to promote gender equality and gender-sensitive development programmes, taking into account, inter alia, the provisions of and complementarity between the Convention on the Rights of the Child and the Convention on the Elimination of All Forms of Discrimination against Women. It recommended that gender concerns be integrated into the national programmes of action as an essential measure for introducing early action to eliminate the discrimination faced by girls and women in the achievement of the mid-decade goals and the universal goals of the World Summit for Children.

125.   Priority will be given to strengthening the integration of gender concerns in country programmes by adopting the life-cycle perspective in addressing gender-based disadvantages and eliminating disparities that exist at each stage of the life-cycle of girls and women, with special attention to development needs of girls in the age groups 0-5 years, 6-12 years and 13-18 years; and the use of the Women's Equality and Empowerment Framework as the conceptual and operational tool in the planning, implementation and evaluation of programmes for mainstreaming gender issues. For this, the ongoing efforts on capacity-building for gender responsive programming through training of professional staff will be intensified both at headquarters and the field offices. During 1993-1994, more than 800 staff were trained and 3,500 counterparts from government and non-governmental organizations have been trained on gender analysis. The country programmes of cooperation include supporting actions and strategies for mainstreaming gender concerns in all sectoral programmes and specific programmes for promoting equality in the family, sharing of parental responsibilities between men and women, gender concerns in emergency situations, and activities for specific target groups of girls and women, such as those in poverty households and in especially difficult circumstances. Priority attention is given to the promotion of gender-sensitive national development through policy-oriented research, the development of gender-sensitive indicators and establishment of age-and-gender-disaggregated data systems, organized participation of women at all levels, and capacity-building and the mobilization of youth for bringing about a more gender-equitable society in the future.

(f)   Institute for Research and Training for the Advancement of Women
126.   INSTRAW has carried out activities to implement the Nairobi Forward-looking Strategies through its training programme. Within that programme it has undertaken activities to promote a more effective use of statistics and indicators on gender issues, including training workshops for users and producers of statistics to address issues and problems of gender statistics and suggest ways to improve relevant concepts and methods of data collection and compilation. A total of 11 training workshops (three subregional and eight national) have been held since 1990.

127.   A major programme on women, water supply and sanitation has been in place since 1984, with INSTRAW taking a lead in this field in the sys-

tem. It developed a training package and has conducted six training seminars using the package at the national, regional and interregional levels. In 1991 the package was updated and, in cooperation with the International Training Centre of the ILO and the Department of Development Support and Management Services of the United Nations Secretariat, training seminars were conducted in five countries using it.

128.   INSTRAW is also the lead agency in the United Nations system in the field of women and new and renewable sources of energy. In cooperation with national counterparts, INSTRAW has utilized participatory and self-reliant techniques in applying a new approach to the organization of new and renewable sources of energy systems in national and regional seminars in six countries.

129.   As part of the follow-up to the United Nations Conference on Environment and Development, INSTRAW, together with the Department of Development Support and Management Services of the United Nations Secretariat organized an interregional workshop on the role of women in environmentally sound and sustainable development, which resulted in 100 replicable project profiles covering 15 areas of Agenda 21, and resulted in a publication and training package.

(g)   World Food Programme
130.   The Commission on Food Aid Policies and Programmes of the World Food Programme adopted in 1987 the Food Aid Strategies for Women in Development and was presented with WFP Sectoral Guidelines on Women and Development: Gender Variables in Food-assisted Projects. The policy directs support to women as equal social and economic contributors to development and resource persons in crisis situations. Strategic interventions include support to women in

(a)   Food production and food security strategies;

(b)   Food for work projects, by creating an enabling environment for the production of assets through reviews of ownership, access and control over resources, review of labour time and labour supply, creation of employment linkages and on-site support services (training and social support);

(c)   Promotion of opportunities for female education and vocational training and sponsoring of community-based skills training for employment, income generation and nutrition improvement.

131.   Particular achievements since 1990 in strengthening of the operational dimensions of WFP include incorporation of women-in-development/gender as integral parts of orientation and training seminars and periodic reviews of WFP's programmes and projects. Various in-depth studies were undertaken to underline the policy of moving from women-in-development to gender-and-development, away from assistance through the formation of women's groups, with little forward or outward-looking perspective on the future. WFP is funding several initiatives with governmental and non-governmental institutions, following an institutional capacity-building approach to sensitize and train professionals, authorities and beneficiaries in rapid appraisals and gender planning.

(h)   Specialized agencies
(i) Food and Agriculture Organization of the United Nations
132.   FAO's project development and monitoring activities to enhance women's roles in agriculture and rural development and increase their access to productive resources are varied. Often, pilot studies and activities are launched; lessons learned are then integrated into follow-up phases or similar projects in other areas. The experience gained is also used to strengthen policy advice activities. Although these efforts are carried out in many fields, four major areas are: credit and banking services; extension and technical training; women, sustainable development, natural resource management and the environment; and nutrition and food security.

133.   Innovative activities where rural women have been beneficiaries include: systematizing loan procedures for simpler and more flexible credit delivery and recovery; establishing revolving loan funds with training components in micro-enterprise and financial management; reducing transition costs through the FAO Microbanking System; in-kind revolving funds and group savings; increasing incomes and savings through income-generating activities; extension training targeted to women professionals and women farmers; reorienting agricultural and home economics curricula and extension; training in marketing, plant nutrient management, horticulture and livestock production; community forestry; and the promotion of non-traditional foodstuffs in household food security.

134.   In the revision of FAO's Plan of Action, efforts will be made to establish an organization-wide monitoring and appraisal system able to identify existing and pipeline regular and field programme activities that are relevant

to women. This will include integrating key gender indicators into the FAO programme and monitoring system and, in particular, incorporating into that system gender-disaggregated data on target groups and a "flag" that indicates the relevance of an activity specifically for women.

(ii) United Nations Industrial Development Organization

135.   UNIDO developed and implemented technical cooperation projects in priority areas for women in industry - i.e., agro-industry, industrial planning, and environment and energy. Particularly successful experiences in project execution have led to the formulation of more systematic and conceptualized programmes suitable for adaptation and replication, utilizing needs assessments and analyses of target groups and country-based socioeconomic environment, across regions and/or industrial subsectors.

136.   UNIDO has prepared a service package, Training Programme for Women Entrepreneurs in the Food Processing Industry. Its main objective is training of trainers and capacity-building at existing training institutions. It targets both potential and existing women entrepreneurs. The package has three modules aimed at upgrading entrepreneurial skills and technology and production skills and one consisting of a workbook for trainers. The programme was originally prepared for the African context; however, it is being adapted and adjusted to the Asian and Central American circumstances.

137.   In order to equip women entrepreneurs/managers in economies in transition with skills and capabilities to cope with the changing economic situation, a training programme has been developed in China, aiming at increasing the participation of women in the newly emerging private sector - i.e., township enterprises in rural areas. This is being done through the development of a tailor-made programme to meet the needs of Chinese women entrepreneurs/managers and through a training-of-trainers course. With adequate adaptation to local conditions, this programme can potentially be replicated elsewhere - in particular in the transitional economies.

138.   In terms of entrepreneurship development for women, targeting existing entrepreneurs, the activity covers all aspects of the production cycle - i.e., market research, product design and development, entrepreneurship and management, production techniques, quality control and marketing with an approach open to both domestic and export markets. It containsan inventive system which is used as a training tool in cash flow analysis.

139.   UNIDO also assisted in the establishment and management of women cooperatives in order to strengthen their capability to provide relevant services for women entrepreneurs. Hands-on practical training in an incubator environment is provided with theoretical classroom training and ongoing consultancy/follow-up at the businesses of the trainees. This is also market-oriented and therefore aims at improving competitiveness.

140.   Development and dissemination of appropriate technologies for women have proved to be an effective tool to improve women's traditional processing activities. In the rural and small-scale industrial sectors, in particular, women users will have to be encouraged to have training on equipment operation, maintenance and repair in order to keep the control over newly introduced and/or improved technology. A pilot project in sub-Saharan Africa combines poverty alleviation, upgrading of living conditions and employment generation, with the primary objective to develop, test and introduce appropriate food-processing technologies and equipment. The project has introduced "multifunctionality" in order to increase the sustainability of the activities undertaken by women, using a mill engine as a power source for several other types of equipment during and outside the harvesting time - e.g., for battery rechargers, water pumps, oil presses, etc.

3. Financial assistance

(a)   World Bank

141.   Over the past two decades, the World Bank has identified and researched major issues with respect to gender disparities, particularly in education and health, drawing attention to the economic costs of under-investment in women and identifying policies and project interventions that can help reduce the disparities. In particular, the Bank has been focusing attention on gender equity issues in its economic and sectoral work and in the design of Bank projects, especially in human resources and agriculture.

142.   The 1994 policy paper on gender, Enhancing Women's Participation in Economic Development, lays out the priorities for the Bank, which include strengthening the implementation of Bank policies on gender. This is to be accomplished by integrating gender issues into the mainstream of the Bank's economic and sector work and lending programmes. The strategic agenda set out by the policy paper calls for the following activities:

(a)   Country-specific analyses of gender issues through poverty assessments, country strategy papers, public expenditure reviews, women-in-development assessments, and other economic and sectoral work;

(b)   Integration of gender issues into the design and implementation of lending programmes, including adjustment operations;

(c)   Explicit demonstration in country assistance strategies of the linkage between gender issues and Bank lending operations;

(d)   Evaluation of the implementation experience on gender equity in the country implementation review process.

143.   Several effective strategies for reducing the barriers to women's economic participation have emerged from the past two decades of project experience. However, there is particularly strong evidence of what works in the five areas discussed below: education, health, wage labour, agriculture and natural resource management, and financial services.

144.   In education, strategies for expanding girls' enrolment include reserving places for girls, establishing single-sex schools or classrooms, recruiting more female teachers, and designing school facilities to conform to the cultural standards of the community.

145.   In health, community-based health services have been cost-effective in improving women's health. Integrated services - which combine nutrition, family planning, maternal and child health services, and primary health care - tend to be the most effective in reaching women.

146.   In wage labour, the principal strategies for increasing women's participation in the formal labour force include removing legal and regulatory barriers, raising women's productivity, easing the constraints on their time, and improving the efficiency of the labour market by providing information on job opportunities.

147.   In agriculture and natural resource management, because most poor rural women work in agriculture, the main strategy is to help women obtain title to the land they farm and to open the door to services and government assistance.

148.   In financial services, innovative programmes have demonstrated that financial services, mainly credit and savings, can be provided to poor women at competitive cost.

(b)   International Fund for Agricultural Development
149.   In view of its mandate for dealing with poverty alleviation, IFAD has, since its inception at the end of 1978, addressed gender issues in programmes for the economic advancement of rural women.

150.   IFAD has adopted a coherent gender strategy on how to address the empowerment of women through its projects. The main elements of the strategy are:

(a)   Improve availability and quality of gender data and analysis;

(b)   Protect and enhance women's access to land and other natural resources;

(c)   Address constraints affecting women's time and labour;

(d)   Improve women's access to rural financial services;

(e)   Address gender issues in agricultural technology systems by facilitating the participation of rural women in technology generation and transfer;

(f)   Provide new skills and information for rural women to enhance their income-generating potential;

(g)   Facilitate communication and information-exchange among poor rural women and between them and other agents of economic change;

(h)   Make increasing use of community-based strategies for par ticipation and involvement of poor rural women in project-induced developmental activities;

(i)   Enhance the effectiveness with which women in resource-poor households contribute to health and household food security.

151.   Women's access to land is an issue that many IFAD projects have to

address, particularly since project interventions can dramatically change land-use patterns. Women's rights to land under customary laws are at best tenuous in most target areas addressed by the Fund.

152.   The strategy underscores the need to address systematically women's labour availability as a project-specific constraint to the implementation of projects promoting increased crop production. In IFAD's project design, an effort is being made to relieve women of their heavy workload through labour-saving technologies or by addressing constraints arising from an absence of drinking water or fuelwood near their homesteads.

153.   The role of IFAD in improving women's access to credit and financial institutions presents a unique development opportunity. IFAD's experience in extending credit and financial resources to the rural resource-poor and in addressing gender-bias in rural financial policies and institutions gives it a comparative advantage in breaking the barriers of formal and informal lending to poor rural women. Many IFAD projects are opening new windows or access to credit and financial institutions in the formal sector. In the past, IFAD projects have for the most part relied on providing revolving loan funds to support women-in-development activities. At present, there is a shift in emphasis to negotiating with formal banking and credit institutions to extend their lending operations to rural women. The ultimate objective is to institutionalize lending and other rural financial services for rural women rather than limiting them to project-based operations whose sustainability is debatable.

154.   IFAD is contributing to the development of agricultural technology responsive to the productive needs of rural women through its technical assistance grant support.

155.   The specific gender issues or questions addressed by the research programmes include among others: women's workload or labour availability as a constraint to be considered in technology selection; women's taste and food-processing or preparation preferences as eventual determinants in whether or not new varieties of crops are likely to be adopted; subsistence food crops produced by women and small livestock and poultry, primarily reared by women and their children; and development of new pre- and post-harvest technology for reducing women's workload. Recently, a recognition

of the gender-differentiated inputs of IFAD target groups at all stages of the crop or livestock production, processing and marketing cycle, led to an examination of the importance of gender issues for all proposed research programmes and towards ensuring that Fund-financed research leads to the generation, development and transfer of technology which is conducive to the specific needs of women beneficiaries and to their positive interaction with the environment.

156.	Training comprises an important critical area for IFAD's technical and institutional support and development activities. Almost all of IFAD's projects have substantial training components that are designed to improve the effective participation of beneficiaries, on the one hand, and the efficient delivery of resources and services by project staff and designated implementing agencies, on the other. Therefore, training is central to the achievement of IFAD's agricultural development and poverty alleviation goals, particularly as they relate to the equitable distribution of these benefits to poor rural women.

157.	The role of development communication in the effective transfer of knowledge and skills to project beneficiaries is increasingly being recognized in IFAD projects. The effectiveness of designing and implementing communication strategies under the projects - by promoting participation of both men and women beneficiaries; by explaining how a project is articulated and how the beneficiaries, including women, can best use new means put at their disposal to maximize the potential benefits; by transferring knowledge and skills; and by providing the beneficiaries with the instruments to guarantee that their voices will be heard - have all been demonstrated in the field.

158.	In the past, many of IFAD's projects with women-in-development components were implemented by ministries of women's affairs and women-in-development units which often lacked sufficient staff, resources or technical skills for effective implementation. Increasingly, there is an emphasis - if not a shift - to implementation and management of women-in-development components by non-governmental organizations and the beneficiaries themselves. Almost all the newly designed projects make provision for the formation of women's groups as an institutional mechanism for implementing productive activities introduced through the project. Women leader/promoters are trained to assist in the monitoring and management of the group's activities.

159.   IFAD's comparative strength lies in its interventions which have a direct bearing on the path from food production or income generation to food availability and household food security. Over the past two years considerable effort has been made by the Fund to refine the conceptual basis of household food security, operationalize it in the context of its loan portfolio and test it through a number of selected investment projects. In so doing, IFAD has gone beyond the mere objective of making food available through production support to also address household access issues, food diversity/dietary aspects within the broader framework of the socio-economic dynamics of prevailing food systems in project areas targeted by the Fund. In recognizing household food security as an immediate outcome objective of its agricultural and rural development initiatives, the Fund has been able to acquire comparative advantage in addressing the broader "nutrition security" issues. This has been a critical step forward in the context of translating project-induced increases in agricultural productivity and often a strengthened resource base into adequate diets for rural poor households.

160.   Finally, IFAD has prepared operational guidelines for project gender analysis including subsector specific guidelines. In addition, IFAD is also working on modules covering specific design elements to facilitate wider replication of participatory approaches based on IFAD's project experience.

(c)   International Monetary Fund

161.   The International Monetary Fund (IMF) provides financial support to the countries implementing comprehensive programmes of economic reform. For the poorest countries, the Fund provides highly concessional resources under the Enhanced Structural Adjustment Facility. Adjustment programmes are designed to promote both macroeconomic stabilization and structural reform, and thereby to lay the foundations for high quality growth - a prerequisite for a sustainable and equitable improvement in living standards. Under the enlarged and extended Facility, which became operational in early 1994, the Fund has placed greater emphasis on social-sector policies. Recognizing the important developmental gains from improving the status and quality of life of women, in the context of both programmes and the policy dialogue with member Governments the Fund has underscored the importance improving women's access to education, health care, and family planning. The Fund is exploring, in close consulta-

tion with the World Bank, the modalities of providing gender-sensitivity training for Fund staff, in order to enhance their effectiveness in both the design of adjustment programmes and the provision of technical assistance.

(d)   Food and Agriculture Organization of the United Nations

162.   While the major portion of FAO's Field Programme is financed from UNDP funds and trust funds from member countries, FAO also provides direct financial assistance to member countries through its Technical Cooperation Programme. Funded from the organization's regular programme, the Technical Cooperation Programme represents about 10 per cent of the Field Programme. It is mainly used as a catalyst to identify and develop programmes for assistance and investment to be funded from other sources. Its funds are also used to respond rapidly to urgent and unforeseen requests for technical and emergency assistance.

163.   A number of projects under FAO's Technical Cooperation Programme are directed specifically to women and include activities to: strengthen women-in-development units, provide policy advice to Governments on gender issues and the integration of rural women into development, provide training in gender analysis, and provide assistance for pilot or experimental programmes for women farmers to improve their agricultural productivity and income.

4. Information and advocacy

164.   An example of how information and advocacy services are provided is found in FAO which considers that the dissemination of information on women's participation in and contribution to agriculture is an important means for mobilizing change in society and for providing an accurate picture of women's roles in a changing world.

165.   Among its activities in this area are: the publication of information materials on rural women's roles in sustainable agriculture and food security; the regular updating and publication of the bibliography of FAO documents on women-in-development and gender issues; the publication of bibliographies of documents on women in development, extracted from the FAO Library's computerized AGRIS/CARIS databases of its collections; the production of audiovisuals on FAO's gender analysis training and on women's roles in agriculture.

D. Coordination in the United Nations system

166.   Throughout the first 10 years of implementing the Nairobi Forward-looking Strategies for the Advancement of Women, the organizations of the United Nations system have utilized a very effective system of linkages for the purpose of coordination. They were built upon networks, processes and institutional structures that were first established during the United Nations Decade for Women.

1. Coordination structures

(a)   Ad hoc inter-agency meetings on women

167.   The formal mechanism for coordination of activities in the area of advancement of women is a network of focal points in the organizations of the United Nations system. These focal points have met annually, on an ad hoc basis, with meetings approved by the Administrative Committee on Coordination each time, for the past 17 years. The meetings have been held at the time of the annual sessions of the Commission on the Status of Women, usually for two days.

168.   The meetings have served as a place to discuss joint activities, such as jointly produced documents (like the 1989 and 1994 world surveys on the role of women in development), joint plans (the system-wide medium-term plans), and common approaches to issues. Starting in 1992, the meetings have produced a joint policy statement to the Commission on the Status of Women on substantive matters of the Fourth World Conference on Women which have affected the preparations for the Conference.

169.   The agendas for the meetings have included coordination of operational activities, but discussion of this issue has not been extensive, in view of the other items on the agenda and the relatively short meeting time.

(b)   Regional inter-agency mechanisms

170.   Three meetings of the specialized agencies and other bodies of the United Nations system at the regional level and intergovernmental organizations on future activities to promote the integration of women into the development of Latin America and the Caribbean were held in preparation for the Fourth World Conference on Women (Santiago, Chile, 3-4 September 1992; Caracas, Venezuela, 26 May 1993; Santiago, Chile, 13 December 1993). It should be mentioned that, after her election, the Regional Coordinator of non-governmental organizations also participated in the meetings in a very vital way. These meetings evaluated the activities of the United Nations to promote the integration of women into development and review inter-agency coordination measures and mechanisms; reviewed regional preparations for the World Conference and made suggestions for the draft of the regional programme of action. The inter-agency meetings have improved communication between regional and subregional bodies of the United Nations system and have undoubtedly permitted more systematic coordination of activities for the advancement of women.

(c)   Other mechanisms

171.   The JCGP Sub-Group on Women-in-Development was established in 1986 and comprises of the women-in-development focal points from UNFPA, UNDP, UNICEF, WFP and IFAD. UNIFEM is also represented in the Sub-Group. In addition to its function for policy guidance, the Sub-Group has identified and promoted special projects on gender analysis training, analysis of macroeconomic policies of structural adjustment and its impact on women and development and more recently, national capacity-building for gender disaggregated statistics. At the forthcoming Conference, a special exhibit will display the framework and results of the project on gender-disaggregated statistics.

2. System-wide medium-term plan

172.   A major innovation of the preparations for the Nairobi Conference was the elaboration of a system-wide medium-term plan for women in development for the period 1990-1995. The purpose of the plan was to

ensure that the implementation of the Nairobi Forward-looking Strategies for the Advancement of Women was included in the plans and programme documents of the organizations of the system, based on consciously designed division of labour. It emphasized both the responsibilities of individual organizations and the need for joint activities. The system-wide plan proposal was extensively discussed at the 1987 session of the Commission on the Status of Women and was accepted by the Economic and Social Council by its resolution 1987/86.

173. In its first report on plans and programmes of the organizations of the United Nations system to implement the system-wide medium-term plan, the Administrative Committee on Coordination stated:

"Since the beginning of the United Nations Decade for Women, a high level of cooperation has existed among the organizations of the system in implementing work for the advancement of women. The preparation of the three world conferences on women, including their documentation, has been a joint effort. There are also examples of joint efforts in current work ... The plan builds on and formalizes this cooperative approach to achieving the objectives of the Nairobi Forward-looking Strategies for the Advancement of Women. Further joint activities are being developed in various inter-agency forums, especially the annual inter-agency meetings on women convened under the aegis of ACC." 3/

174. In his report on implementation of the system-wide medium-term plan for women and development in 1991, the Secretary-General concluded:

"The system-wide medium-term plan has raised the awareness of programme planners of the organizations of the United Nations system of the need to identify activities related to women and development. This is reflected in a higher level of reporting for regular budget activities during 1990-1991 as compared with 1988-1989 ..." 4/

175. In anticipation of this result, the Council had requested, by its resolution 1988/59, that the Secretary-General, in his capacity as Chairman of the Administrative Committee on Coordination, initiate the formulation of a system-wide medium-term plan for the advancement of women for the period 1996-2001. On that basis, a draft was prepared by the Secretariat and submitted to the Council (E/1993/43). However, the report noted that the

plan could not take into account the results of the Fourth World Conference on Women.

176.   After consideration, the Economic and Social Council, by its resolution 1993/16, endorsed the system-wide medium-term plan as a general framework for the coordination of system-wide efforts and requested organizations of the United Nations system to use it in formulating individual medium-term plans for advancement of women. However, it also requested the Secretary-General, in his capacity as Chairman of the Administrative Committee on Coordination, to arrange for a revision of the system-wide plan after the platform for action has been adopted by the Fourth World Conference on Women.

177.   The process of revising the system-wide medium-term plan began in 1995.

Notes

1/	E/1991/16, table 1.
2/	E/1993/84, table 4.
3/	E/1989/16, para. 8.
4/	E/1991/16, para. 4.

Annex

Preparation of National Reports
for the Fourth World Conference on Women

Introduction

The Fourth World Conference on Women, to be held in Beijing in September 1995, should be the culmination of a process that begins with the national preparations. The Commission on the Status of Women has underlined the importance of these national-level preparations. According to Commission resolution 37/7, they should lead to the production of a national report. National machinery for the advancement of women, together with other technical ministries, governmental agencies and non-governmental organizations have the opportunity to take stock of the present situation of women, analyse the progress made since the Nairobi Conference and prepare for future action.

The Commission, recognizing that this is a complex exercise, requested the United Nations Secretariat to assist countries by providing guidelines for the preparation of national reports. It was also felt that some standardization between reports would increase their analytical value and their capacity for building consensus at both the regional and global conferences. This would contribute greatly to building both regional and international consensus for the Conferences.

The suggestions presented here also bear in mind that an important purpose of the national reports is to help shape future national action.

General Suggestions

In order to ensure broad national and international dissemination, the main body of each national report should be short, usually not more than 50 pages. It should feature the most important national priorities and issues for the advancement of women.

Existing national reports on the situation of women can serve as inputs and thus reduce resource requirements as well as ensure consistency. These can include reports prepared for the Committee on the Elimination of Discrimination against Women (CEDAW), for the World Conference on Human Rights and for the International Conference on Population and Development, as well as reports prepared for specialized organizations of the United Nations system. These reports often contain data and analysis in various areas which can be helpful.

In order to reinforce the government offices formally responsible for the report, it is advisable to involve the national statistical office as well as national research and academic talent in various fields such as law, economics, statistics or sociology to collect, analyse and write up the information necessary for the report.

A calendar of work for the preparations would be useful. Although the first beneficiaries of the report are at the national level, countries would obtain an additional benefit if the report were ready in time to be used by and presented at the regional preparatory conference. The dates for the regional conferences are:

7-14 June 1994, Jakarta, Indonesia	Asian and Pacific Preparatory Conference
26-30 September 1994, Mar del Plata, Argentina	Latin American and Caribbean Preparatory Conference
17-21 October 1994, Vienna, Austria	European Regional Preparatory Conference
6-10 November 1994, Amman, Jordan	Western Asian Regional Preparatory Conference
16-23 November 1994, Dakar, Senegal	African Regional Preparatory Conference

For national reports to be useful in regional reviews and appraisal, they should be available to the respective regional commissions well in advance of the date of the regional meeting.

The themes of the United Nations Decade for Women - equality, development and peace - remain valid today. In preparing for the 1995 review and appraisal of the Nairobi Forward-looking Strategies, rather than simply describing changes under each theme, the Commission on the Status of Women has identified eight "critical areas of concern" for future action. National reports can usefully be built around these critical areas. The outline suggested below is based on these areas.

In order to produce a document that will serve to mobilize women and men for action in the critical areas of concern and thus have maximum impact, emphasis should be placed on:

(a)   Quantitative indicators as a basis for the analysis of the situation and changes;

(b)   In each area, the most interesting programmes and experiments implemented for and by women for their advancement. These would include activities of public, private or non-governmental organization origin.

National reports developed in this way can also be of direct interest to other countries to study and compare with their own experience. The full set of national reports can present a sum of experience as well as a global catalogue of pilot projects and experiments which will serve as an important input for the Platform for Action.

As requested, a core set of indicators is suggested below. A few words of explanation are necessary about these indicators. Effective advocacy requires facts; planning and programming require facts; action requires facts. Facts can largely speak for themselves. The emphasis placed on indicators is one of the innovations of the Beijing Conference. Indicators and facts which measure present status and change over time can be of considerable assistance in debates and decision-making.

Most countries already have the data necessary for the national report. The suggested indicators have been selected on the basis of their common availability in the international system because they were provided by the countries themselves. Generally, the main difficulty in using these indicators is locating where they can be found in each national circumstance.

Many are collected by the national statistical office, some other government agency or a periodic survey. Some of the indicators proposed are not commonly available in the traditional statistical system, but can be obtained from some public source, usually through a certain amount of research. They have been suggested because of their significance for the areas of concern.

The preparation of the national report is an opportunity to discuss the relevance of new indicators for national action and to introduce them into the routine data collection or disaggregation if they are already collected, but not separated by sex.

The selection of indicators has been also guided by their sensitivity to change over time. For example, many of the indicators are based on specific age groups rather than covering the entire population.

Presentation of the indicators should be accompanied by a discussion on the implications for action. This can also lead to the presentation of national targets in the critical areas of concern.

Outline Of A National Report
Overview
This section should be limited to one page, highlighting the major features of the report, including major accomplishments and new priorities for action. If possible, a translation should be provided in the United Nations official languages in order to enable use by delegations of other countries.

Introduction
A brief presentation of the most relevant global or regional changes relevant to the advancement of women taking place from the national perspective. This should provide a framework for examining how national change is taking place.

Review and appraisal at the national level
Situation in the early 1980s
A brief section should recall what the national situation of women was like in the early 1980s - i.e, prior to the Nairobi Conference. If possible it should refer to the national review and appraisal report prepared for the Nairobi Conference. The section should highlight what were considered the major remaining problems at that time.

Changes since the early 1980s
The Commission on the Status of Women has identified eight critical areas of concern:

1. Inequality in the sharing of power and decision-making at all levels;

2. Insufficient mechanisms at all levels to promote the advancement of women;

3. Lack of awareness of, and commitment to, internationally and nationally recognized women's rights;

4. Poverty;

5. Inequality in women's access to and participation in the definition of economic structures and policies and the productive process itself;

6. Inequality in access to education, health, employment and other means to maximize awareness of women's rights and the use of their capacities;

7. Violence against women;

8. Effects on women of continuing national and international armed or other kinds of conflict.

For each of these areas, a section should analyse the changes since the early 1980s as well as the present situation, using, wherever possible, statistical indicators as suggested in the annex. Another section in each area should present and evaluate the most innovative and interesting programmes, pilot projects or activities organized by the public, private sectors or by women themselves and discuss the possibilities of extension in the country.

Review and appraisal of international support
In this section emphasis should be placed on technical cooperation and assistance in relation to the critical areas of concern, the successes, the problems encountered.

355

Future strategic goals and objectives and corresponding financial arrangements
In this section, future plans should be outlined (corresponding to the areas of concern) by defining goals (e.g., overcoming the feminization of poverty) and quantitative targets (e.g., achieve equality in the ratio of girls to boys at university level by 2000). The kind of measures necessary to achieve these goals or targets should be indicated. In order for such plans to be successful, indications on the political commitment, the institutional mechanisms to implement measures and the availability of resources should be provided.

Key National Indicators
The statistical and other indicators used in the national reports should be those that permit examination of the situation of women in terms of the eight critical areas of concern. They should also show the changes that have occurred, but comparing situations at different points. The comparison points that are suggested include 1980 (the midpoint of the United Nations Decade for Women and the Copenhagen Conference), 1985 (the end of the United Nations Decade for Women and the Nairobi Conference), 1990 (the year of the first review and appraisal of the Nairobi Forward-looking Strategies) and the most recent date for which statistics are available. These dates need not be exact, and data that were obtained close to those dates can also be used (e.g., 1979 or 1981 would do for a 1980 comparison).

1.   *Inequality in the sharing of power and decision-making at all levels*
Women by virtue of their gender, experience discrimination in terms of denial of equal access to the power structure that controls society and deter-mines development issues and peace initiatives. This discrimination pro-motes an uneconomic use of women's talents and wastes the valuable human resources necessary for development and for the strengthening of peace. Women need to be involved in order to bring their interests and aspi-rations into the societal agenda.

The indicators listed below can show the level and the evolution of women's and men's participation in political and economic decision-making bodies.

  Indicators
  (a)   Participation in parliamentary assemblies: number of women and men. 1980, 1985 and the latest available year. Sources: election statistics, usually maintained by central electoral boards or similar institu-tions;

(b)   Participation in Government (highest levels; e.g., ministers, deputy, vice- or assistant ministers, secretaries of state or permanent secretaries, deputy secretaries or directors of Government Departments): number of women and men. 1980, 1985 and the latest available year.
Sources: government directories or lists of public officials (requires counting by level, sex and ministries grouped by type - e.g., prime ministry, economic, social, legal, defence and foreign affairs);

(c)   Participation in foreign affairs: number of women and men ambassadors. 1980, 1985 and the latest available year. Sources: Ministry of Foreign Affairs;

(d)   Participation in local representative bodies (highest levels in municipalities or state legislatures - e.g., mayor, state legislator, municipal councilperson): number of women and men. 1980, 1985 and the latest available year. Sources: lists of public officials or central electoral boards;

(e)   Employers and own account workers (indicator of women as economic decision makers in the private sector): number of women and men in that category of occupation. 1980, 1985 and the latest available year. Sources: national statistical office from national labour statistics or national censuses;

(f)   Administrative and managerial workers (indicator of women in decision-making in the labour force): number of women and men in that type of occupation. 1980, 1985 and the latest available year. Sources: national statistical office from national labour statistics or national censuses;

(g)   Proprietors in business establishments (indicator on women as economic decision makers in the private sector): number of business establishments registered to women, to men or jointly. 1985, current year (1993). Sources: industrial statistics and/or commercial registries.

2.   *Insufficient mechanisms at all levels to promote the advancement of women*
Appropriate governmental machinery needs to be established at a high level and endowed with adequate resources, commitment and authority to advise on the impact on women of all government policies. To be effective, such machinery should disseminate information to women on their

rights and entitlements, collaborate with various ministries and other government agencies and with non-governmental organizations.

The indicators listed below can show the evolution of general and specific institutional arrangements for the advancement of women, at the governmental and non-governmental levels as well as at the national, subnational and local levels.

Indicators

(a)   National machinery at the national, subnational (state or province or region) and local levels (indicating the institutional existence, outreach and resource levels for it); existence and form (e.g., ministry, office, non-governmental organization), status within governmental structure, mandate and percentage of national budget allocated.1980, 1985 and 1993. Sources: government budget documents and information provided by the national machinery for the advancement of women;

(b)   Focal points for the advancement of women in technical ministries (indicating the extent to which a coordinating mechanism has been set up and its level in decision-making terms). Existence, level of decision-making and mandate. 1980, 1985 and 1993. Sources: ministries;

(c)   Non-governmental organizations for the advancement of women at the national and subnational levels (indicating the extent to which these organizations are working in the country): number and principal areas of activities. 1980, 1985 and the latest available year. Sources: non-governmental organizations themselves or national machinery for advancement of women if they keep lists of non-governmental organizations.

3.   *Lack of awareness of, and commitment to, internationally and nationally recognized women's rights*

The United Nations system has worked for four decades to establish international standards to prevent discrimination on the basis of sex. Although much progress has been made in ensuring that the provisions of the Convention on the Elimination of All Forms of Discrimination against Women and of other international instruments lead to legislative changes, measures are necessary for effective implementation and enforcement.

In some countries, discriminatory legislative provisions still exist, including civil, penal and commercial codes and certain administrative rules and regulations. The indicators listed below can show us the evolution of the legal basis for de jure equality of women and men. The elimination of de facto discrimination requires as a fundamental step the dissemination of information on women's rights. For the most part, these indicators are qualitative.

Indicators

(a)　Main legal instruments for women's rights (description of the main legislative provisions guaranteeing women's rights, including constitutions, equal opportunity laws, whether the country has ratified or acceded to the Convention on the Elimination of All Forms of Discrimination against Women and whether this has been without reservations. The analysis should indicate when this took place, in terms of the comparison dates. 　　　Sources: Parliament or/and Ministry of Justice or/and national machinery for the advancement of women;

(b)　Main measures taken to increase awareness among women and men of women's rights. This should indicate whether there are active efforts to inform women and men about rights and efforts to make it easier to exercise those rights. These might include the existence of information campaigns, efforts to make the judiciary more accessible, the creation of ombudspersons or other institutional arrangements to implement anti-discrimination laws. It can also include efforts in the education system, such as adding human rights to the school curriculum and changing textbooks. The comparison dates could enable tracing the evolution of these efforts. Sources: national machinery for the advancement of women.

4.　*Poverty*

It is widely assumed that the burden of poverty falls disproportionately on women and that in many circumstances those women are heads of households with children. It has also been found that women's experience of poverty is different and more acute than that of men because of gender-based forms of discrimination. The burden that women in poverty carry forces them to transfer part of their workload to other women, such as daughters, mothers or sisters. This has, in most cases, serious implications for the inter-generational transmission of poverty.

Poverty is experienced mostly by households. While there are a number of traditional indicators of poverty, based on the ability of the household to purchase a defined "basket of goods", these figures are not always available. If such figures are available, they should be used, but they may not distinguish by sex. Bearing in mind the close association between female headship and low incomes, the proportion of women-headed households and the change in this over time, is considered one of the best indicators of poverty. Another approach is to examine whether programmes and facilities exist that would provide means by which women could escape from poverty. This constitutes the basis for the other proposed set of indicators: the existence of programmes, services and facilities that could ease women's double burden.

Indicators

(a)   Women-headed households (usually an indicator that the household has no more than one major income earner and therefore at risk of poverty): percentage of households headed by women. 1980, 1985 and the latest available year. Sources: national statistical office from national censuses or from specific population surveys;

(b)   Urban unemployment (indicating whether unemployment and its consequent income reduction affects women more than men): percentage of women and men unemployed in urban areas. 1980 and the latest available year. Sources: national census, labour force surveys, unemployment office statistics;

(c)   Public day-care centres for children (indicating whether alternative, public-supported facilities exist that can allow a woman with children to hold a job): number of centres (nurseries and kindergartens), by rural/urban area. 1980, 1985 and the latest available year. Sources: statistics on education, specific surveys, health surveys;

(d)   Vocational training (indicating whether job training exists for women and men on an equal basis: number of students, by sex and by field of study. 1980, 1985 and the latest available year. Sources: Ministry of Education or Labour.

5. *Inequality in women's access to and participation in the definition of economic structures and policies and the productive process itself*

As a result of cultural, institutional, behavioural and attitudinal discrimination, women world wide suffer a lack of access to land, capital and other productive resources. This gender bias excludes women from most policy-making bodies which have an impact on development agenda. It also has an impact on poverty. There are few standard indicators of access that would normally be classified by sex. However, by a relatively simple study of existing records using sampling, estimates can be obtained which could indicate the degree of inequality present. If the data are too cumbersome to collect for an entire year or for the entire country, samples should be used (e.g., registration of urban properties during the month of January 1993 in the capital and selected large, medium and small cities). If possible, the same should be done for a previous year in order to compare the change over the time.

Indicators

(a)   Credit in public banks (indicating the extent to which women have access to publicly provided or guaranteed credit): number of public loans granted to women, to men and jointly (man and woman in a household).To the extent possible, the loans should be divided between rural and non-rural. Current year (1993). Sources: national public banks (sample of persons to whom loans were granted);

(b)   Rural land-ownership (indicating whether there is access by women to land-owning): number of rural properties registered, by sex. During the current year (1993). (If possible the average area registered by women and men should be compared.) Sources: national land registry (sample of titles registered) and/or Ministry of Agriculture/Rural Development (sample of titles or data from most recent agricultural census);

(c)   Real estate tenure in urban areas (indicating whether women have access to urban property): number of urban properties registered by women, by men and jointly (woman and man in a single household). During the current year (1993). Sources: national registry of deeds or registry in the largest cities (sample of registrations).

6.   *Inequality in access to education, health, employment and other*
        means to maximize awareness of rights and the use of their capacities
To achieve the goal of de facto equality of women and men special efforts
should be made in order to increase the status of women. Access to education, health services and to income-generating activities in the formal and
informal sector, are the basic factors to reach it. For women, they represent
the principal means for their self-empowerment. For the society, they represent an investment in human resources with very high level of returns. The
indicators listed below under the chapters on education, health and employment can show us the investment gap between women and men, girls and
boys and their evolution over the time. Most are standard statistical indicators routinely collected and presented by national statistical authorities.

Indicators
   Education
   (a)   Illiteracy (indicating the extent to which past discrimination
in educational access is reflected in present inability to read and write): percentage of women, of men illiterates (by age group) 15-24 years; 25-44 years;
over 45 years. 1980, 1985 and the latest available year. Sources: national census and/or specific surveys and/or Ministry of Education;

   (b)   Enrolment ratio (indicating to what extent girls and boys are
able to start school on an equal basis). First-level enrolment ratio by sex.
Second-level enrolment ratio by sex. 1980, 1985 and the latest available year.
Sources: Ministry of Education, often reported to national statistical offices;

   (c)   Schooling completed (indicating the extent to which girls
and boys complete schooling on an equal basis): number of boys and girls
receiving diplomas from or otherwise completing first and second levels of
education. 1980, 1985 and the latest available year. Sources: Ministry of
Education;

   (d)   Graduation in third-level (indicating whether boys and girls
have equal access to entry-level jobs in the professional and managerial levels); number of boys and girls graduated, by field of study. 1980, 1985 and the
latest available year. Sources: Ministry of Education;

   (e)   Technical graduation (indicating the extent to which women
have equal access to non-traditional fields): number of women and men

graduating with an engineering degree or diploma. 1980, 1985 and the latest available year. Sources: Ministry of Education;

(e)   Teachers (indicating the extent to which women participate among those teaching): number of women and men teaching at first, second and third levels. 1980, 1985 and the latest available. Sources: Ministry of Education.

Health

(a)   Life expectancy at birth (indicating the probable life-span of a person born in a given year, which summarizes all of the factors, influencing life-span): life expectancy for women, for men. 1980 and the latest available year. Sources: national statistical service;

(b)   Maternal mortality per 100,000 births. 1980 and the latest available year. (If the data are too cumbersome to collect for an entire year or for the entire country, samples should be used (e.g., registration of these data during any month in the capital and selected large, medium and small cities). If possible, the same should be done for the previous years, in order to compare the change over the time.) Sources: national statistical service or Ministry of Health;

(c)   Infant mortality rate: annual number of deaths of male and female infants (under one year of age) per 1,000 live births. 1980 and the latest available year. (If the data are too cumbersome to collect for an entire year or for the entire country, samples should be used (e.g., registration of these data during any month in the capital and selected large, medium and small cities). If possible, the same should be done for the previous years, in order to compare the change over the time.) Sources: national statistical service or Ministry of Health;

(d)   Child mortality per 1,000: mortality rate for boys, for girls aged from one to four years. 1980 and the latest available year. (If the data are too cumbersome to collect for an entire year or for the entire country, samples should be used (e.g., registration of these data during any month in the capital and selected large, medium and small cities). If possible, the same should be done for the previous years, in order to compare the change over the time.) Sources: national statistical service or Ministry of Health;

(e)   Total fertility rate: 1980 and the latest available year. Sources: national statistical service;

(f)   Percentage of women using contraceptives: proportion of women of child-bearing age (15-49) currently using contraceptives, either traditional or modern. 1980 and the latest available year. (If the data are too cumbersome to collect for an entire year or for the entire country, samples should be used (e.g., registration of these data during any month in the capital and selected large, medium and small cities). If possible, the same should be done for the previous years, in order to compare the change over the time.) Sources: Ministry of Health or specific survey - e.g, demographic and health surveys;

(g)   Prevalence of anaemia: percentage of women aged 15-49 with haemoglobin levels below 12 grams/dl for non-pregnant women and 11 grams/dl for pregnant women. 1980 and the latest available year. Sources: Ministry of Health or specific surveys;

(h)   Malnutrition in children under-five years of age: percentage of girls, of boys with mild-moderate/severe malnutrition. 1980 and the latest available year. Sources: Ministry of Health or specific surveys;

(i)   Sex-differentials in immunization rates: percentage of girls and boys one year of age fully immunized (TB, DPT, polio and measles). 1980 and the latest available year. Sources: Ministry of Health;

(j)   Percentage of pregnant women fully immunized against tetanus (TT2 or booster): 1980 and the latest available year. Sources: Ministry of Health;

(k)   Service availability: percentage of births attended by trained personnel (doctor or the person with midwifery skills). 1980 and the latest available year. Sources: Ministry of Health;

(l)   HIV positive women: percentage of women, by age group, found HIV positive in maternity clinics/wards (specify geographic area covered). Most recent five years. Sources: national AIDS programme or Ministry of Health.

Employment

(a)   Economically active population: percentage of women and men in each sector of activity (primary, secondary and tertiary). 1980, 1985 and the latest available year. Sources: national census and/or labour surveys;

(b)   Characteristics of employment: percentage of women and men in part-time employment. 1980, 1985 and the latest available year. Sources: national census or labour surveys.

7.   *Violence against women*

Violence against women exists in all regions, classes and cultures. Physical violence against women, which derives from their unequal status in society, has been acknowledged as hindering their full integration and equal participation in the society. This issue has grown in importance in the last few years and has been considered at numerous national and international meetings. The indicators listed below are primarily qualitative and show which policies and measures the Government and other agencies are being undertaken to prevent, control and reduce the impact of violence on women.

Indicators

(a)   Specific measures taken to ensure the elimination of violence against women in all its forms: legal measures, national plans of action, training to sensitize law enforcement officers and public officials. If a comparison is desired, it could be based on whether these measures were in place in 1980, 1985 and the latest available year. Sources: parliamentary or/and Ministry of Justice or/and national machinery for the advancement of women;

(b)   Protective measures taken to assist abused women: number of public shelters, shelters sponsored by non-governmental organizations' shelters and other services (including an indication of how many persons were attended). 1980, 1985 and the latest available year. Sources: social statistics or specific surveys;

(c)   Women in the judicial system (indicating the extent that women, who are usually more understanding of violence against women, are found in decision-making positions): number and percentage of women and men at the professional level (judges, lawyers, prosecutors and attorneys). 1980, 1985 and the latest available year. Sources: Ministry of Justice or of Interior;

(d)   Women in police forces (indicating the extent that women, who tend to be more understanding of the problem of violence, are available in the forces): percentage of women. 1980, 1985 and the latest available year. Sources: Ministry of Interior.

8.   *Effects on women of continuing national and international armed or other kinds of conflicts*

The international community recognizes a humanitarian responsibility to protect and assist refugees and displaced persons. In most cases, the affected are women and children exposed to a variety of difficult situations. There are few indicators about the affected population, either in the countries where the conflicts occur, the countries receiving or assisting refugees or among the international agencies involved. If figures are available in countries experiencing armed conflicts about the proportion of women among refugees and displaced, these should be reported. One indicator, however, of a probable understanding of the extent to which armed conflict is seen a male issue is the extent to which women are included in national military formations. The existence of a high proportion of women would probably mean that those formations would be more sensitive to gender violence.

Indicator

Women in the military: percentage of women in the armed forces. 1980, 1985 and the latest available year. Sources: ministries of defence.

Notes

1 /   The text for this section has been derived from a contribution prepared by UNESCO for the 1994 World Survey on the Role of Women in Development in light of its relevance for the review and appraisal.

93670 – AUGUST – 1995 – 1,500^{M}